Jim

With very best wishes

Kevin Rathburn

August 2018

SHIPWRECKS

and

SALVAGE

on the

EAST AFRICAN COAST

The Globe Star – Mombasa's most notorious wreck

KEVIN PATIENCE

Second Edition
Published by the Author
2018

Copyright © Kevin Patience
saburi@hotmail.com

ISBN No. 978-1-5272-1430-9

Ships are all right – it's the men that's in them
Joseph Conrad

Take it all in all, a ship is the most honourable thing man has ever produced
John Ruskin

**Sometimes it is more important for a navigator to know where his ship is not,
rather than where it is**

**Navigation - The art of conducting a vessel from one place to another by sea,
safely, expeditiously and efficiently, without actually hitting anything !**

Printed by
Short Run Press Ltd,
Exeter, Devon. EX2 7LW, United Kingdom

**Dedicated to the memory of Captain Keith Trayner, Extra Master, 1929-2011,
who played a large part in the maritime history of the East African coast**

The British India Line passenger ship Kenya alongside Berth No. 1 Kilindini

Mombasa Old Harbour c. 1900

The British India liner Matiana in the Old Harbour, Mombasa

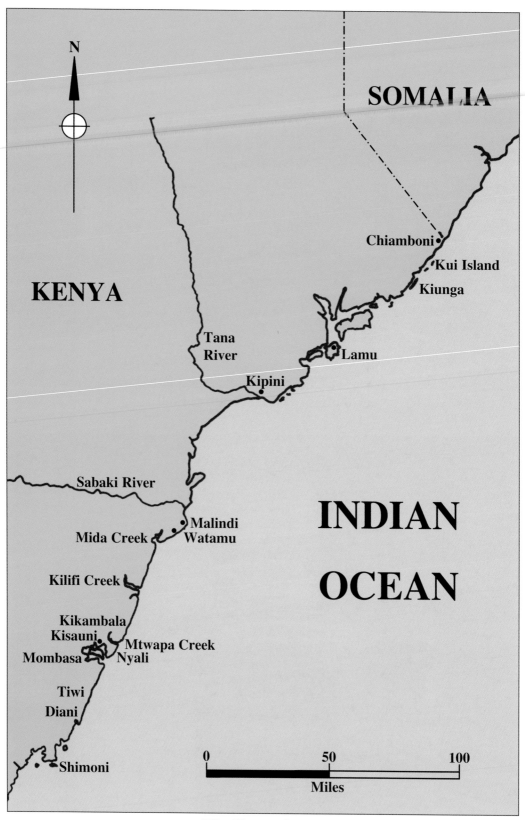

The Kenya Coast

Contents

Foreword

Preface

Part One

Shipwrecks on the Kenya Coast 1698 - 2014

Strandings and Salvage on the Kenya Coast 1799 - 2017

Part Two

Shipwrecks on the Tanzania Coast 1499 - 2012

Strandings and Salvage on the Tanzania Coast 1883 - 2013

Part Three

Shipwrecks and Strandings on the East African lakes 1896 - 2010

Tugs in East Africa

Postscript

Acknowledgements

Bibliography

About the Author

Index

Foreword

There is something about shipwrecks which is of enduring interest, not only to the seafarer but also to others. Added to this is the fascination of the waters of the East African seaboard, seen by most to be azure, serene and basking in the scents of the spice islands that lace the coastline. To those who know these waters, the scene is very different, waters lashed by monsoon storms and strewn with reefs and shallows, some only recently charted, that have become the grave of vessels since early mariners probed the coast in search of spices, slaves and trade. In this book the author has utilised an in depth knowledge of both the waters of the East African coast and of the ships which have sailed through them. A keen interest in maritime matters commencing in his childhood in Kenya and fuelled through his profession as a salvage diver over twenty-five years, has led to this publication, linking his origins, interests and prime profession.

Kevin originally embarked on the considerable task of documenting the then known vessels that have succumbed to Neptune's grasp on this coast and also those which have, through dint of effort or sheer luck, narrowly evaded a watery grave and survived to sail on. His tenacity in continued research has led him to further information now resulting in this enhanced second edition. This improved edition of the work continues to be of considerable fascination, academic interest and reference, it now includes not only previously unrecorded events but is now presented with greatly improved photography in both colour for more recent events and black and white for earlier mishaps. Resulting from the popularity of the first edition, seafarers world wide have contributed additional eye witness information and memories of their experiences thus giving a rare insight into the events and circumstances surrounding the incidents the author has so accurately and lucidly recorded.

Peace and war, commerce and pleasure, accident and intent, have all made contributions to this ever enlarging marine jigsaw, now increasingly researched and accurately pieced together.

An ongoing mutual interest in research and a love of maritime matters, railways, wrecks and salvage has forged a friendship with Kevin that has lasted for over 40 years and encompassed numerous countries for us both.

For me, this second edition recalls events of close a half century ago when, as a young Royal Navy Lieutenant, seconded to the infant Kenya Navy in command of the patrol boat 'KNS Chui', in 1967, my small vessel was the first to reach the stricken Panamanian freighter "Paraportiani" in the Pemba Channel. Little did I think, in those halcyon days, that the event and the eventual fate of 'K.N.S.Chui', my first command, would be so well documented and illustrated, initially in 2006 and now again in 2018!

Captain Michael Bowman
Master Mariner, E.S.M., J.P.
Darwin,
Northern Territory
Australia

Preface to the Second Edition

The first edition proved a success and in the intervening eleven years there have been further incidents and casualties giving an opportunity to update and publish a second edition in colour. I am indebted to the following who kindly allowed me to use their colour paintings, photographs, postcards and slides : Terry Bagworth, Maurice Barasa, John Batchelor MBE, Captain Mike Bowman, Ron Bullock, Juanita Carberry, Peter Chantry, Tony Chetham, Gordon Davies, Rob Dickinson, Steve Farrow, Henry Gunston, Ian Hay, Lorenz Kaestner, Bernard Kunicki, Malcolm McCrow, Ian Marshall, Iain Mulligan, Jan Nielsen, Captain Mark Oatley, Bruce Phillips, Peter Phillips, Simon Phillips, Robin Piercy, Anton Rijsdijk, Dave Ruddock, Robin Schalch, Lt. Col. Harjit Kelly Singh, Chip Vincent,Chris White, Captain Bryan Woods and the Comarco Group formerly Eagle Tugs and Diving Contractors Ltd, referred to as Divecon in the text. In particular Anne Cowne, Information Advisor of Lloyds Register Foundation, London for answering innumerable requests for help.

The East African coastline stretches some 4,000 miles from Cape Guardafui in Somalia to the Mozambique Channel. It is a rugged and inhospitable shore swept by the monsoons, with few safe anchorages, miles of treacherous coral reefs and a strong northerly current. It is a ship's graveyard for the unlucky ones, and a dire warning to those that have gone aground and were subsequently refloated.

Seafarers have travelled and traded along this coast for hundreds of years and until the late 19th century, Zanzibar had been the centre of a major trading empire based on slavery, spices, coal and fresh water. Many vessels came to grief along the coast but the most catastrophic incident was the loss of over one hundred and fifty vessels in the great hurricane of 1872.

With the signing of the Treaty of Berlin in July 1890, the vast tract of East Africa ruled by the Sultan of Zanzibar was divided to become British and German East Africa, now Kenya and Tanzania together with Uganda.

These territories soon saw the arrival of missionaries, engineers to build the railways and settlers. Referring to Steve North's new book 'Europeans in British Administered East Africa - 1888-1910' it is surprising to see how many there were in the territory in these early days, all of whom had travelled by ship to Dar es Salaam, Mombasa and Zanzibar.

This publication covers most of the known recorded casualties, wrecked, stranded or salvaged along the Kenya, Tanzania and Zanzibar coastlines over the years, a distance of 1,400 miles and conveys some idea of the hazards faced by mariners in this part of Africa. The great lakes of Africa tend to get overlooked but Lake Albert, Tanganyika and Victoria have been the scenes of many fatalities and are also included.

Shipwrecks on the
Kenya Coast
1698 - 2014

Agia Marina	1982	Mombasa
Ahmadi	1909	Mombasa
Alfa Kilimanjaro	1994	Mombasa
Arab Trader	1951	Nyali
Aventura	1983	Mombasa
Bente Dania	1992	Kiunga
Calicut	1928	Mombasa
Dania	2002	Nyali
Derna	1956	Mombasa
Fish Eagle	2014	Mombasa
Funguo	2002	Diani
Globe Star	1973	Mombasa
Harrier	1988	Pemba Channel
Highland Lassie	1879	Kisauni
H.M.S. Hildasay	1945	Tiwi
Impala	1984	Mombasa
Kota Menang	1975	Nyali
Lavest	1994	Malindi
Mirage	1997	Mombasa
Mtongwe	1994	Mombasa
Nairobi	1922	Malindi
Ngamia	1981	Mombasa
Rafaela	1984	Mombasa
Rafiki	1981	Mombasa
Ramora Bay	1994	Kiunga
Said Mohamed	1993	Mombasa
Saint Michael	1996	Mombasa
Santo Antonio	1698	Mombasa
Shakwe	1989	Watamu
R.F.A. Spapool	1983	Mombasa
Sussex	1909	Nyali
Tembo	1973	Chiamboni

Agia Marina

Builders	:	Werft Nobiskrug, Rendsburg, Germany. 1956
Length	:	234 feet
Beam	:	35 feet
Displacement	:	1,380 tons
Machinery	:	M.A.N. 7 cyl. diesel. 1,470 hp.
Position	:	04°.03'.55" S 39°.35'.06" E

The Cyprus registered vessel arrived at Mombasa in September 1982 with a general cargo including 1,900 tons of salt from Alexandria. 1,100 tons had been discharged when the port stopped the offloading due to non-payment of port and stevedoring charges. The vessel was arrested and laid up in Port Reitz awaiting settlement of dues when she caught fire on 4 October. The Murri International tug Bison 1 arrived on the scene and commenced fire-fighting operations but the vessel was declared a total loss when the after end of the ship including the accommodation, was destroyed. The ship was abandoned in Port Reitz and sank on 8 August 1985. Two years later the wreck was sectioned by a floating crane using an anchor chain as a saw and dumped ashore where it was cut up for scrap in February 1990. The ship had been launched as the Pasajes for the German company Oldenburg-Portugiesische. After two sales in 1971-2 the ship was renamed Rasajes and after four further sales named Agia Marina by Braham Maritime in 1982.

Ahmadi

Builders	:	Robert Stephenson, Newcastle, England. 1888
Length	:	290 feet
Beam	:	40 feet
Displacement	:	2,518 tons
Machinery	:	Single triple expansion. 250 nhp
Position	:	04°.04'.30" S 39°.40'.80"E

One of the most prominent wrecks on the East African coast is the Ahmadi, whose remains have lain below the lighthouse at Ras Serani, Mombasa just over a hundred years. She was launched as the Endeavour for McIntyre Brothers of Newcastle and after twelve years service sold to the Bombay and Persia Steamship Navigation Co. Ltd and renamed Ahmadi. The ship grounded while entering Kilindini from Zanzibar on the evening of 16 November 1909 under the command of Captain T.L. Green while carrying 343 passengers and 71 crew. At the time of stranding it was not practice to have the leading lights lit as ships generally entered during daylight. However the Master knowing he would be arriving late had asked the ships agents to telegram Mombasa and ensure the lights were lit. On arrival a blue flare was lit indicating the need for a pilot although there were no certificated pilots available and pilotage was not compulsory. A local native was used more for his knowledge than his navigating skill. The tide was in accordance with the East African Pilot and with a moon and the weather clear Captain Green headed in on the compass course indicated on the chart hoping to pick up the pilot. On reaching the turning buoy he ordered 'hard a port' and the helm was put over but there was little change in heading. Realizing something was amiss he ordered 'slow ahead' and then 'stop' and finally 'full astern'. Four minutes later the ship gently grounded. The soundings showed 11 feet forward, and 42 feet aft. The engine was run full astern while cargo was shifted from the forward to the aft hold and the ballast tank emptied. A kedge anchor was laid to keep the stern in deep water but the hawser parted when the tide was running in and the ship swung broadside on to the reef. The passengers were landed and cargo and baggage

Discharging coal into dhows

loaded into lighters. The following day The Times of London reported the ship aground with a total value of £150,000. Two more anchors were laid out to stabilize the vessel while three other company vessels the Africa, Nadri and Tima attempted unsuccessfully to refloat the ship. Five days later another report stated the ship was leaking badly and hundreds of bags of cloves were thrown overboard and the ship's agents offered one rupee per bag delivered to the old port jetty. There was fierce competition between boat owners who rushed up and down the harbour collecting the floating jetsam. Dhows were brought alongside and tons of coal discharged but to no avail: the ship remained stuck fast. No. 2 hatch was now flooded and the collision bulkhead buckled. The crew left on the 25th and the Master the following day. On the 27th the port authority divers confirmed severe damage to the hull caused by the strong winds and heavy seas, and the surveyors reported the pumps were unable to keep the water out and it was unlikely the ship would be refloated. By the 29th the agents recommended the ship and cargo be sold by auction but

'The Elephant wreck'

Aerial view of the wreck in 1974

the owners had already contacted the Perim Salvage Co. whose vessel Meyun arrived from the Red Sea on 18 December and discharged the remaining cargo. Despite their efforts the ship remained firmly on the reef and was declared a total loss. The remains were sold in auction to Hassanali Jevanjee for £225 and stripped of all useful fixtures and fittings with some of the timber being used in a house in Nyali. A Court of Enquiry held in Bombay on 23/24 December concluded that the Master and crew had acted correctly and attributed the stranding to the strong currents from the old port and Kilindini channels preventing the ship from answering the helm. The triple expansion engine remained upright for many

The author cutting the propeller shaft with a thermic lance, 1984

The 5 ton propeller shaft

years and due to the steam pipe projecting from one end became known as the 'Elephant Wreck'. Eventually with the passage of time the engine fell over and the name faded into history. In 1984 the author was tasked with recovering a section of propeller shaft. Around thirty foot was cut using thermic lances and after machining the corroded layer, the steel was found to be in excellent condition. Today the rusting remains of the two boilers and engine still lie on the foreshore below the lighthouse.

The wreck today

Alpha Kilimanjaro

Builders	:	Australian Shipbuilding, Freemantle, W. Australia. 1988
Length	:	90 feet
Beam	:	25 feet
Displacement	:	197 tons
Machinery	:	Caterpillar V12 diesel. 632 hp.
Position	:	04°.04'.35" S 39°.39'.65" E

The Alpha Kilimanjaro was a locally owned trawler undergoing repair alongside the jetty at Southern Engineering Ltd. in Mombasa when she sank on 24 July 1994. On 5 August, Divecon International were awarded the salvage contract and mobilised a team of divers and equipment, together with a heavy lift crane on a barge. The trawler's stability caused a number of problems during the salvage operation and it was not until a second shore based crane was used in conjunction with the floating unit that the vessel was refloated on 3 September and laid up.

Arab Trader

Builders	:	Cook, Welton & Gemmel, Beverley, Yorkshire, England. 1943
Length	:	150 feet
Beam	:	27 feet
Displacement	:	456 tons
Machinery	:	Single triple expansion. 850 ihp
Position	:	04°.02'.50" S 39°.43'.57" E

The Arab Trader was one of a number of Isles class armed trawlers built for the Royal Navy during the Second World War for a variety of tasks. Launched as the Gulland with the pennant number T 365, the ship was placed on the disposal list after the war and sold to Belgian owners in March 1946. The following year the ship changed hands and was renamed Henken and two years later sold to Arab Navigation & Transport Co. in Aden and renamed Arab Trader. On 13 April 1951 the ship grounded three miles north of Mombasa on a voyage from Aden to Mauritius with a cargo of lentils and within a day or two the heavy seas flooded the engine and boiler room. The wreck settled on the reef and the main deck was awash at high water. With a cargo that was now worthless and no one in Mombasa capable of salvaging the ship, she was abandoned as a total loss. The wreck broke up in the surf and at a later date the remains were demolished with explosives. What was left of the wreck was rediscovered in the 1970s on an extremely low tide in front of the Reef Hotel consisting of a pile of steel plate and machinery on the edge of the reef.

Aventura

Builders   : Craig Shipbuilding Co. Long Beach, California. U.S.A. 1931
Length   : 147 feet
Beam   : 23 feet
Displacement : 273 tons
Machinery   : Twin Winton 6 cyl. diesel. 1,000 hp

Position   : 04°.04'.30" S 39°.39.30" E

The Aventura arrived in Mombasa after an engine failure off the Somali coast in 1972 during a round the world voyage. The passengers departed and the vessel was laid up in Mtongwe awaiting spares. A year later she was sold for £35,000 to local interests who began an overhaul with a view to local charter work. A 1974 survey showed the vessel required extensive repairs to the shell plating along the waterline and a number of internal tank tops and bulkheads. After dry-docking at African Marine the projected venture fell through and the vessel was laid up. In January 1977 after further repairs, the ship was cleared for sea trials along the coast but failed to attract a business venture and in December after a further trial the ship was laid up once more. Two years later a proposal to turn the ship into a floating hotel was accepted by the Port Authority but never carried out. The ship

was sold in 1982 and the name changed to Emissary. A year later while moored in Liwatoni Creek, Mombasa the vessel was accidentally damaged and sank leaving the bows above the surface. Until recently, various salvage efforts had been unsuccessful and the vessel remained in situ. However, as of 2013 dredging operations in the vicinity meant the vessel required removal and it was removed the following year. Aventura was built as the private yacht Pudlu and during the Second World War requisitioned for service with the U.S. Coast Guard as the U.S.S. Amethyst. At the end of hostilities she reverted back to civilian ownership and was renamed Samona II, Explorer and finally Aventura.

Bente Dania

Builders	:	Batservice Verft, Mandal, Norway. 1968
Length	:	180 feet
Beam	:	30 feet
Displacement	:	835 tons
Machinery	:	B & W Alpha 6 cyl. diesel. 500 hp.
Position	:	01°.44'.90" S 41°.32'.90" E

The Bente Dania was built for the Danish company Riis Shipping of Copenhagen who sold her to Arne Stecher of Copenhagen in 1972. Later she changed owners to Dania Shipping of Copenhagen before being sold to a Moroccan company and renamed Tayysir trading in the Mediterranean. In 1990 she was sold to Trident Trade of St. Vincent and named Bente Dania trading on the East African coast. On 18 August 1992 the vessel sank on a voyage from Mombasa to Brava in Somalia with general cargo. The day after leaving Mombasa the vessel was hit by a freak wave and developed a 15° starboard list. Despite jettisoning some of the cargo and pumping the double bottoms, the list remained. The Master radioed for help saying the ship was listing and taking on water near Kiwayu Island north of Lamu. At two in the morning the crew took to the life rafts and drifted northwards. Sometime during the night the ship sank leaving the bow protruding above the surface which was spotted by a Kenya Navy helicopter. A motor boat succeeded in rescuing the entire crew later that afternoon and returned them to Kiunga. A later search by the helicopter showed no sign of the ship which was presumed to have sunk about six miles south of the Kenya/ Somalia border. The crew were later flown back to Mombasa in the same helicopter.

Calicut

Builders	:	Hall Russell & Co. Aberdeen, Scotland. 1910
Length	:	134 feet
Beam	:	23 feet
Displacement	:	273 tons
Machinery	:	Single triple expansion. 65 nhp
Position	:	04°.04'.27" S 39°.41'.99" E

The Calicut was the former Admiralty trawler Coalaxe, later renamed Seis and after service in the First World War as a mine-sweeper, was sold to A.M. Jevanjee and sailed to Mombasa to be used as a coastal trader. The vessel was laid up in Mombasa for five years having proved a commercial failure due in part to the large bunker capacity that left little space for cargo. In 1927 she was sold to N. Dosajee in Bombay and prepared for a delivery voyage. While leaving the old port on the afternoon of 21 April 1928, the ship grounded

on Leven Reef and a signal from the port enquired if the Master wished to abandon ship. Having received an affirmative, the tugs Mvita and Nguvu were sent to help, but the running sea and nightfall made any rescue attempt impossible. In the early hours of the next morning when the sea had moderated, the thirty-nine crew took to the boats and landed on Nyali beach. A salvage attempt by the Nguvu was called off when it was apparent that if the ship refloated, she would most likely have sunk. An enquiry at Mombasa showed the vessel had been surveyed and pronounced fit for the voyage but was beset with legal difficulties. As the enquiry had not been gazetted according to a government ordinance, it was considered invalid and later reported that, *'There will be no need to publish the findings at all, since the evidence clears those concerned of any attempt to scuttle the ship'*. The wreck was abandoned and broke up and today the boiler and engine can be seen on the reef at low water.

Dania

Builders	:	Hatlo Verksted, Ulsteinvik, Norway. 1965
Length	:	248 feet
Beam	:	36 feet
Displacement	:	1,215 tons
Machinery	:	M.A.K. 8 cyl. diesel. 1,400 hp
Position	:	04°.01' S 39°.43' E

The Dania was built for the Dutch company Nieuwe Kustvaart Maats and traded in European waters for some years before being sold to a Norwegian company and renamed Kviksholm in 1976. Six years later the ship changed hands and sailed to Mauritius and was renamed Rodriguez. In 1993 she was sold and the name reverted to Dania and six years later the decks were converted for livestock carriage, trading between Mozambique, South Africa and Mauritius. Later that year she was chartered by a Mombasa shipping company but with a decline in the cattle trading industry, was laid up pending sale to India for scrap. A local scuba diving company, Buccaneer Diving, purchased the vessel to use as an artificial reef and dive site to the north of Mombasa. Weeks of preparation followed while fuel and oil were pumped out, and the ship stripped of fixtures and fittings, prior to its inspection and approval by Kenya Wildlife Services. Finally when the ship had been cleaned, holes were cut throughout the ship to ensure a safe passage for divers entering the wreck and on 27 October 2002 the ship was towed out and anchored fifty yards outside the reef at Bamburi Beach. After the final openings were cut in the hull, water was pumped

into the ship to control the sinking and two hours later she settled upright in ninety feet to become a new dive site on the coast.

Derna

Builders	:	Cochrane & Sons, Selby, Yorkshire, England. 1907
Length	:	120 feet
Beam	:	21 feet
Displacement	:	236 tons
Machinery	:	Single triple expansion. 70 nhp
Position	:	04°.04' S 39°.38'.50" E

The Derna arrived in Dar es Salaam in 1948 having been purchased by East African Fisheries for a trawling venture along the coast. A year later the vessel was sold, the venture having proved a costly failure with damage to nets and fishing gear. The new owners based in Mombasa converted the vessel to carry cargo and the Derna took on a new role as a coaster running between Mombasa and ports in Tanganyika. On 21 July 1954 the ship grounded on Niule Reef outside Tanga while entering the port with a cargo of 400 drums of petrol. A week later the cargo had been recovered by floating the drums ashore and the ship abandoned with a flooded engine room. A salvage team headed by Tony Bentley-Buckle from Southern Line, Mombasa arrived having signed a Lloyds Open Form on a '*no cure, no pay*' basis, and set about refloating the vessel two hundred yards from the sea at low water. After patching the leaks and pumping, the vessel was nearly afloat on the high tide. Using two heavy anchors as ground tackle and wires from the salvage vessel Southern Cross, wrapped around the Derna's superstructure she was slowly hauled off the reef. On 27 August the ship refloated and was towed via Tanga to Mombasa. Two weeks later while anchored at Mtongwe, the Derna sank in unexplained circumstances, leaving the funnel and mast tops above the surface. The age of the vessel and extent of repairs required after the grounding meant further salvage operations were abandoned and the ship left where it lay. Over the years the mast collapsed and the hull settled into the mud leaving the funnel top just below the surface. For years this served as a reference point for divers. In 1974 the wreck was rediscovered by the author with only the upper deck and remains of the superstructure visible above the seabed. The galley on the after deck was inhabited by a large grouper which appeared out of the gloom to watch the occasional visitors with interest. Correspondence with the previous owners regarding the stranding and subsequent loss were interesting but inconclusive. The ship became a regular dive site for a number of years, but has since slipped back into obscurity. Launched as the Dewsland for W. Jenkins in November 1907 she was based at Milford for nearly twenty years before being sold and based at Fleetwood. During the Second World War she moved to Hull and was renamed Derna in 1945 before leaving for East Africa.

Fish Eagle

Builders	:	J.G. Hitzler, Germany. 1967
Length	:	174 feet
Beam	:	36 feet
Displacement	:	812 tons
Machinery	:	Twin MWM 16 cyl. diesel . hp
Position	:	03. 74' S 39°. 85' E

Fish Eagle was built as the offshore supply vessel Fangturm for the German company OSA and served in the North Sea. In 1984 the ship was bought by Eagle Tugs renamed Fish

23

Eagle and based in Mombasa. During the next thirty years, operated by Comarco, Fish Eagle served in in a variety of roles including diving support vessel, offshore supply vessel, tug and accommodation ship in many African countries as well as Malaysia, Indonesia, Singapore and Thailand. As the vessel was nearing the end of its useful life it was decided to sink it as an artificial reef and dive site. Months of preparation and cleaning of the vessel and negotiations with Kenya Wildlife Service resulted in an agreement to add the vessel to a growing number of specially sunk vessels off the Kenya coast. On the evening of 28 December 2014, Fish Eagle began its final voyage to a pre planned position for its sinking towed by two Comarco tugs. The following morning the vessel was on site and the flooding commenced and two hours later Fish Eagle lay upright on the seabed in ninety feet, the latest dive site on the coast.

Funguo

Builders	:	Donghae Shipbuilding Co., Ulsan, Korea. 1980
Length	:	146 feet
Beam	:	26 feet
Displacement	:	385 tons
Machinery	:	Makita 6 cyl. diesel. 750 hp
Position	:	04°.19' E 39°.35' S

The Funguo was a tuna trawler built for Kenya Fishing Industries arriving in Mombasa in March 1980. For the next seventeen years the vessel fished off the coast until June 1997 when she grounded on the reef close to Shelly Beach, a mile south of Mombasa. A salvage operation by Southern Engineering Ltd. refloated the ship after which she was laid up. In 2001 the vessel was purchased by the local diving consortium Dive the Crab to be sunk as an artificial reef and dive site off Diani beach south of Mombasa. Preparations prior to sinking included liaison with the Kenya Wildlife Services in whose marine park the ship would be sunk, and the complete removal of all fuel, oil, wood and insulation, together with doors and hatches. Finally at midday on 21 February 2002 the trawler arrived on site off Diani reef towed by the Comarco tug Privateer and seven hours later disappeared from view to sit upright on the seabed as one of the latest wrecks on the Kenya coast and attractions for the local dive shops.

Globe Star

Builders	:	Short Brothers, Sunderland, England. 1952
Length	:	451 feet
Beam	:	57 feet
Displacement	:	11,100 tons
Machinery	:	Doxford 4 cyl, diesel. 3,000 hp.
Position	:	04°.04'.48" S 39°.42'.30" E

The Globe Star became one of the most notorious wrecks off Mombasa following the death of five salvage crew in November 1973. She was launched as the Burutu Palm, for the Palm Line of Liverpool, and the first ship built specifically for the company trading to and from West Africa, carrying general cargo and 1,100 tons of bulk palm oil in deep tanks aft of the bridge. The ports of call were Dakar for bunkers, and Freetown, where the ship took on Kroo boys to handle the cargo. Then on to Takoradi, Lagos, Apapa, Accra, Victoria, and up the creeks to Sapele, Warri, Port Harcourt and Calabar where a quite unconventional method of navigation was used to negotiate the tight turns. At low revolutions the African pilot pointed the bow into the bank, which had many 'V' indentations, and the stern swung round before backing off and heading up river. After fifteen years service the bell was removed and she was transferred to Astrocid Naviera of Piraeus and renamed Tyhi. While on a voyage from Shanghai to Bangladesh on 27 July 1970 she grounded within the port but refloated the same day. Three years later the ship was sold to Globe Navigation of Singapore and renamed Globe Star. Approaching Mombasa for water on a voyage from Iskenderun to Karachi with 10,000 tons of malt wheat, she ran aground on Leven Reef at 05.30 on the morning of 27 April 1973. A Lloyds Open Form was signed with the Port Authority and an attempt by their tugs to free the ship the following afternoon failed and the task was abandoned. A new salvage operation was mounted by Murri International in conjunction with Southern Engineering and the Port

Taking to the water for the first time

Abandoned and off limits to all

Authority to offload the wheat using suction pumps. The removal of cargo into the landing craft Citadel and Rampart continued for some time until the engine room flooded and operations ceased while repairs were made to the pipe tunnel. This was a covered

Rotting wheat in No. 4 hold

Damage to the hull in No. 3 hold

passageway that ran forward from the engine room through No. 3 hold containing electrical wiring, ballast and fire lines. The engine room was pumped dry and after the generators had been overhauled, the operation continued. Heavy seas split the hull in No. 3 hold, and salvage was abandoned in June when the engine room flooded for a second time. The stranding was attributed to a navigation error in that the ship approached too close to the harbour entrance prior to picking up a pilot and having been advised to return to the anchorage, turned to starboard instead of port and ran aground. In November there was a tragic accident when two divers and three surface personnel died in No. 3 hold during a second salvage attempt to seal the pipe tunnel. The accident was attributed to toxic gas on the surface of the water from the rotting wheat. The divers having come to the surface removed their mouth pieces and while giving instructions to the support crew on

The bow and after end, 1977

Cutting the aft end, 1978

Demolition of the engine room

the t'ween deck inhaled the fumes and drowned. Three support crew then went to their aid, who in turn died. The ship was declared off limits to all and the forward section gradually began to break up. In December 1975 the author carried out a toxic gas check on board the vessel on behalf of Murri International in preparation for the possible salvage of the after end that was still intact. The survey showed large quantities of carbon monoxide and hydrogen sulphide in various spaces, and in particular petroleum gases venting from a swan neck ventilator on deck. This was caused by fermenting wheat in No. 4 hold now open to the elements, boiling the fuel oil in the double bottom. The attempt was abandoned and the ship left to break up. In late 1978 Divecon were awarded the contract to demolish the wreck. The coaster Five Oceans was brought alongside and in the next few weeks the wreck was cut down to the low water mark. What was left was flattened with explosives leaving only the engine block known locally as the 'Four Apostles'. In 1984 the four ton spare propeller tail shaft was recovered by the author after cutting open the shaft tunnel using oxy thermic Kerry cable. Today the remains are a popular dive site, with extensive fish life amongst the large sections of broken steel on the seabed.

The 'Four Apostles'

Harrier

Builders	:	Kabushiki Kaisha Ishii, Futtsu Chiba, Japan. 1977
Length	:	47 feet
Beam	:	13 feet
Displacement	:	28 tons
Machinery	:	Hanshin 6 cyl. diesel. 320 hp
Position	:	Unknown

The Harrier was the former harbour tug Jacaranda brought to Mombasa in 1977 by the Japanese company Sumitomo Ltd. for the construction of the new Nyali Bridge. On the completion of the bridge, the tug was purchased by Divecon in October 1978 and renamed Harrier. She proved to be an extremely versatile vessel performing a variety of small towing and salvage jobs including refloating the fishing trawler Kivuna in 1980. Eight years later on the evening of 5 August, the tug departed Mombasa with supplies for a Pemba contract, and was supposed to make a radio call twelve hours later. The following morning when no response was received from the vessel, a large air to sea search of the coast and Pemba Channel commenced. No sign of wreckage or crew was ever found and the search was eventually called off. An enquiry attributed the loss to the tug capsizing in inclement weather.

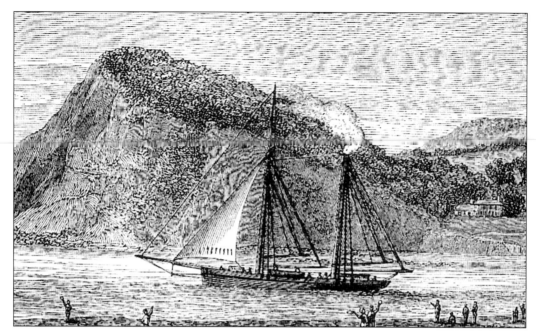

Highland Lassie

Builders	:	Lobnitz, Colbourne & Co., Renfrew, Scotland. 1865
Length	:	66 feet
Beam	:	16 feet
Displacement	:	80 tons
Machinery	:	Single compound. 15 nhp
Position	:	04°.02'.44" S 39°.40'.48" E

In 1873 the British government despatched the politician Sir Bartle Frere to Zanzibar to negotiate the closure of the slave market with the ruler, Sultan Bargash bin Said. He was unsuccessful and the treaty was concluded by Sir John Kirk, the British Consul after a threat to blockade the island. Two years later an area at Kisauni on the mainland north of Mombasa Island was set aside for freed slaves, with a church built and staffed by missionaries from the Church Missionary Society in London. Since Zanzibar was the main trading and religious centre on the East African coast, the C.M.S. required a vessel to maintain communication between the two places. A wooden schooner was presented to the Society in 1876 by the society's secretary, the Rev. Henry Wright. She had been launched as the Maighdeann na Herradh and fitted with an auxiliary steam engine using the hollow steel after mast as the funnel. After weeks of preparation the ship left Teignmouth for East Africa on 11 March 1876 under the command of Lieutenant Shergold Smith. The voyage was not without incident, when off the Spanish coast they lost part of the bowsprit and on arrival in Malta the forepeak deck required caulking. They eventually arrived in Zanzibar and carried the first passengers, mail and stores between the island and the mission. Mr R. J. Canham was appointed its first Master but failed to keep her clean and tidy and the Rev. E.A. Praeger wrote, '*Everything on board is in a fearfully dirty and deplorable condition*'. He later reported seeing the ship being careened for cleaning on the seashore at Mombasa in September 1879. After a year in service it was apparent the schooner was unsuitable for the hundred and fifty mile trip between Zanzibar and Mombasa, especially during the monsoons. By the end of 1879 a decision was made to replace the Lassie with a larger vessel. Although not mentioned officially, story has it the ship was sunk in Tudor Creek not far from the mission, when the mate, Antonio Martini dropped an iron bucket that holed the hull. He subsequently left the employment of the C.M.S., changed his name to James Martin and became a caravan leader for the explorer Joseph Thompson. In 1881 a collection was started for the new vessel to be named Henry Wright after the secretary who had drowned the previous year. The new ship built by Green & Co. on the River Thames was delivered in 1883, and shortly after sailed for East Africa. The Admiralty chart for Mombasa shows a wreck believed to be the Highland Lassie situated in the creek not far from the present Emmanuel church.

H.M.S. Hildasay

Builders	:	Cook, Welton & Gemmel, Beverley, England. 1941
Length	:	164 feet
Beam	:	27 feet
Displacement	:	452 tons
Machinery	:	Single triple expansion. 850 ihp
Armament	:	1 x 12 pdr. gun. 3 x 20 mm anti aircraft guns
Position	:	04°.13' S 39°.37' E

H.M.S. Hildasay was commissioned on 29 September 1941 with the Penant No. T173, one of a number of Isles Class armed trawlers ordered in 1940, that became the maids of all work for the Royal Navy during the Second World War. In January 1942 she was fitted with ASDIC for anti-submarine work together with thirty depth charges and mine sweeping gear. After five months service in home waters the ship served as a convoy escort to Cape Town and West Africa. From May 1942 she was based in the Indian Ocean spending a considerable period based at Diego Suarez in Madagascar. In July 1943 she had a refit at Mombasa and spent some time in the Seychelles. By March 1945 the

Three months later

Hildasay was based at Mombasa together with a sister ship H.M.S. Shapinsay. On 21 June, Shapinsay was returning to Mombasa from Tanga with a lighter laden with cases of petrol. Twenty miles south of Mombasa the ship radioed for assistance in heavy weather and Hildasay was despatched to take the tow. After handing over the line, Shapinsay headed for Mombasa leaving the Hildasay to follow. Shortly afterwards the barge capsized and the tow line wrapped itself around the propeller. Unable to manoeuvre, the ship drifted ashore and grounded on the reef at Tiwi, some ten miles south of Mombasa. Within hours the ship flooded when the hull was damaged. Six days later a salvage party had patched the holes

Six months later

A year later

and placed pumps aboard but their efforts were unsuccessful. The wreck was stripped of all useful fittings and abandoned as a total loss on 9 July. Numerous four gallon tins of petrol drifted ashore and were put to good use at a time when petrol was still rationed. In some ways it was reminiscent of the S.S. Politician that became famous as the '*Whisky Galore*' wreck in Scotland. A month after the ship was abandoned, two young boys, Francis and Robert Foster came to stay with their uncle some two miles from the wreck. The wreck intrigued them and they were soon on board collecting souvenirs. As the weeks went past, the ship gradually broke apart in the pounding surf until one afternoon the wooden bridge structure drifted ashore. With the help of oil drums, it was floated along the coast and mounted in their garden. Later it was incorporated into the house as a bedroom, where it can still be seen today complete with some of the original electrical fittings. A year after the stranding the wreck had broken up, leaving only the boiler, engine and stern visible. Today only the boiler is occasionally visible at low tide, the remainder lies broken up, hardly recognisable under the coral growth.

The wheelhouse today

Impala

Builders	:	Böhme Werft, Cuxhaven, Germany. 1952
Length	:	75 feet
Beam	:	20 feet
Displacement	:	81 tons
Machinery	:	Motorenfabrik Damstadt, 5 cyl. diesel. 150 hp
Position	:	04°.16' S 39°.37' E

The Impala was the former KW 9, a steel framed wooden planked patrol boat used by the German Navy and in 1963, together with three others of the class presented to the newly formed Tanzanian Navy. The boat was renamed Uhuru (Freedom) and in 1973 sold out of service, renamed Impala and used as a coastal trader running between Mombasa, Tanga and Dar es Salaam. On 27 April 1984 the boat left Dar es Salaam for Mombasa with a general cargo that included tea and Makonde wood carvings. While on passage along the Kenya coast, the engine room developed a leak and the water rose rapidly. Unable to stem the flow, the crew abandoned the engine room and within a matter of minutes the engine seized. As the boat drifted towards the reef the crew signalled to a passing coaster which was unable to help. Cargo was thrown overboard in an attempt to lighten the vessel but it was eventually driven on to the reef and became a total loss. The crew made their way to safety through the surf .

Kota Menang

Builders	:	Noordseewerke, Emden, Germany. 1956
Length	:	503 feet
Beam	:	62 feet
Displacement	:	13,465 tons
Machinery	:	M.A.N. 7 cyl. diesel. 6,300 hp.
Position	:	04°.03'.09" S 39°.43'.34" E

The Kota Menang like the Globe Star was another prominent wreck visible on the reef for many years after she ran aground. The ship was the former Claere Hugo Stinnes named after Clare Wagenknecht, wife of Hugo Stinnes, who died in 1924. Built for the Stinnes

Discharging cargo into the landing craft Rampart

37

Discharging water from No. 2 hold

Loading cargo into a skip

Line of Hamburg with a strengthened hull for navigation in ice she was the subject of an article in the publication *'The Motor Ship'* in November 1956. Eight years later she was sold and renamed Cimbria and on 1 December 1971 sold to Pacific International Lines of Singapore who renamed her Kota Menang. On the morning of Sunday 10 August 1975 on a voyage from the Far East to the Red Sea via East Africa, the vessel grounded on the reef opposite Nyali Beach Hotel, much to the surprise of some guests who were having breakfast. The Port Authority mobilised two tugs to secure the vessel but were unable to prevent the ship swinging starboard side onto the reef. Murri International were awarded the salvage contract and operations commenced immediately using two landing craft, the Citadel and Rampart to discharge the general cargo. Eight days later due to the exposed position on the edge of the reef, the ship hogged and broke her back across No. 3 hold.

Recovering water logged cargo from No. 2 hold

Scrap railway line was purchased from Kenya Railways and welded across the break in the hull to hold the vessel together. In the meantime No. 2 hold also flooded, and the cargo including cases of padlocks, T shirts, blue machine dye, tyres and canned food was removed down to the low water level. The latter consisting of corned mutton, peas and beans turned the water black and produced an indescribable smell. Prior to diving operations the water was analysed and found despite the colour and smell, to be safe to swim in. To improve the visibility a number of six-inch electric pumps were mounted in the t'ween deck to change the water. One noticeable side effect was a strange black fungus that grew on deck where the water discharged over the side. The author and a team of divers began the unpleasant task of removing the remainder of the cargo in zero visibility. Cargo removal from holds 1, 4 and 5 continued for some weeks until the engine room flooded and the generators stopped. The machinery space was sealed and the generators

Abandoned to the elements, 1976

Breaking up 1982

Two years later

The aft end, 1984

overhauled and the operation continued. Over four hundred tons of fuel oil were removed before the ship was abandoned in December 1975 after two attempts to refloat her failed. An enquiry attributed the stranding to steering failure. On 9 September 1976 the ship was declared a total loss and later set on fire to burn the woodwork and prevent debris from floating ashore. The ship's bell was recovered by the author and now hangs outside the Coast Academy in Mombasa. Over the next ten years the wreck broke up with the forward section collapsing first. Today large quantities of flattened broken steel litter the seabed around the main engine block that can still be seen on the edge of the reef.

The engine block today

Lavest

Builders	:	Astilleros Espanoles, Bilbao, Spain. 1974
Length	:	525 feet
Beam	:	75 feet
Displacement	:	20,950 tons
Machinery	:	Sulzer 6 cyl. diesel. 9,900 hp
Position	:	Aground : 04°.04'.26" S 39°.43'.02" E
		Sunk : 03°.11'.21" S 40°.29'.80" E

The Lavest was built as the Aegis Heroic for the Greek company Andromache Shipping. Eleven years later the ship changed hands and was renamed Alpha Heroic and after two further sales and name changes became the Lavest in 1992. The following year the Cypriot registered bulk carrier was on a voyage from Maputo in Mozambique to Turkey with 17,000 tons of steam coal. On the morning of 18 April the vessel ran aground on Leven Reef close to the wreck of the Kota Menang, while on the approach to Mombasa to take on water. An hour later three port tugs arrived but were unable to help, having insufficient horsepower to pull the vessel clear. That evening on the high water the ship endeavored unsuccessfully to free itself. Over the next two days further attempts also failed and the Master eventually signed a Lloyds Open Form with Smit Tak on the 23rd. The following evening the tug Steve-B connected a towline and commenced pulling. Worsening weather broke the line twice and fouled one propeller. A second tug, Fast Fox owned by Cory Towage anchored in Mombasa, was also chartered and took on the tow. In the meantime a sounding survey in the bow showed water in the forepeak and forward ballast tanks. An attempt to regain buoyancy using compressed air was unsuccessful and the bows remained stuck fast. With the help of the Steve-B, the ship refloated on the 25th but was heavily trimmed by the bows. The strong northerly current swept the casualty and tugs up the coast and by midday they were twenty miles north of Mombasa. During the course of the day the bows sank deeper, such that by that evening the water had reached halfway along No. 2 hatch. Twenty-four hours later the bow had sunk even further and with the weather worsening, the crew were evacuated on to the Steve-B. The tow was disconnected that evening when the propeller appeared above the surface. Some hours later the stern rose into the air and the vessel sank in 1,000 feet of water, twenty miles east of Malindi. The stranding was attributed to poor navigation during the approach to Mombasa.

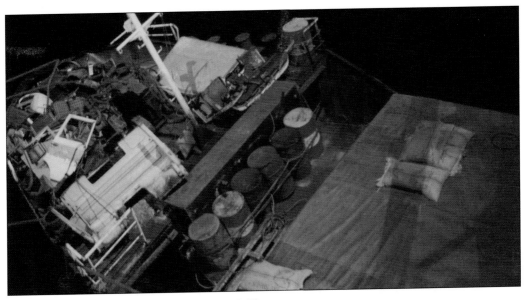

Mirage

Builders	:	De Groot van Slikkerveer, Vliet, Holland. 1960
Length	:	158 feet
Beam	:	25 feet
Displacement	:	480 tons
Machinery	:	Bolens 6 cyl. diesel. 390 hp.
Position	:	04°.03'.20" S 39°.38'.20" E

The Mirage was the former Bonsella trading with new owners following a rebuild in September 1997 after capsizing at Tanga. On 27 June 1998 the ship had completed loading general cargo for Somalia at Berth No. 4 in Kilindini when she slowly listed to port, and came to rest with the superstructure leaning on the quay wall at an angle of thirty-five degrees. On the upper accommodation deck was a cargo of thirty-five tons of chlorine in drums that commenced leaking producing a toxic gas that hampered operations while on the fo'csle was a large collection of car and truck parts. As attempts were made to remove some of the deck cargo, the stern began to settle as water gradually filled the engine room through an open water-tight door on the after deck. Within twenty minutes the ship sank leaving the masts and aerial protruding above the surface. The next few days were spent gathering the loose cargo that floated to the surface. The Merchant Shipping Superintendent examined the relevant bills of lading and concluded the vessel had been overloaded by some forty-five tons, thirty-five of which had been loaded above the deck line. The salvage contract was awarded to Divecon International who commenced work on 17 July removing the cargo that included tons of vehicle spares. By 12 August the cargo had been cleared and a 150 ton steel pontoon and barge prepared for the salvage operation. The pontoon was secured in the cargo hold to obtain the necessary lift with the barge alongside for stability. The bows surfaced on the 15th and the vessel was redelivered afloat to the owners on 22 September. The ship was rebuilt a second time and traded as the Siyama. Twenty years later and the ship has probably been scrapped.

Mtongwe

Builders	:	African Marine and General Engineering Co. Mombasa. 1970
Length	:	50 feet
Beam	:	14 feet
Displacement	:	10 tons
Machinery	:	Gardener 5 LW 78 bhp diesel.
Position	:	04°.03'.90" S 39°.38'50" E

The Mtongwe was a steel launch built to carry 150 passengers across Kilindini Harbour, Mombasa. On the morning of 29 April 1994 the launch was crowded with an estimated 370 people and set off from Mtongwe jetty, on the south side of the harbour for the Mombasa jetty. Within minutes of leaving, the vessel veered and listed due to an apparent steering failure. The passengers moved towards the opposite side and the vessel righted itself and quickly rolled the opposite way and sank leaving around seventy people struggling for their lives. The remainder were trapped and drowned inside the cabin. Rescue operations were quickly mounted by divers of the Kenya Navy and Divecon International but torrential rain made the task more difficult, while hundreds of curious bystanders and relatives stood and watched. Over the next three days over one hundred bodies were recovered, while efforts were under way to mobilise a crane and barge to lift the sunken launch. Finally on 4 May the vessel was brought to the surface and the remaining bodies recovered. An enquiry put the final death toll at 276 and the apparent cause of the accident to overloading affecting the vessel's stability.

Nairobi

Builders	:	Cook, Welton & Gemmel, Beverley, England. 1918
Length	:	125 feet
Beam	:	23 feet
Displacement	:	290 tons
Machinery	:	Single triple expansion. 480 ihp
Position	:	03°.12'.40" S 40°.08' E

The Nairobi was one of a large number of Castle Class minesweeping trawlers used by the Admiralty during the First World War. Launched as the John Gauntlett with the Pennant No. FY3779, she was sold to A.M. Jevanjee of Bombay on 11 May 1920 and renamed Nairobi. Together with a sister ship Calicut, they were brought to East Africa but were found to be unsuitable as coastal cargo vessels due in part to the large coal bunker capacity that left little space for cargo. Correspondence in Lloyds Register of Shipping, London shows the Lloyds Agents in Mombasa had written to the owners about the tail shaft survey that was due in March 1922, but since the vessel was laid up it was never completed. On 2 December 1922 the vessel ran aground on Pillar Reef at Malindi and abandoned five days later under protest from Lloyds in London. Heavy seas pounded the vessel on the reef and a week later was listing 45 degrees with the engine room flooded, the bilge keels damaged and the stern tube fractured. The East African Standard reported '*the ship was in a bad way with little hope of refloating. With the freshening monsoon the chances are the Nairobi will find a permanent home on Malindi Reef*'. Four days later she was declared a total loss, the stern had sunk leaving the bows wedged in the coral above the surface. Some items were recovered before a tender was issued for the salvage but there were no takers, and by 5 March further advertisements for the sale of the wreck produced no interest in what was now a pile of scrap. The boiler can still be seen today on the reef at low tide.

Ngamia

Builders	:	James Lamont, Scotland. 1969
Length	:	115 feet
Beam	:	30 feet
Displacement	:	298 tons
Machinery	:	Twin Crossley 6 cyl. diesel. 2,500 hp.
Position	:	04°.03'.80" S 39°.39'.10" E

The Ndovu and Ngamia were a pair of general purpose berthing and fire fighting tugs built for the East African Railways and Harbours and based at Mombasa. After twenty years service Ngamia was withdrawn in 1980 and laid up alongside the dockyard jetty where she sank the following year. Divecon were awarded the salvage contract and the tug refloated using two shore based and one floating crane. The hulk was handed over to the Kenya Navy for use as a target and sunk by an Israeli built Gabriel missile fired from one of the patrol boats.

Rafaela

Builders	:	Chantiers Navals de la Ciotat, La Ciotat, France. 1959
Length	:	515 feet
Beam	:	65 feet
Displacement	:	9,128 tons
Machinery	:	Sulzer 10 cyl. diesel. 13,450 hp
Position	:	04°.04'.35" S 39°.39'.65" E

The ship was launched as the Martinquais, one of four sister ships for the French company Messageries Maritimes. In March 1967 the ship developed engine trouble and returned to Marseilles for repair and in April 1970 collided with the Polish vessel Galczinski, requiring dry docking at Antwerp. Eight years later she was bought by the Mediterranean Shipping Company and named Rafaela after the owner's wife. In November 1981 the vessel docked at Mombasa on a voyage from Antwerp to Maputo with a cargo of cars, chemicals, containers and textiles. On the 19th a major fire broke out in No. 4 and 5 holds and firemen from the port, Mombasa Fire Brigade and the Kenya Navy battled the blaze while the two adjacent ships were moved to other berths. The following evening the ship was towed to Port Reitz while teams aboard the harbour tugs Ndovu, Nyangumi and Tewa fought the fire. Despite their efforts the flames spread to the accommodation and bridge. The fire also spread below deck and the ship's side glowed red. Water directed on to this area turned to steam. Fire fighting continued throughout the night and in the early hours of the 21st, portholes were broken for water to be directed inside the accommodation. Later that day holes were cut in the deck and the fire extinguished in No. 4 hold. The accommodation burnt out and the fire in No. 5 was brought under control that evening. An estimated six hundred tons of cargo and twenty-six cars had been destroyed in the blaze. The following day a floating crane discharged the containers and shortly after the ship was declared a total loss and sold to local ship breakers. The hull was cut down and berthed alongside Southern Engineering jetty at Mbaraki Creek, where while awaiting final demolition the remainder of the hull sank in 1984.

Rafiki and Salama

Builders	:	Böhme Werft, Cuxhaven, Germany. 1952
Length	:	75 feet
Beam	:	20 feet
Displacement	:	81 tons
Machinery	:	Demag 5 cyl. diesel. 150 hp
Position	:	04°.05'.20" S 39°.40' E

The Rafiki ex KW 4, like its sister ship Impala was one of four ex German wooden patrol boats presented to the Tanzanian Government shortly after independence in 1963. After a period in service all four vessels were sold to local ship owners and the Rafiki was registered in Mombasa and traded along the coast for many years. On 26 May 1981 on a voyage from Zanzibar to Mombasa, the boat grounded on the reef near Shelley Beach on the south side of the entrance to Kilindini. The hull quickly broke open and became a total loss. The Demag engine was later recovered as spares for another vessel.

The Salama was another sister vessel that sank in Mombasa old port close to the jetty in the early 1970s. The hull eventually broke up and the remains settled into the mud.

Ramora Bay

Builders	:	G. Renck, Hamburg. 1950
Length	:	135 feet
Beam	:	25 feet
Displacement	:	415 tons
Machinery	:	Callesen 6 cyl. diesel. 480 hp
Position	:	01°.70' S 41°.80' E

The Ramora Bay was the former Welle built for a private owner Captain Rahmstorf, and engined with a 250 hp Deutz diesel. Sixteen years later he sold her to a Norwegian who re-engined her with a 425 hp Aabenraa unit and renamed it Sortun. Nine years later she was sold and renamed Oddtun and in 1990 sold and renamed Ramora Bay having been re-engined for a third time. In June 1994 the ship loaded a cargo of containers at Mombasa reportedly containing beer and beverages destined for Mogadishu, and sank some distance north of Lamu. All but one crew member returned to Mombasa with a tale of inclement weather and the vessel listing. The latter was possibly due to a movement of cargo within the containers that resulted in a loss of stability.

Said Mohamed

Builders	:	
Length	:	70 feet
Beam	:	20 feet
Displacement	:	125 tons
Machinery	:	
Position	:	04°.30'.20" S 39°.40'.80" E

The Said Mohamed was a Somali coaster outbound from the old port of Mombasa on the morning of 17 May 1993 when she slowly rolled over and floated upside down opposite Fort Jesus with the loss of four lives. The vessel had loaded eighty-five tons of general cargo including mattresses, soap powder, soda ash, tea and tents for Mogadishu. Three dhows immediately sailed across to help and shortly afterwards boats from the Kenya Navy and Port Authority arrived to assist. Some survivors were picked up while others struggled ashore. An enquiry found the vessel to be overloaded and top heavy and carrying eighteen crew and sixty-two passengers. The hulk was subsequently beached and abandoned in the upper reaches of Tudor Creek.

Saint Michael

Builders	:	African Marine & General Engineering Co., Mombasa. 1969
Length	:	139 feet
Beam	:	34 feet
Displacement	:	50 tons
Machinery	:	Twin Gardner diesels, Voith Schneider propellers. 1,140 hp
Position	:	04°.04'.68" S 39°.39'.45" E

The motorised ferry across the harbour entrance at Kilindini is the only means of access to the coast south of Mombasa. In the early days the ferry consisted of little more than a pontoon with ramps propelled by two wooden motor boats. As traffic increased the pontoon was replaced by the newly built self propelled ferry Saint Christopher which in turn was replaced by the Saint Michael in 1969. The ferry continued in service until 1975 when it too was superseded by the larger Safina. The Saint Michael was modified to become a passenger ferry with the removal of the vehicle ramps and used across the harbour until laid up in 1993. Three years later while moored close to the Divecon International premises at Likoni the hull sank on 3 October 1996. Divecon were tasked with the salvage and using a 150 ton pontoon attached to the deck filled with compressed air, the vessel surfaced and was later beached and scrapped.

Santo Antonio de Tanna

Built	:	Basein, near Bombay. 1680
Length	:	120 feet
Beam	:	25 feet
Displacement	:	500 tons
Armament	:	42 muzzle loading cannons
Position	:	04°.03'.70" S 39°.40'.75" E

The Portuguese first came to East Africa in 1498 but it was not until 1593 that they established a base at Mombasa with the construction of a large fort known as '*Jesus of Mombasa*'. Within a few years they gained control of the lucrative spice trade from the Far East and in due course the Omani Arabs set about dislodging them from their monopoly. In March 1696 the Arabs laid siege to the fort but it was not until Christmas Day that a relief force consisting of two frigates and two galliots with seven hundred men, arrived from the Portuguese colony of Goa on India's west coast. The flagship was the Santa Antonio de Tanna under the command of General Luis de Mello Sampiao. They did little to aid the situation and sailed south to Mozambique. Having received news that the fort was still under siege some months later, they arrived back on 15 September 1697. The Santa Antonio was anchored close to the fort and subjected to a withering fire from the Arab batteries ashore while supplies were landed under cover of darkness. A month later on 20 October an anchor rope parted and the ship grounded on the mainland opposite the fort. With the incoming tide the ship refloated, but with a damaged rudder was unable to manoeuvre and grounded again near the fort. The ship was fired on again until the enemy battery was quickly eliminated by a raiding party from the fort. The ship was then towed along the rocky foreshore to a position in front of the fort where the inmates could recover the remaining stores. As late as December, gunpowder was still being recovered from the ship. A year later the fort was overrun and Portuguese rule in East Africa came to an end. The ship is believed to have been scuttled by the Arabs about the same time. The wreck was rediscovered in 1970 by scuba divers and artifacts recovered bore a similarity to those excavated within the fort. In 1977 the first of three major excavations took place uncovering fifteen metres of the hull. Today some of the artifacts recovered from the wreck are on display in the fort while others remain in long term preservation.

Shakwe

Builders	:	African Marine & General Engineering Co. Mombasa. 1969
Length	:	72 feet
Beam	:	20 feet
Displacement	:	122 tons
Machinery	:	Kelvin 8 cyl. diesel. 320 hp
Position	:	03°.24'.40" S 39°.58'.84" E

The Shakwe was a stern trawler owned by the Kenya Ministry of Tourism and Wildlife, Fisheries Department and operated along the East African coast on research projects for some years. On 26 April 1986 the vessel was returning to Mombasa from Malindi in heavy weather with some three tons of prawns and eight tons of fish, when water began to fill the after peak and steering compartment. The bilge pump failed to keep up with the ingress of water and the ship began to settle by the stern with a starboard list. The Master decided to beach the vessel that evening on the reef near the entrance to Mida Creek close to Watamu. As the vessel grounded the main engine and generator failed. At first light the crew took to the liferafts and abandoned ship, and shortly after the trawler slid off the reef into thirty feet of water. The wreck was located a day later after a life raft surfaced still attached to the ship. An enquiry attributed the loss to water ingress into the after peak due to corrosion on the after deck. Today it is a regular dive site for the Watamu based diveshops.

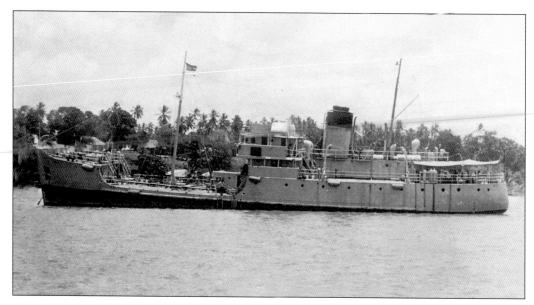

R.F.A. Spapool

Builders	:	Charles Hill & Co. Bristol, England. 1946
Length	:	172 feet
Beam	:	21 feet
Displacement	:	672 tons
Machinery	:	Single triple expansion. 850 ihp
Position	:	04°.04'.35" S 39°.39'.65" E

The Spapool was one of the Spa Class water replenishment tankers built for the Royal Fleet Auxiliary after the Second World War and delivered in June 1946. After home service the ship was based in Mombasa until 1956 when she was transferred to Malta. Nine years later the ship sailed to Singapore and in 1967 returned to Mombasa, having been

Raising the bows and preparing to rotate the ship

Upright with lift bags in place around the aft end

commissioned into the Royal Navy for the delivery voyage. The ship took part in the Beira Patrol in the late 1960s supplying water to the ships on station in the Madagascar Channel. By the mid 1970s she was no longer required and sold to local interests in July 1976. Later that year Divecon chartered her as the support vessel for the salvage of the tanker Southern Pioneer sunk at Tanga. When the boiler was eventually condemned, the ship was towed round the harbour as an oil fuel bunker barge. In the early 1980s the ship was laid up alongside Southern Engineering jetty at Mombasa, when over the 1983 Christmas period, she sank and lay on her port side. The author was tasked with the salvage operation. Sealing all the deck hatches, fitting air hoses and cutting holes at the lowest extremity of each of the six cargo tanks took two weeks. These were filled with compressed air and

Under tow by the tug Betty

within a day the bows rose to the surface and the ship rolled upright using three ten ton lift bags attached to the bridge wing. The stern was still embedded in the mud, but as there were too many entrances and apertures to make the aft end watertight, it was decided to lift the stern using all the available lift bags. Fifteen bags totalling one hundred and ten tons of lift were secured around the aft end and the stern rose out of the mud. The ship was beached and later cut up for scrap. Two sections of the forward hull were saved and today serve as water tanks for the supply of vessels alongside the jetty.

Sussex

Builders	:	Barclay Curle & Co. Glasgow, Scotland. 1866
Length	:	230 feet
Beam	:	35 feet
Displacement	:	1,341 tons
Position	:	04°.04'.16" S 39°.41'.14" E

The Sussex was an iron hulled three masted fully rigged ship built for George Marshall & Sons of London and used on the Calcutta jute trade. In 1883 the ship was sold to G.G. MacFarlane and the yards on the aft mast were removed converting her to a barque. Dismasted in a gale in the 1880s she was towed into Falmouth for repairs and ten years later sold to R. Barr & Co. After a further sale in the 1890s she passed to Prospero Schiaffino of Camogli, Italy in 1908. Under the command of George Schiaffino, the ship loaded 1,500 tons of coal at Cardiff and set sail for East Africa on 26 December 1908. The morning of 11 April 1909 saw both the Sussex and a British India Line ship approaching Mombasa. The pilot set out for the Sussex but boarded the B.I. ship since it was closer. Schiaffino decided to bring the ship into the old port himself but misjudged the current and tide and was soon in close proximity to Leven Reef. Realising his predicament he signalled the B.I. ship for assistance but was refused with regrets. Both anchors were dropped but dragged in the sand. The Port Officer who had been watching the proceedings put out in a boat to assist but was too late. The ship was four hundred yards off course and grounded on the Nyali shore and slowly swung round in the current until she was almost at right angles to the beach. Members of the Mombasa Club were taking breakfast when the vessel drifted into view and ran aground and the eleven crew were brought ashore later that day. The Lloyds surveyor visited the ship and cabled London advising of a total loss, and The Times of London reported the ship ashore and that she should be sold as soon as possible. The hull was balanced on the edge of the reef with the stern in deep water. Discharging commenced but as the tide receded the ship took on a list and the following day rough seas were sweeping over the deck at high water. The holds flooded on the 19th when the port side was split below the waterline by an eleven foot hole. Attempts to refloat the ship were abandoned. The East African Standard wrote, '*It is a distressful sight to the passer by*'. Lloyds of London had insured the cargo and declared the ship a total loss. On the morning of 20 April under instructions from the Lloyds agents an auction was held in Jubilee Hall in Mombasa and the wreck sold to two Indian businessmen, the hull fetching 3,000 Rupees and the coal 1,900 Rupees. Within a week the foremast and mainmast had broken through the bottom and four ballast tanks were open to the sea. Over the next few weeks, the masts and yards collapsed and the hull broke up. Sixty three years later divers found the remains of the ship. The bow had broken off leaving the anchor windlass upright on the seabed next to the large triangular plate through which the bowsprit passed. Both anchor chains ran backwards into deep water. The hull had collapsed outwards leaving tons of rusted overgrown steel plate lying on the reef. The hollow masts lay in the sand and the aft end with its clipper stern sat upright in thirty feet of water. In 1973 the stern capstan was found by the author protruding from the sand complete with brass builders plate and the hull number 149. Details were passed to Barclay Curle who identified the ship from their records. The builders plate together with a painting and photographs of the wreck are now on loan to the Mombasa Club, and presently hang on the wall of the upstairs verandah overlooking the site.

Tembo

Builders	:	Eriksbergs M/V A/B, Gothenberg, Sweden. 1943
Length	:	381 feet
Beam	:	51 feet
Displacement	:	6,055 tons
Machinery	:	Twin B & W 6 cyl. diesel. 4,100 hp
Position	:	01°.43'.30" S 41°.32'.80" E

The Tembo was the former ice strengthened cargo ship Bullaren, one of four sister ships built for the Norwegian company Rederei Transatlantic of Gothenburg. In 1971 the ship was sold to Poship Navigation of Piraeus and renamed Tembo. Two years later on the evening of 9 August 1973 on a voyage from Bombay to Mombasa with a cargo of 5,700 tons of bulk oil cake, she grounded on a reef opposite the village of Chiamboni on the Kenya - Somali border. A sounding survey showed damage to the starboard wing tanks, rudder and starboard propeller. Later the seas swung the ship through ninety degrees and swept the vessel further onto the reef. A distress call was picked up by the Kenya Navy and the Indian ship Vishva Jyoti who between them took off twenty-one crew. Further rescue attempts of the remaining five were abandoned for the time being when rough seas capsized the navy's inflatable boat. The Smit tug Mississippi arrived from Mombasa but was unable to approach close enough to assist and after standing by for twenty-four hours returned to Mombasa. The ship was high and dry at low water but developed a list and settled when the tide rose. Heavy seas swept over the after deck and within a few days split the hull and flooded the engine room and holds, and cargo was seen floating in the surf. Murri International expressed an interest and their salvage master flew over the wreck on the 17th. There was a proposal to use the landing craft Rampart alongside but the exposed position and damage to the ship made the operation questionable. The following day the remaining crew were taken off and repatriated. Further damage to the hull led to the ship being abandoned as a total loss. Three years later when the author visited the site there was nothing left other than a large quantity of broken steel plate strewn across the reef. An enquiry in Mombasa attributed the stranding to a damaged rudder and steering due to rough weather, and an inoperative radar preventing the crew fixing their position.

An unidentified wreck
Position : 01°.49'.83" S 41°.26'.83" E

Kui Island is a coral outcrop north of Lamu, against which are the remains of a steamship. The wreck is completely broken up with the boiler, triple expansion engine and part of the bow lying in the sea while an iron four bladed propeller lies on the island partly grown into the coral with part of the windlass close by. A search of the Hydrographic Department records in Taunton showed no mention of the vessel. From the available records of the period and having examined the vessel loss reports for the area, it is possible this may be the remains of the Cetriana. She was a 900 ton steamer owned by Cowasjee Dinshaw of Zanzibar on a voyage from Zanzibar to Kismayu via Lamu. The ship left Lamu on 31 July 1923 with a general cargo and shortly afterwards the Chief Engineer reported a major leak under the port boiler. The pumps were started but the water reached the engine room and the vessel was turned to shore. The ship came to rest on the reef and both anchors were let go. The crew and passengers took to the boats and were transferred to Mombasa. As there were no salvage facilities available and after removal of the small valuable items the ship was abandoned. Two weeks of rough weather carried away the deck house and broke open the hull. The cargo washed out of the wreck and within a month the vessel was a total loss. She had been built by the Grangemouth Dockyard in 1891 for the Norwegian company Dampskbsselskbet Faerder with a length of 203 feet, a beam of 30 feet and powered by a 122 nhp triple expansion engine. In 1911 she was sold to W. Eadie of Glasgow who in turn sold her in 1917 to Luke Thomas & Co. of Vancouver. A little over a year later she sailed to East Africa for her new owners.

The triple expansion engine and boiler

The iron propeller grown into the coral

Part of the bows

Strandings and Salvage on the Kenya Coast
1799 - 2017

Adhara	1969	At sea
Afton	1901	Mombasa
Al Amin	1966	Mombasa
Ann W	1956	Mombasa
Aspia	1989	Mombasa
Atlantic Maru	1988	Mombasa
Baron Cawdor	1957	At sea
Bateleur	1983	Mombasa
Bernora	1990	Mombasa
Berwick Castle	1919	Mombasa
Burma	1943	Nyali
Buyuk Anna	1995	Mombasa
Chakdara	1966	At sea
H.M.S. Chatham	1914	Mombasa
Chenab	1972	Mombasa
Cheog Yang 31	1980	Mombasa
Chrysovalandou Dyo	1980	Mombasa
K.N.S. Chui	1969	Shimoni
City of Agra	1965	At sea
City of Shanghai	2013	At sea
Costoula	1967	Malindi
No. 203 Dong Sung	1981	Nyali
H.M.S. Durban	1942	Mombasa
Ekali	1967	At sea
El Moaiz	1966	Mombasa
Eva	1982	Mombasa
T.C.G. Gökçeada	2010	Mombasa
Highly 1	1969	Nyali
Indian Resolve	1974	Mombasa
Jean Laborde	1931	Mombasa
Johangella	1986	Mombasa
J S Danube	2015	Mombasa
Kestrel	1983	Tiwi

Khalaf	1992	Mombasa
Khandalla	1949	Mombasa
Lagada Star	1978	Mtwapa
Langleescot	1952	Mombasa
H.M.S. Leopard	1799	Malindi
Lion 1	1992	Malindi
Mansoor	1971	Mombasa
Margo	1977	Mombasa
Maria Bourbolulis	1963	Mombasa
Marina	1963	Mombasa
Melbourne	1909	Mombasa
Minerva	1898	Mombasa
Miramichi	1916	Mombasa
Modasa	1952	Mombasa
Negba	1979	Kilifi
Nooreen	1996	Mombasa
Olympic Rider	1976	Mombasa
Pacific Express	2011	At sea
Parkgate	1960	At sea
Patna	1895	Malindi
Pelion	1958	Malindi
Putiala	1907	Lamu
Rogo	1966	Kilifi
H.M.E.A.S. Rosalind	1962	Mombasa
Sanko Cherry	1983	Mombasa
Si-Kiang	1964	Mombasa
Silago Express	1987	Nyali
Southern Baobab	1973	Mombasa
Stolt Dimitris	1975	Malindi
Sunetta	1993	Mombasa
Tenyu Maru 58	1978	Mombasa
Thorland	1970	At sea
HMS Turquoise	1889	Mombasa
Winnie	1901	Malindi
Yung Hsaio	1974	Kikambala
Zanzibar	1900	Mombasa

Adhara

Builders	:	Odense Staalskibs, Odense, Denmark. 1939
Length	:	484 feet
Beam	:	59 feet
Displacement	:	9,100 tons
Machinery	:	Twin B & W 7 cyl. diesel. 5,050 hp

The ship was built as the Laura Maersk with limited passenger accommodation for the Danish owners A.P. Moller. With Denmark under German occupation at the outbreak of the Second World War, the ship was requisitioned by the United States Maritime Commission and renamed Day Star. At the end of hostilities she was returned to Moller and renamed Laura Maersk. Eleven years later the ship stood by following the collision between the Italian passenger ship Andrea Doria and the Swedish passenger ship Stockholm off New York. After three more owners she was named Adhara and registered in Cyprus. On 11 January 1969 while on a voyage from India to the United Kingdom, the ship developed engine trouble off the Kenya coast. A radio message for assistance was picked up by the lighthouse at Ras Serani and the two port tugs Nguvu and Marie Felling assisted the vessel into Mombasa where African Marine carried out repairs. Two years later in November the ship was sold to Chinese breakers at Whampoa.

Afton

Builders	:	R. Duncan & Co Ltd. Port Glasgow. 1901
Length	:	365 feet
Beam	:	48 feet
Displacement	:	4,434 tons
Machinery	:	Single triple expansion. 400 nhp.

The ship was built as the Afton for McLaren & McLaren of Port Glasgow. In March 1901 the ship was chartered by the Uganda Railway Committee to carry materials for the building of the Uganda Railway now nearing completion. The railway was under construction across the plains of British East Africa now Kenya from Mombasa to Kisumu on Lake Victoria. At this point the line had crossed the great Rift Valley and was now in its final stages from the Mau Hills towards the Kavirondo Gulf.

The Afton grounded in the entrance to Kilindini in March 1901 when the Master having arrived in the afternoon decided to bring the ship in without a pilot. He failed to realise the strength of the flood tide and ran aground on the foreshore at Ras Serani at the south east corner of Mombasa island. Thomas White the senior railway storeman who had previously recovered the cargo from the S.S. Minerva was placed in charge of the salvage operation and using the railway tug Percy Anderson laid out three anchors and had the cargo off loaded into lighters. With a less exposed position and shorter distance to the port than the Minerva all 1,800 tons were put ashore in five days with nothing lost or damaged. Once the spring tides came round the ship pulled herself off the rocks and steamed into port. White was awarded £100 for his efforts and received his payment within a year.

The ship was sold in 1903 and renamed Solveig by the Norwegian owners Dampsk Solveigs Rederi, Bergen. Twelve years later the ship was seized at Marseille when the Danish buyer, A. Jensen was suspected of having German interests. Sold to the French government the ship traded as the La Marne until 1920 when she was sold to a second French company in Marseille renamed Vauclin and eventually scrapped at Copenhagen in mid 1934 by Petersen & Albeck.

Al Amin

Builders	:	California Shipbuilding Corp. U.S.A. 1943
Length	:	441 feet
Beam	:	57 feet
Displacement	:	10,777 tons
Machinery	:	Single triple expansion. 2,500 ihp

The Al Amin was a Liberty ship launched as the Samson Occum on 31 August 1943, and renamed Samarinda in September as part of Britain's lease lend program under the management of T & J Harrison of Liverpool. In 1947 she reverted to the U.S flag and was immediately purchased by Harrison's for £139,183 and renamed Student. While anchored off Beira in 1949 the Chief Officer accidentally fell overboard, and was swept aft but managed to hold on to the stern frame until eventually a ladder was lowered and he climbed back on board. On 15 January 1963 she was sold to Parthenon Shipping of Monrovia for £40,500 and renamed Parthenon. A year later she was bought by the Lebanese company Midsutra Shipping Ltd. and renamed Al Amin. On 17 January 1966, approaching Mombasa loaded with 10,000 tons of sugar, she had a boiler water feed pump failure. The boilers were shut down and both anchors dropped while the tugs Nguvu and Marie Felling were summoned to assist. Lines were connected to the stern of the ship and the Nguvu pulled her clear of the reef. The feed pump was repaired and the ship escorted into Kilindini where her cargo was discharged. Later that year she was sold to Ionia Shipping of Panama and renamed Fortune Sea and on 21 April 1967 started her final voyage from Hong Kong to the breakers Chiu Ho Fa Steel Co. at Khaosiung, Taiwan, where she arrived four days later.

Ann W

Builders	:	Isaac Pimlott & Co. Northwich, England. 1947
Length	:	85 feet
Beam	:	20 feet
Displacement	:	180 tons
Machinery	:	Lister 4 cyl. diesel.
Position	:	04°.03'.00" S 39°.40'.75" E

The Ann W capsized in front of Fort Jesus on the 15 September 1956. Members of the Mombasa Club watched with interest as the vessel sailed towards the entrance of the old harbour and slowly rolled over. The crew jumped overboard and as the vessel continued to float upside down they clambered onto the upturned hull and waited for assistance. The cargo of flour, potatoes and steel fell to the seabed. The steam tug Nguvu towed the vessel back to port and secured her alongside. Ten days later the vessel had been righted and under repair while the cargo was recovered by a local scuba diver. The accident was attributed to the incorrect stowage of the steel cargo on deck instead of in the hold. The ship had been launched as VIC 67, one of many small compound steam engined cargo vessels known as Victualling Inshore Craft based on the Scottish 'Clyde Puffer'. The design was adapted for wartime mass production to service Royal Navy vessels and facilities, and the first of sixty-four VICs was built by Richard Dunston of Thorne, Yorkshire. The original length was sixty-six feet but later increased to eighty-five. VIC 67 was placed on the disposal list and sold to Greenwood Shipping of Liverpool in 1948 who renamed her Ann W. In 1954 the steam machinery was replaced by a diesel engine and two years later she was bought by the Zanzibar Transport Co. and sailed for East Africa. After the unfortunate mishap, the ship returned to service, and in 1959 on instructions from the owners, the class was withdrawn. Later she was sold to R.J. Galidari and remained listed in Lloyds Register until 1964 although she was reported scrapped in 1962.

Aspia

Builders	:	J. J. Sietas Schiffwerke, Hamburg, Germany. 1974
Length	:	423 feet
Beam	:	60 feet
Displacement	:	9,560 tons
Machinery	:	Twin Deutz 8 cyl. diesel, single propeller. 6,400 hp
Position	:	04°.03'.30" S 39°.40'.53" E

The Aspia was one of a number of bulk cement ships on charter to Bamburi Cement Ltd, Mombasa and sailing to Indian Ocean ports. The shipping of bulk cement from silos at English Point in Mombasa old port first started with the Southern Line vessel Southern Baobab in December 1960 when she carried 2,000 tons to Mauritius. Over the years a number of new build vessels have continued the trade that is still a major revenue earner for the country. In February 1989 the Aspia berthed at the silos having completed a voyage to the Seychelles and loaded a cargo for Colombo in Sri Lanka. While un-berthing on the afternoon of the 26th, the bows grounded on the edge of the channel. Ten minutes after grounding, soundings showed water in the forepeak and deep tank. The ballast pumps were started but the water level remained static. Two port tugs Duma and Simba II were called but were unable to free the ship. The following morning, having been engaged under a salvage contract by Owners, Comarco divers repaired holes in the shell plate and the two tanks were pumped out. To help trim the ship by the stern, the after peak ballast tank was filled with water. Lightening operations started that afternoon with the transfer of 460 tons of cement from No. 1 hold into 3 and 4, and 360 tons into a barge alongside. The ship was refloated on the evening of 1 March and after repairs at African Marine sailed for Colombo. The enquiry found the cause of the grounding to be poor navigation by the master and pilot while turning the vessel in the narrow confines of the old port. The vessel was sold for breaking at Alang, India, on 9 May, 2009.

Atlantic Maru

Builders	:	Sumitomo Heavy Industries. Yokosuka. Japan. 1980
Length	:	769 feet
Beam	:	138 feet
Displacement	:	81,248 tons
Machinery	:	Sumitomo / Sulzer 6 cyl. diesel. 15,000 hp
Position	:	04°.05' S 39°.42'.20" E

The Japanese owned tanker Atlantic Maru laden with 77,190 tons of crude was on a voyage from Jebel Dhana in the United Arab Emirates to Mombasa and arrived off the port on 9 December 1988. The following day the ship was requested to proceed towards the channel entrance to pick up the pilot and on the approach grounded on the southern end of Leven Reef. A sounding survey showed her aground on the starboard side between No. 1 and 4 tanks. Two of the port tugs Chui and Duma arrived and pushed on the bow but with little success. Two more tugs Faru and Nguvu II arrived and stood by at the stern. That evening the port ballast tanks were filled with 2,300 tons of water and on the evening of the 11th with all tugs pulling the ship refloated and proceeded into Mombasa where a diving inspection showed no damage. The stranding enquiry showed the crew had been navigating with photocopies of the Mombasa approach chart and had approached too close to the channel entrance without waiting for the pilot. They were positioned too far north and the northerly current and wind combined to put the ship aground. The following year the ship was sold and renamed Oppama Spirit. In 1997 the ship was sold and renamed Legaspi and on 2 September 2003 sold for breaking at Alang, India.

Baron Cawdor

Builders	:	D.&W. Henderson Ltd. Glasgow. 1935
Length	:	401 feet
Beam	:	53 feet
Displacement	:	7,539 tons
Machinery	:	Single triple expansion. 3,400 ihp.
Position	:	04°.03'.35" S 39°.35'.27" E

The Baron Cawdor was one of three sister vessels built for H. Hogarth & Co. of Glasgow and carries the distinction of being the last coal burning tramp steamer under the British flag. In 1956 on a voyage from Canada to Manchester with iron ore the ship was damaged by heavy seas off the Irish coast and after requesting assistance eventually arrived in Manchester. In August the following year on a voyage to Mombasa with a cargo of coal, she discharged the cargo into lighters and departed on the 24th for Lourenco Marques. Two days later the ship returned and signalled the lighthouse for two stowaways to be taken off. A day later a boiler valve gasket blew and both boilers were shut down for the repair. The ship drifted north out of control while the joint was repaired. The boilers were relit but developed steam leaks in the back ends and had to be shut down again on the 27th. That afternoon the Master called for assistance giving his position as twelve miles off Kilifi. The tug Simba under the command of Captain Trayner sailed and that night located the ship off Malindi with the international signal of two vertical red lights on the masthead indicating 'not under command'. A towline was connected and the two vessels headed for Mombasa. On the morning of the 29th they entered Kilindini, where the tugs Tiddler and Toroka assisted with mooring her on the buoys at 'A' anchorage. New tubes were fitted to the boiler and repairs completed on 19 September when the vessel sailed for Mozambique. Three years later she was sold to Eisenberg Limitado, Goa and handed over to breakers at Hirao, Japan on 17 March 1960.

Bateleur

Builders	:	F. Schichau Gmbh, Bremerhaven, Germany. 1956
Length	:	130 feet
Beam	:	28 feet
Displacement	:	287 tons
Machinery	:	Klockner Humboldt Deutz, 6 cyl. diesel. 1,900 bhp
Position	:	04°.04'.90" S 39°.39'.80" E

The Bateleur was launched as the tug Hermes for the German salvage and towing company Bugsier-Reederei - und Bergungs A.G. in July 1956. On 8 May 1965 the tug was summoned to assist the Pakistani ship Yousufbaksh on fire in the English Channel. A Lloyds Open Form was signed and the tug beached the vessel that evening in Sandwich Bay and started fire fighting with the help of a sister tug Wotan. The fire spread throughout the ship destroying the accommodation but was finally extinguished on the 12th. After a number of unsuccessful attempts to refloat the vessel, part of the cargo was discharged and the ship refloated on the 28th. After a second grounding the ship was towed by the Hermes and Wotan to Holland for discharging, and eventually to Hamburg for scrap. A year later the tug was chartered to tow the British India ship Chakdara from Suez to Glasgow. In 1976 the tug was sold to C. J. King & Sons of Bristol and renamed Sea Queen and four years later sold to Eagle Tugs Ltd, Mombasa and renamed Bateleur. In February 1981 the tug went to the assistance of the Tanzanian cargo vessel Lindi with engine trouble off Mombasa. Later that year while towing a barge into Mombasa the tug grounded at Likoni but refloated on the high tide after the removal of fuel. Two years later she sank off the Madagascar coast on 10 October 1983, during a salvage operation to refloat the stranded landing craft Vatsy 2 at Ile Saint Marie, with the loss of three lives.

Bernora

Builders	:	Onomichi Zosen, Onomichi, Japan. 1976
Length	:	730 feet
Beam	:	118 feet
Displacement	:	82,279 tons
Machinery	:	Sulzer 7 cyl. diesel. 20,300 hp
Position	:	04°.04'.90" S 39°.42'.10" E

Launched as the Manhattan Duke for Deborah Maritime of Monrovia she was renamed Duke in 1983 and six years later renamed Bernora when purchased by the Norwegian company Bergshav a/s. On the afternoon of 8 July 1990 the ship was inbound to Mombasa from Jebel Dhana in the Persian Gulf, when she stranded on Leven Reef close to No. 1 channel marker buoy. That afternoon the Port Authority tugs Chui, El Lamy and Kiboko were secured to the ship in preparation for the rising tide. There was no movement and the attempt was abandoned until the following day. In the meantime cargo was transferred from No. 1 to 4 tank to trim the vessel by the stern. That afternoon with the Chui and Kiboko secured on the starboard side, the Nguvu II on the port and the Mwokosi on the stern, together with the main engine running astern, the ship refloated and proceeded in to discharge. The underwater inspection showed only a small amount of scoring to the paintwork. The stranding was attributed to the ship being too far north when approaching the channel entrance marker buoys. Two years later the ship was renamed Venture and on 21 August, 2002 the ship was sold for breaking at Alang, India.

Berwick Castle

Builders	:	William Beardmore & Co. Glasgow. 1902
Length	:	398 feet
Beam	:	50 feet
Displacement	:	8,000 tons
Machinery	:	Twin triple expansion. 3,400 ihp.
Position	:	04°.03'.35" S 39°.35'.27" E

The ship was one of two sister vessels built for the Union Castle Line and used on the west coast run to South Africa and Mauritius. On 8 March 1904 under the command of Captain Cruise, the ship left Southampton for Hamburg and was proceeding down the Solent when a lookout spotted an object in the water ahead. The helm was put hard over and the engine telegraph to full astern but collision was inevitable and there was a vibration as the hull struck. Believing it to be a torpedo on trial, Cruise sent a signal to the Royal Navy. Two

hours later when the submarine A1 failed to surface the situation became clear and it was realised that a disaster had occurred. Eleven men lost their lives in the tragedy, which caused great concern throughout the country. A1 was located on the seabed with damage to the conning tower and four weeks later salvaged and returned to service. The submarine had been dispatched to attack a battleship during manoeuvres against the Fleet. The submarine was lost in 1911 during an exercise and rediscovered in 1988. In 1915 with the build up of Allied forces in British East Africa prior to the invasion of German East Africa, the Berwick Castle brought part of the Nigerian Brigade to Mombasa. Four years later on 16 October the ship caught fire in Kilindini, on a voyage to Beira with general cargo and was beached in Port Reitz. Three days later the fire was extinguished and on 1 November the ship was refloated and laid up pending disposal. Five months later she sailed for Durban and was sold in December to buyers who intended to use her as an emigrant ship to South America. In June 1921 she was renamed Andora Star and laid up in Italy before being scrapped at La Spezia in June 1925.

Burma

Builders	:	William Denny & Bros. Dumbarton, Scotland. 1914
Length	:	465 feet
Beam	:	48 feet
Displacement	:	15,130 tons
Machinery	:	Single triple expansion. 347 nhp
Position	:	04°.03'.18" S 39°.43'.38" E

The Burma was ordered for the British & Burmese Steam Navigation Co. in September 1913 and launched on 21 August 1914 at a cost of £128,910. On trials in November she reached 13.93 knots and when delivered was fitted with a fore and aft schooner rig. There was accommodation for 102 passengers with a crew of 111. After fifteen years service the ship returned to Denny for overhaul and the fitting of an Oertz balanced rudder and in 1940 was requisitioned as a troop ship between India and Suez. On 26 December 1943 while approaching Mombasa, the ship grounded off Nyali damaging the double bottom in No. 3 hold. Pumps were placed on board and both the Royal Navy and the port services attempted to refloat the ship on 1 January. After a second attempt a week later both parties abandoned the ship and in a report to London stated the task was impossible due to the extensive damage. In the meantime despite the boiler and engine room being flooded, the cargo and 300 tons of coal were discharged into lighters. By 21 January the Lloyds surveyor, Ministry of War Transport engineer and a Dutch salvage superintendent had carried out a detailed inspection and concluded the vessel was salvageable. The latter offered to use his best endeavours on a '*no cure, no pay*' agreement for the sum of £34,000, and deliver her in Mombasa with repairs sufficient for a temporary certificate of seaworthiness. Heavy salvage equipment arrived on 8 March and on 13 April the ship was refloated and towed into Kilindini for repair. On 8 May a report to Lloyds stated the ship had completed sea trials satisfactorily, and the numerous cement repairs to the hull and tank tops were sound. Four days later the ship left for dry-docking and returned to service. In 1949 she was sold and renamed Florentia and used on the immigrant run to Australia. Four years later she was bought by Pan Islamic Shipping of Karachi and renamed Safina-E-Nusrat for the Karachi - Persian Gulf service before being scrapped in September 1957.

Buyuk Ana

Builders	:	Astilleros Espanoles, Seville, Spain. 1973
Length	:	600 feet
Beam	:	72 feet
Displacement	:	26,643 tons
Machinery	:	Sulzer 6 cyl. diesel. 9,900 hp
Position	:	04°.04'.90" S 39°.39'.90" E

The ship was the former Cunard Calamanda, one of eight bulk carriers built for the Cunard Shipping Group. After five years service the ship was sold and renamed Ionian Carrier and after two further sales in 1987 she became the Turkish owned Buyuk Ana in 1995. On a voyage from Maputo in Mozambique to the Black Sea with 27,000 tons of steam coal, the ship experienced engine trouble north of Pemba on 30 December 1995. A radio call for assistance was picked up by the Mombasa signal station, and the tugs Simba II and Nguvu together with the Murri International tug Barbara were despatched to assist. With the Barbara leading and the other two tugs alongside, the vessel was escorted into Mombasa on 4 January. While entering Kilindini close to Shelly Beach there was a main engine crankcase explosion followed by a fire. The steering failed and the vessel veered to port and grounded on South Reef. The Barbara was swung round and narrowly avoided being run aground. Refloated later that day the ship was anchored in Port Reitz pending the arrival of spares. Repairs were completed by the 26 February when the ship departed, but two years later she was the subject of class suspension by Lloyds. Laid up, she was sold for breaking and arrived at Alang on 8 December 2001.

Chakdara

Builders	:	Barclay Curle & Co., Glasgow, Scotland. 1951
Length	:	465 feet
Beam	:	62 feet
Displacement	:	9,650 tons
Machinery	:	Doxford 6 cyl. diesel. 6,800 hp

The Chakdara was one of nine 'C' Class passenger cargo vessels built for the British India Line after the Second World War. On 15 May 1966 while on a voyage from England to Dar es Salaam, she radioed for assistance following a main engine crank case explosion off the Somalia coast. The Danish salvage tug Svitzer based in Aden was summoned to tow the ship to Mombasa where they arrived on 27 May. The tugs Marie Felling and Simba assisted her to the anchorage for survey. The engine was opened and the cause found to be fractured scavenge pump mounting bolts. The bedplate had also been severely damaged and it was suspected the crankshaft could be misaligned. The repairs were beyond the capability of local yards and the Svitzer was chartered to tow the ship to Suez. A General Average was declared and the ship berthed along side the City of Hull to transfer cargo. On 26 June the two vessels left Mombasa for the long tow back to Britain. At Suez the tow was passed to the Bugsier tug Hermes later to be lost off Madagascar as the Bateleur. The ship arrived in Glasgow on 9 August for a major engine rebuild and six years later was sold and renamed Fortune Navigator. In May 1974 she was sold and broken up at Kaohsiung in September.

H.M.S. Chatham

Builders	:	Chatham Dockyard, Chatham, England. 1912
Length	:	457 feet
Beam	:	50 feet
Displacement	:	5,400 tons
Machinery	:	Four steam turbines. 25,000 shp.
Armament	:	8 x 6 inch guns. 4 x 3 pdr. guns
Position	:	04°.06' S 39°.41' E

H.M.S. Chatham was one of six Chatham class cruisers built for the Royal Navy shortly before the First World War. At the outbreak of war Chatham under the command of Captain Drury-Lowe was on convoy duty in the Red Sea when he was ordered to East Africa, following the destruction of the cruiser H.M.S. Pegasus at Zanzibar on 20 September 1914 by the German cruiser Königsberg. During the course of returning to Mombasa for refuelling in the early hours of 2 October 1914, the ship grounded on a reef south of Mombasa. The engines were run full astern but the ship remained fast. At daybreak the collier Banffshire arrived from Mombasa and a towline was passed to the ship. A lighter and tug arrived and 650 tons of water, oil fuel, coal and ammunition were off loaded. Early the following morning with the assistance of the Banffshire and both engines running astern Chatham floated off and sailed into Mombasa where the ship's diver reported damage to two oil fuel compartments. Shipwrights were put to work and repaired the leaks. The stranding was attributed to poor navigation and the navigating officer was cautioned for sleeping in his cabin instead of the duty bunk on the bridge. The ship sailed on the 15th and two weeks later discovered Königsberg six miles upstream in the Rufiji Delta, after an intensive search with the cruisers H.M.S. Dartmouth and Weymouth. It was Drury-Lowe who suggested the use of aircraft to locate and plot the raider's position in the delta. Chatham left East Africa in May 1915 and served at Gallipoli and the North Sea, until placed in reserve at the end of hostilities. On 11 September 1920 the ship was re-commissioned for the Royal New Zealand Navy and returned in 1924 to become flagship of the 4th Cruiser Squadron in the East Indies. After thirteen years service the cruiser was paid off at Devonport in November 1925 and sold to Messrs. Ward of Pembroke for scrap in July 1926.

Chenab

Builders	:	Brodogradiliste, Split, Yugoslavia. 1965
Length	:	508 feet
Beam	:	62 feet
Displacement	:	10,747 tons
Machinery	:	Sulzer 6 cyl. diesel. 9,000 hp

The Pakistani owned Chenab departed Karachi on 21 April 1972 with a general cargo bound for Djibouti, Mombasa and European ports. After loading linseed oilcake at Djibouti the ship sailed for Assab to collect a further 1,400 tons before continuing to Massawa and Mombasa. On arrival at Kilindini the ship anchored in mid stream and discharged salt and on 17 May moved to the jetty where four days later smoke was observed coming from No. 3 hold. The hatch was closed and carbon dioxide released into the hold. The ship was moved to Port Reitz and cargo discharged from the hold to find the source of fire. On the 24th smoke increased and the hold was flooded. The next morning flooding was stopped and the discharge continued. Four days later smoke began to appear from No. 4 hold and carbon dioxide was released and the ship moved to Mbaraki wharf to expedite the discharge. No. 4 hold was reopened and discharge continued until the 31st when an explosion caused a fire that burnt the stevedores. The flooding continued until a second explosion lifted the steel hatch covers and caused a severe fire in the t'ween deck. The fire fighting tug Ngamia arrived and together with the port fire brigade fought the blaze. The ship was removed from the berth and beached in Port Reitz where the fire destroyed the accommodation and damaged the shell plating. The fires in the holds were eventually extinguished and the ship refloated on 10 June after tons of water had been pumped out. The balance of cargo was discharged over the next three weeks. After a survey of the hull and machinery, the damage was considered repairable and on 19 July she left for Karachi towed by the tug Euroman. On arrival she was drydocked and on 16 December towed to Shimonseki in Japan for repair. Three months later the ship left for Singapore and returned to service. The fire was attributed to poor stowage and spontaneous combustion of the oilcake due to inadequate ventilation. Some of the oilcake cargo loaded aboard the cargo ship Efploia later caught fire when the vessel docked at Lorenco Marques on 22 July, but was extinguished without damaging the vessel. In 1979 the Chenab was sold to Pakistan National Shipping Co. and in 1985 made her last voyage to Gadani Beach for breaking.

Cheog Yang 31

Builders	:	Miho Zosensho, Shimitsu, Japan. 1967
Length	:	180 feet
Beam	:	27 feet
Displacement	:	371 tons
Machinery	:	Niigata 6 cyl. diesel. 1,300 hp
Position	:	4°.05'.70" S 39°.41'.20" E

The Cheog Yang 31 a Korean owned long line trawler carrying 250 tons of fish for processing in Mombasa, ran aground at 06.40 on 10 March 1980 on the eastern extremity of Andromanche Reef. An hour later the Murri International tug Barbara arrived by which time the vessel had developed an eight degree list to starboard and was pitching and pounding in the ten foot swell. A Lloyds Open Form was signed and a line passed to the trawler using an inflatable boat. The ship was pulled off shortly after 09.00 with the help of the main engine and towed into Mombasa where a diving survey showed damage to the hull and propeller. The vessel was later drydocked for repairs at African Marine.

Chrysovalandou Dyo

Builders	:	Swan Hunter Ltd. Wallsend on Tyne, England. 1959
Length	:	481 feet
Beam	:	62 feet
Displacement	:	12,875 tons
Machinery	:	Doxford 5 cyl. diesel. 5,600 hp
Position	:	04°.04'.75" S 39°.40'.40" E

Built as the Eastern Trader for the Indo-China Steam Navigation Co. in Hong Kong, the ship was sold to the Cypriot company Santiren Shipping in 1972. While entering Mombasa on the evening of 24 April 1980 she grounded close to the Florida Night Club on a voyage from Nagoya to Dar es Salaam carrying 460 cars, some of which were destined for Mombasa. The tug Harrier attended the vessel on initial grounding but failed to refloat it. The salvage was awarded to the Port Authority and Murri International and during the operation the tug Nguvu also grounded but refloated on the incoming tide. The Barbara and Bison 1 refloated the ship on the 25th and the cars were discharged before dry-docking on 10 May at African Marine. The stranding had caused extensive bottom damage and misaligned the main engine crankshaft. The rudder skeg was twisted and two of the four steering crossheads cracked. Details of the damage were sent to two dock yards in South Africa, but the cost was considered uneconomic and the ship declared a total loss and laid up in Port Reitz. In January 1981 she was sold to Pakistani ship breakers and arrived at Gadani Beach on 3 April.

K.N.S. Chui

Builders	:	Vosper Ltd., Portsmouth, England. 1966
Length	:	103 feet
Beam	:	19 feet
Displacement	:	96 tons
Machinery	:	Twin Paxman Ventura V12 cyl. diesel. 2,800 hp
Armament	:	Twin 40 mm Bofors guns
Position	:	04°.39' S 39°.23' E

Naval defence of the Kenya coast prior to independence was the responsibility of the Royal East African Navy, formed during the Second World War. Two of its early patrol vessels had been the two armed trawlers H.M.S. Hildasay and Shappinsay, the former being wrecked on the coast south of Mombasa in 1945. These were followed by another armed trawler, H.M.S. Rosalind in service until 1963, when the R.E.A.N. was disbanded. With the country attaining independence from Britain later that year, the new Kenya Navy was presented with the Seaward Defence Vessel H.M.S. Aberford by the Royal Navy as their first naval vessel. Renamed Ndovu she saw service for some years before being laid up and scrapped in the 1970s. Three new patrol boats named Chui, (Leopard) Ndovu (Elephant) and Simba (Lion) where ordered from Vosper in October 1964 and commissioned between May and July 1966. They left Portsmouth on 4 October for Mombasa via the Suez Canal and were used on general patrol work along the coast and in particular near the Kenya-Somali border during the Somali Shifta campaign. While on a routine visit to Shimoni, on the south coast, Chui struck an uncharted rock on 15 May 1969 and damaged the hull and propellers. The vessel was refloated and towed to Mombasa by the tug Ndovu and dry docked at African Marine for repair. All three ships have since been disposed of and replaced by newer vessels.

City of Agra

Builders	:	William Denny & Bros, Dumbarton, Scotland. 1936
Length	:	459 feet
Beam	:	56 feet
Displacement	:	9,500 tons
Machinery	:	Triple steam turbines. Single propeller. 1,350 shp

The ship was ordered by Ellerman Lines on 20 August 1935 at a cost of £149,940 and the keel laid on 25 November. Launched on 2 October 1936 she entered service in December as a passenger cargo ship with an unusual profile of having the third hatch on a raised deck in front of the bridge. At a time when oil firing was common she was coal fired requiring ten stokers for her three boilers but was later converted to oil. On 27 February 1965 the ship left Mombasa for Djibouti and England having loaded 3,500 tons of cargo. Some sixty miles out to sea the main engines had to be shut down following an overheated bearing. The ship drifted slowly to the south attempting repairs before calling for assistance from the Mombasa port authorities. The tug Nguvu sailed on 1 March and brought the casualty back to Mombasa after a Lloyds Open Form had been signed and the tug Marie Felling assisted the vessel into harbour the next day. On 13 March the ship completed repairs and sailed. By 1966 the ship was the oldest in the fleet and on 10 May she was sold to Spanish breakers at Bilbao.

City of Shanghai

Builder	:	Xiamen Shipbuilding Industry, Xiamen, China. 2009
Length	:	695 feet
Breadth	:	95 feet
Displacement	:	34,269 tons
Machinery	:	Sulzer 7 cyl. diesel. 28,900 hp

On 1 December 2013 a radio call was received in Mombasa from the German owned 2,600 teu container vessel City of Shanghai some thirty miles off the Kenya coast of a main engine failure and a request for assistance. Terms of towage were agreed with the owners and the Comarco Mombasa based tug KMC Rhino was despatched to the casualty the following day. By the time the tug reached the ship the vessel had drifted in an easterly direction towards the coast at around two knots and was now around twenty five miles off shore. The tow was connected that evening and the two vessels arrived off Kilindini harbour on the evening of the 3rd where they were instructed to wait until the next morning to enter port. The tow was finally handed over mid afternoon of the 4th with the vessel safely berthed alongside. The vessel had been launched as the City of Shanghai but in May 2012 the name had been changed to Emirates Mombasa and just over a year later reverted to its original name and continues to trade.

Costoula

Builders : New England Shipbuilding Corp. Portland, Maine, U.S.A. 1944
Length : 441 feet
Beam : 57 feet
Displacement : 10,750 tons
Machinery : Single triple expansion. 2,500 ihp

Position : 03°.16' S 40°.10' E

The Costoula was a Liberty ship built for the U.S. War Shipping Administration and launched as the Samwye. After war service with the British Government the ship spent nine years with the Bank Line as the Willowbank before being sold and renamed Cavala in 1956. During the next ten years the ship changed hands three times. On the 10 September 1965 as the Kimon she was driven ashore during a hurricane at New Orleans, but was repaired and aground a year later after which she was sold and renamed Costoula. On the evening of 2 August 1967, she grounded on Leopard Reef, Malindi on a voyage from Bombay to Mombasa in ballast. A radio message from the Master was received in Aden and the Tsavliris salvage tug Nisos Kerkyra, the former Turmoil of Flying Enterprise fame, sailed from Mombasa but the Master refused assistance. The vessel was high and dry at low tide and after the Lloyds surveyor found the ship making water in No. 5 hold and damage to the main engine mountings, he recommended the ship accept immediate assistance. On the 8th the Master signed the Lloyds Open Form and a line was passed to the ship. After eight days of unsuccessful pulling on the high water, the tug returned to Mombasa. On the 17th salvage operations ceased and the crew repatriated to Greece. The Merchant Shipping Superintendent in Mombasa issued a salvage statement saying that the vessel was insured for £140,000 but after deducting salvage and repair costs it was unlikely to be a worthwhile undertaking. The current value of a Liberty ship at the time being around £50,000 and the scrap value £40,000. On 7 September the abandoned vessel floated briefly and moved two hundred yards further on to the reef. During this period the ship proved to be a huge attraction to holiday makers, with hundreds walking out at low water. One such group was Monty Brown and his family who posed by the propeller. Eventually Southern Line in Mombasa were asked if they would quote for the removal of 200 tons of bunker oil and inspected the vessel early in September and shortly after signed a Lloyds salvage agreement to refloat the vessel. A preliminary inspection showed the engine room and shaft tunnel partially flooded with insufficient fresh water on board to fire up the boiler. In view of her position it was decided to lay a steel pipe across the seabed and supply the ship with some 200 tons of fresh water from a second vessel. The Rafiki, an ex patrol boat became the support vessel and towed a pontoon to Malindi loaded with two inch pipe. After laying was completed, the tanker Southern Pioneer supplied the ship. The ships anchors were laid out ahead and a portable diesel pump connected to the ship's ballast lines and water discharged from No. 5 and 6 double bottoms together with the engine room and shaft tunnel. The forepeak and No. 2 hold were filled to trim the ship by the head. In the meantime a boiler was lit and steam supplied to the windlass. On 6 October Costoula began to move as both anchors were hauled in and by late afternoon the vessel was afloat. The bulk cement carrier Southern Baobab towed the ship to Mombasa where it was anchored in Port Reitz. Legal proceedings with the owners took eighteen months to resolve before the vessel was sold to Palma Shipping for scrap. On 3 May 1969 negotiations were completed, with the ship being resold to Lee Sing Co. for breaking. The Costoula left on 8 May behind the Japanese tug Tokyo Maru and arrived in Hong Kong on 13 June.

On tow to the breakers

The Brown family poses beside the Costoula's rudder and bronze propeller

No. 203 Dong Sung

Builders	:	Niigata Engineering Co. Niigata, Japan. 1976
Length	:	145 feet
Beam	:	25 feet
Displacement	:	380 tons
Machinery	:	Niigata 6 cyl. diesel. 760 hp
Position	:	04°.02'.30" S 39°.43'.30" E

The Dong Sung and a sister vessel were two Korean trawlers inbound to Mombasa to discharge a cargo for processing. The duty pilot departed for the first vessel lying in the anchorage on the morning of 11 March 1981 and reported to the lighthouse at Ras Serani that the Dong Sung was aground on the reef between the remains of the Globe Star and Kota Menang. Within an hour the tug Jacaranda from Divecon arrived and stood by the casualty. As the tide went out the ship listed to starboard but remained stable. That afternoon with the rising tide, the ballast was pumped out and a line passed to the trawler and with the help of the ship's engines the Dong Sung refloated and sailed into Mombasa with little damage to show.

H.M.S. Durban

Builders	:	Scott, Greenock, Scotland. 1918
Length	:	471 feet
Beam	:	45 feet
Displacement	:	5,870 tons
Machinery	:	Twin steam turbines. 40,000 shp.
Armament	:	6 x 6 inch guns. 2 x 3 inch guns
Position	:	04°.04'.50" S 39°.40'.48" E

During the Second World War, Mombasa became one of the strategic ports for the Royal Navy in the Indian Ocean. The entrance to Kilindini was protected by two steel wire anti-submarine nets controlled by boom defence vessels to allow vessels in and out. There was also a battery of 6 inch guns set in concrete emplacements on the seafront controlled by a gunnery director near the lighthouse. In 1942 the port contained three battleships H.M.S. Resolution, Revenge and Warspite. Many warships stopped at Mombasa for refuelling and one of these was H.M.S. Durban on passage from South Africa. On the afternoon of 8 December the cruiser had completed gunnery exercises and approached the channel leading towards the lighthouse at Ras Serani. A signal alerted the boom vessels and the net was opened. Both captain and navigating officer were on the bridge with the latter in charge of bringing the ship in. For reasons unknown the ship turned to port on to the Likoni transits before the black turning buoy and when the error was noticed a hurried starboard correction was made. But it was too late and the ship grounded on the northern end of Andromache Reef. Half an hour later the harbour master arrived followed by the pilot. The two tugs Marie Felling and Nguvu were made fast astern and pulled for over an hour before returning to port. Work parties arrived from the three battleships while an inspection and soundings were carried out around the ship. Shortly after three in the morning the two tugs returned and within an hour together with the ship's engines refloated the cruiser. Later that morning divers inspected the hull and arrangements made for dry docking in Bombay. The court martial was held a week later on board H.M.S. Warspite. At the end of a gruelling session in which a number of officers and the captain were cross examined, the court retired and later returned their verdict. The captain was severely reprimanded and rejoined the ship and the navigating officer was posted to another ship two days later. The cruiser sailed shortly after for Bombay and drydocked on 5 January for two months repair work. On completion the ship returned to Mombasa and this time collected a pilot before entering harbour. In 1944 Durban was stripped of her fittings and sunk on the 9 June as part of Gooseberry 5 sea defences at Ouisterham, Normandy. After the war she was salvaged and scrapped.

Ekali

Builders	:	Bethlehem Fairfield, Baltimore, U.S.A. 1943
Length	:	441 feet
Beam	:	57 feet
Displacement	:	10,920 tons
Machinery	:	Single triple expansion. 2,500 ihp

The Ekali was a Liberty ship launched with the unusual name U.S.O. 54. She was sold in March 1947 and again in 1954 and renamed Columbella under the Panamanian flag. In 1962 she was bought by Naftilos Shipping of Piraeus and renamed Ekali. Two years later on a voyage from Argentina to Japan via Mombasa with a cargo of grain, one of the main engine bearings overheated. A message for assistance was answered by the tugs Marie Felling and Simba that escorted the ship into Mombasa. Repairs were carried out by African Marine and the ship departed a week later. A year later the ship was sold to Peggy Navigation of Monrovia and renamed Loyal Fortunes. On 6 November 1967 while on her last voyage from Da Nang to Kaohsiung, the ship grounded on Pratas Reef in the South China Sea during the typhoon Emma. The Royal Navy minelayer H.M.S. Manxman picked up the distress signal but was unable to help suggesting the use of a helicopter and the American carrier U.S.S. Coral Sea airlifted the thirty-five crew to safety. Within a day the boiler and engine room flooded and with the main boiler steam line fractured, proposed salvage operations were abandoned and the ship later scrapped.

El Moaiz

Builders	:	W. Holst, Hamburg, Germany. 1952
Length	:	206 feet
Beam	:	33 feet
Displacement	:	1,810 tons
Machinery	:	M.A.K. 8 cyl. diesel. 1,400 hp
Position	:	04°.04'.35" S 39°.39'.60" E

The El Moaiz grounded on the Mombasa seafront in June 1966, not far from the Likoni ferry with a cargo of cement for Berbera and Djibouti. The ship was outbound from Kilindini when a fuse blew in the electrical steering gear and the ship veered across the channel. The Master dropped an anchor and the ship swung in the current until the aft end grounded. On the rising tide and with the aid of the anchor windlass the ship refloated itself and the tug Nguvu assisted her back into port where after repairs the vessel sailed. Launched as the Monsun for the German company Ahrenkiel & Bena, she was sold in 1956 to the Yemeni company Ali Mohammed Jabarly and renamed El Moaiz. Five years later she was bought by the Arabian Gulf Navigation Co. who sold her in 1969 to Yemen Navigation. A year later she was shown in Lloyds Register as the Alsalam. Twenty six years after she was built she was sold to the Egyptian company Tartour Co. of Suez for breaking on 14 November 1978.

Eva

Builders	:	Astilleros y Talleres, El Ferrol, Spain. 1981
Length	:	800 feet
Beam	:	130 feet
Displacement	:	80,000 tons
Machinery	:	Sulzer 7 cyl. diesel. 16,800 hp
Position	:	04°.04'.95" S 39°.42'.23" E

On the afternoon of the 9 May 1982, the Greek owned tanker Eva grounded off Mombasa carrying 80,000 tons of Arabian Light Crude from Yanbu in Saudi Arabia. Two Port Authority tugs, Kiboko and Nyangumi were despatched but failed to move the vessel. The following morning five tugs, three from the Port Authority, Chuchunge, Kiboko and Nyangumi together with two tugs from Murri International, Barbara and Bison 1 secured to the vessel and commenced pulling at high water. The attempt was abandoned as the tide fell. A sounding survey showed the ship to be a metre out of draft and at least 12,000 tons of cargo would have to be removed to refloat her. Meanwhile marine brokers located the tanker Thiaki available for charter. Two additional tugs, Marterstack and Woona from the Great Lakes Dredging Co. were brought in on the 12th and together with the other five connected to the ship for an attempt at high tide. There was no movement and the two extra tugs were laid off. In preparation for the transfer of cargo to the lightening tanker, 13,000 tons of sea water was pumped into the double bottom tanks as ballast. The Thiaki arrived on the 14th but was unable to berth due to bad weather. An additional 6,000 tons of ballast was also loaded to help keep the ship steady on the reef. By the evening of the 16th, over 12,000 tons of cargo had been transferred and deballasting started to coincide with the following days high water. With four tugs pulling, Eva refloated at midday and proceeded in to discharge the remaining cargo. There was only minor damage to the frames in No. 4 port tank. Seven years later the ship was sold and during the next six years had two further ownership and name changes until 1995 when she became the Panos G under the Cypriot flag and the Zhen Hua 10 of Shanghai Zhenhua Shipping Co. in April 2005. That same year she was converted to a heavy lift ship and on 2 February 2008 ran aground off Rotterdam carrying container cranes. The ship was refloated three days later and continues to trade.

T.C.G. Gökçeada

Builders	:	Todd Pacific Shipyards, San Pedro, California. U.S.A. 1980
Length	:	453 feet
Beam	:	45 feet
Displacement	:	4,200 tons
Machinery	:	Twin G.E. gas turbines driving a single propeller. 41,000 s.h.p.
Armament	:	One OTO Melara Mk 75 76 mm/62 caliber gun
	:	One Vulcan Phalanx CIWS;
		Four .50-cal (12.7 mm) machine guns.

The Gökçeada was the former United States Navy frigate U.S.S. Mahlon S Tisdale (FFG -27) commissioned on the 27 November 1982. After fourteen years service with the fleet the ship was decommissioned on 27 September 1996 and struck off two years later. Through the Security Assistance Program the ship was part of a sales program of warships to Turkey in 1999. Turkey acquired eight Oliver Hazard Perry class frigates from the United States. TCG Gaziantep (F-490), TCG Giresun (F-491) and TCG Gemlik (F-492) were commissioned in 1998 and the TCG Gelibolu (F-493) and TCG Gökçeada (F-494) the following year. All underwent extensive modernisation programs, and are now known as the G Class frigates. The Class have an additional Mk 41 Vertical Launch System for the Evolved Sea Sparrow missiles for close-in, as well as their longer range SM-1 missiles. The ship was part of the Somali anti-piracy patrol and called into Mombasa for supplies. On 6 September 2010 while departing Kilindini, the Captain asked the pilot, an ex Kenya Navy officer, to disembark from the ship at Likoni ferry as he was confident of taking the ship out, possibly to impress the Admiral on board. On a transit of 238 degrees, heading 058 degrees and passing No 8 red buoy the ship turned right towards the open sea and grounded on a sand bar north of Andromache Reef. With the help of the port authority tugs Simba and El-Lamy she was towed back into harbour after an hour where divers inspected the propeller and found two of the blades missing. These were subsequently recovered. A second frigate the Gaziantep arrived to offload the ammunition prior to the Gökçeada being towed back to Turkey by the Turkish naval tug Inebolu. The ship was repaired and continues in service.

Highly 1

Builders	:	Korean Shipbuilding Co. Pusan, S. Korea
Length	:	116 feet
Beam	:	21 feet
Displacement	:	320 tons
Machinery	:	Niigata 6 cyl. diesel. 760 hp
Position	:	04°.04'.20" S 39°.42'.80" E

The Taiwanese fishing vessel Highly 1 stranded on Leven Reef on the morning of 20 July 1969, laden with thirty tons of fish and an injured seaman for treatment. The tug Nguvu arrived and passed two ropes to prevent the ship moving further on to the reef in the breaking surf. While salvage operations were in hand, ten crew abandoned the trawler and attempted to swim to the pilot boat Malkia which was also standing by. Eight succeeded while two others were washed over the reef. They were subsequently rescued by Kenya Navy sailors in inflatable boats, one of which overturned in the surf. The following day the attempt was renewed and the remaining crew also abandoned the ship swimming along a lifeline to the pilot boat. The vessel was eventually refloated on the 23rd and towed into Mombasa for dry-docking at African Marine. An enquiry into the stranding showed the vessel's crew had been navigating on a small-scale chart of the East African coast covering Mozambique to Cape Guardafui.

Indian Resolve

Builders	:	Howaldtswerke, Hamburg, Germany. 1956
Length	:	536 feet
Beam	:	63 feet
Displacement	:	11,776 tons
Machinery	:	Twin steam turbines. 9,300 hp
Position	:	04°.04'.70" S 39°.40'.42" E

The Indian Resolve was one of two sister ships built for the Indian Steam Ship Co. of Calcutta. On the morning of 4 July 1974 while outbound from Mombasa the ship developed engine trouble and called the signal station. The two tugs Ngamia and Simba were despatched to the ship and towed her back to the anchorage for repairs. The ship continued to trade until sold to Haryana Steel of Bombay for breaking on 3 August 1978.

Jean Laborde

Builders	:	Messageries Maritime, La Ciotat, France. 1929
Length	:	463 feet
Beam	:	61 feet
Displacement	:	11,414 tons
Machinery	:	Twin Schneider 8 cyl. diesel. 1,303 hp
Position	:	04° 04'.35" S 39°.40'.80" E

The Jean Laborde was built for the French company Messageries Maritimes for their Marseilles to Madagascar service, with accommodation for 138 First, 92 Second, 76 Third Class and 594 passengers in steerage. Less than a month after entering service she grounded on 6 April 1931 on the Mombasa seafront not far from the wreck of the Ahmadi due to a steering servo motor failure. Later that day a telegram arrived at Lloyds in London advising them of the stranding and the ship should be afloat on the evening tide. With the help of the tug Marie Felling the ship was pulled off that afternoon with a slight starboard list and proceeded into Kilindini. As no divers were available the ship sailed the following day. Two months later on the return voyage to East Africa, the ship lost a propeller and dry docked at Marseilles on 18 June. In 1933 the route was extended to include Indo China, and with an increase in cargo and passengers the ship underwent a major refit in 1936. An additional twenty-six feet was inserted to the forepart in front of the bridge, and the Schneider main engines replaced with more powerful Burmeister and Wain units. With the fall of France to the Germans in 1940, the ship was laid up in Dakar, West Africa but later sailed for Marseilles where she became a nautical training school until set on fire and scuttled on 19 August 1944 by the retreating enemy. Two years later the salvaged wreck was towed to La Seine for survey, but proved beyond economical repair and scrapped.

Johangella

Builders	:	Schiffs. U Masch. Kiel, Germany. 1968
Length	:	250 feet
Beam	:	40 feet
Displacement	:	2,127 tons
Machinery	:	M.A.K. 8 cyl. diesel. 1,500 hp
Position	:	04°.03'.78" S 39°.40'.86" E

The ship was launched as the Winnetou for the German company Paul Lindeman & Co. and twenty four years later sold to Atlantic Rhederei of Hamburg and renamed Johangella. Four years later the ship was trading out of Mombasa as a bunkering tanker, when on the afternoon of 1 January 1996 she grounded in the old port while underway to refuel the bulk cement carrier Aspia alongside the Bamburi English Point terminal. A Lloyds Open Form was signed with the port, and the ship refloated later that afternoon using two tugs. The stranding was attributed to the inexperience of the Master in not allowing for the current after he stopped the vessel due to numerous swimmers in the channel. While awaiting the swimmers to clear, the current grounded the ship on the foreshore near Fort Jesus. The ship continued to trade and was still in Lloyds register in 2004 but has since been deleted.

J S Danube

Builders	:	Dayang Shipbuilding, Yangzhou, China. 2012
Length	:	660 feet
Beam	:	100 feet
Displacement	:	63,500 tons
Machinery	:	M.A.N. / B&W 5 cyl. diesel. 11,285 hp
Position	:	04°. 03' S 39°. 43' E

The Singapore registered JS Danube grounded on Nyali Reef three miles north of Mombasa harbour at 22.40 on the evening of the 27 April 2015 while in bound to pick up a pilot at the time. The Master advised the port of the situation and the first unsuccessful attempt at refloating took place at 03.00 hrs the following morning. A second attempt later that day with two Kenya Port Authority tugs Nyamgumi and Kiboko was also unsuccessful and a joint venture with the Dutch salvage company Smit was signed. Around 3,000 tons of coal was discharged into the chartered vessel m/v Andrea to lighten the forward end of the ship to assist with the refloating. Low tides of 2.3 metres for four days hampered the salvage operation and it was not until midday on 2 May the ship was refloated using four tugs. After engine trials the ship entered Kilindini that afternoon under its own power where it anchored in Port Reitz awaiting a diving inspection and to discharge the remaining cargo of coal. There was some damage to the underside of the bow and the stranding was attributed to poor navigation at night in adverse weather conditions. The ship sailed on 21 May for dry docking in China. The JS Danube had loaded 46,000 tons of coal at Richards Bay, South Africa destined for one of the Kenya cement works and continues to trade.

Kestrel

Builders	:	Asia Pacific Shipyard, Singapore. 1975
Length	:	135 feet
Beam	:	35 feet
Displacement	:	450 tons
Machinery	:	Twin Deutz 12 cyl. diesel. 520 hp. Schottel units
Position	:	04°.10'.02" S 39°.37' E

The Kestrel was the former landing craft GMZ-7 built for Gray Mackenzie, Bahrain, operating in the Arabian Gulf. Seven years later the vessel was purchased by Eagle Tugs, Mombasa, and renamed Kestrel. On 10 September 1983 on a voyage from Tanga to Mombasa with twenty containers of coffee, tea and sisal, the vessel encountered heavy weather and a number of container lashings parted. The ship was turned to enable the crew to secure the lashings but the pitching and rolling worsened and the vessel took on a list. Since the ship was running parallel with the reef south of Mombasa, the Master called the office and advised them of the situation and his decision to put the vessel on the reef to prevent a possible capsize. Laying out his stern anchor he drove the vessel through the surf and successfully grounded the ship a mile north of Black Cliff Point, and awaited assistance. Comarco were awarded the contract and mounted a salvage operation with a barge and crane to offload the containers. The vessel was refloated on the 17th and towed back to Mombasa for repair where the underwater inspection showed the bottom plating heavily indented. The ship was lifted out the water on a flat top barge modified as a floating dock. On completion of repairs the barge was submerged and the Kestrel returned to service. The vessel was sold in the 1990s.

Khalaf

Builders	:	Luerrsen Werft, Bremen, Germany. 1962
Length	:	275 feet
Beam	:	38 feet
Displacement	:	1,597 tons
Machinery	:	Sulzer 5 cyl. diesel. 1,520 hp
Position	:	04°.03'.18" S 39°.43'.38" E

The Khalaf was launched as the ice strengthened reefer vessel Sote Jarl for the Norwegian company Torkei Alendai Rederi. After twenty-eight years service the ship was sold and renamed Jarl and a year later sold to Ajman Foodstuffs of Qatar and renamed Khalaf. On the afternoon of 8 November 1992 on a voyage in ballast from Mogadiscio to Mombasa, she ran aground close to the wreck of the Kota Menang, despite the arm waving of some fishermen standing on the reef. The Master refused any assistance and attempted to refloat the ship on the high water but failed. On the 12th the ship was driven further over the reef on the high tide. The following day with the arrival of the owner's superintendent, a Lloyds Open Form was signed with Murri International and the tug Bison 1 put a line aboard. An attempt to pull the ship off on the next high water failed when the ship's aft bollards were ripped out of the deck. While waiting for the next suitable high water the vessel was ballasted down with both anchors laid out astern and eighty tons of fuel off loaded. In the early hours of the 24th the ship refloated and was towed in to Mombasa by the Bison 1. An investigation into the stranding found the ship to have no charts of the Kenya coast and the Master had navigated from Mogadishu to Mombasa using a GPS and the Admiralty Hydrographic Chart catalogue. He then mistook the engine block of the Kota Menang to be a channel marker buoy and ran aground. The ship returned to service and between 1994 and 2000 changed owners and names four times and was shown on Lloyds Register as the Natasha in 2005. In recent years the existence of the vessel has been in doubt and she has since been deleted from the Register.

Khandalla

Builders	:	Swan Hunter, Newcastle, England. 1923
Length	:	425 feet
Beam	:	55 feet
Displacement	:	7,018 tons
Machinery	:	Twin triple expansion. 5,800 ihp

The Khandalla was the last of four sister ships ordered by the British India Line for service on its premier Bombay - Durban run. She was a modern looking vessel with a cruiser stern and a service speed of 15 knots carrying 60 First, 68 Second Class and 1,061 deck passengers. They were well appointed with all the First Class cabins outboard and an option of one, two or three berths. Launched on 16 February 1923 she ran trials on 31 May at 17 knots in part due to eight forced draft coal fired Scotch boilers. A week later she sailed on her maiden voyage for Bombay arriving on 1 July before leaving for Durban and returning on 29 August. Five years later the ship arrived at Mombasa from Bombay with an outbreak of smallpox in her passengers and was ordered to Zanzibar for quarantine. An unusual occurrence to the ship was the loss of her starboard anchor while at Victoria in the Seychelles. The cable parted as the anchor was let go and the port anchor used instead. Eight months later the ship returned and succeeded in hooking and recovering her lost anchor when she came to sail. In June 1932 she and her sister ship Karagola were replaced on the Africa service and sailed for Calcutta to serve on the Straits run. After the outbreak of the Second World War a large number of British India ships were requisitioned for war service and in November 1940 the Khandalla returned to a limited Bombay - Durban service, which she continued until 1947 when she was transferred to the East Africa run. On 7 April 1949 at Mombasa a fire broke out in No. 3 hold containing 300 bales of cotton that burnt for seven hours and delayed departure by six days. Her last East Africa run was in December 1950 and on 26 October the following year she left for London and was sold to the breakers for £75,000 and partially dismantled at Dalmuir before final demolition at Troon.

Lagada Star

Builders	:	Werft Nobiskrug, Rendsburg, Germany. 1954
Length	:	376 feet
Beam	:	49 feet
Displacement	:	6,049 tons
Machinery	:	Twin M.A.K. 5 cyl. diesel, single propeller. 3,600 hp
Position	:	03°.58'.07" S 39°.45'.09" E

The Lagada Star was launched as the Troyburg for Partenreederei of Hamburg and sold in 1966 to F.N. Vinnen and renamed Cristel Vinnen. She was sold eleven years later to Kaspana Cia Nav. and renamed Nahost Transporter and a year later sold and renamed Lagada Star. In September 1978 the vessel was on a voyage from Umm Qasar in Iraq to Tanga with 5,500 tons of powdered sulphur in bulk. Due to adverse weather the ship required additional fuel and planned to call at Mombasa, but on the evening of 23 September stranded on the reef seven miles north of Mombasa. The following morning the two port tugs Chuchunge and Ngamia tried unsuccessfully to refloat the ship. The salvage contract was awarded to Murri International and the tug Barbara and LCT Rampart were placed on standby. An initial attempt to refloat on the high water by the Barbara was unsuccessful and both anchors were laid out astern to prevent the vessel moving further inshore. Calculations showed that as the vessel was eight feet out of draft at the bows, around 900 tons of cargo would have to be carefully removed to avoid a possible explosion in the dust laden atmosphere. Grabs were used to remove the sulphur and by the 29th, five hundred tons had been discharged from No. 1 and 2 holds into the Rampart and a barge. Two days later the ship refloated using her main engine, Barbara and the port tug Ndovu and proceeded to Mombasa to reload the discharged cargo. The diving report showed a slight setting up of the bottom between the frames from the engine room forward. On 20 October the ship resumed her voyage to Tanga and Maputo. The stranding was attributed to an inoperable radar and lack of detailed charts and navigational directions of the Mombasa area. The ship continued to trade for a further seven years before being sold for scrap to Mansoor Tayerbhai in January 1985.

Langleescot

Builders	:	Blythswood Shipbuilders, Scotstoun. Glasgow. 1947
Length	:	483 feet
Beam	:	62 feet
Displacement	:	10,235 tons
Machinery	:	Doxford 6 cyl. diesel. 6,800 bhp

The ship was built for the Medomsley Steam Shipping Company. Co Durham, one of nine ships named Langlee. After the Second World War the company was bought by the Dutch ship owner Van Ommeren and the Langleescot entered service in 1947 in the new owners colours. On the morning of 12 June 1952 a fire broke out in No. 2 hold while the ship was alongside in Mombasa. Hundreds of gallons of water were poured into the hold by firemen from the port and municipal fire brigades. The fire was attributed to self combustion in the cargo of eighty tons of copra that spread to the cotton and sisal also stowed in the same hold. The fire was extinguished after two hours and pumps were lowered into the hold to drain the water from the fire pumps. Later the fire damaged cargo of copra and cotton was discharged and the vessel sailed. A search of the Kenya Gazette for references to the fire showed only that a case of vintage port was listed as uncollected cargo in store at Mombasa which was subsequently sold. Later that year she was sold to Ellerman Lines of London and renamed the City of Bath and in 1969 sold to Cypriot owners and renamed Lena. On 26 March 1972 the ship was sold to breakers at Castellon in Spain.

H.M.S. Leopard

Builders	:	Portsmouth Dockyard, Sheerness Dockyard. 1790
Length	:	146 feet
Beam	:	30 feet
Displacement	:	1,045 tons
Armament	:	22 x 24 pdr. cannon, 22 x 12 pdr. cannon, 4 x 6 pdr. cannon
Position	:	03°.17' S 40°.05' E

H.M.S. Leopard was laid down at Portsmouth Dockyard in 1775 but ten years later while still incomplete was towed to Sheerness and completed in 1790. Designed by Sir John Williams, Leopard was a compromise between a frigate and the larger ships of the line but well armed with 50 guns. During the next twenty years the ship saw action in the Mediterranean and North America stations as well as running aground off Malindi on the 15 February 1799. She was sailing in a south westerly direction when land was sighted at three in the morning, The wheel was put hard over to port with a new course to the south east when there was an ominous grinding as the keel hit the edge of the reef. A signal lamp was lit to warn H.M.S. Orestes following astern, to stand off while sails were furled and the jolly boat lowered to take soundings. The tide was ebbing and it would be a six hour wait until she floated off with the help of the boats from Orestes which laid out a stern kedge anchor. The reef was later named after the ship. Eight years later Leopard was involved in an incident off the American coast when she intercepted the U.S.S. Chesapeake outward bound for the Mediterranean with instructions to search for British deserters. A boarding party was sent over, but the Captain, Commodore James Barron refused the request and prepared for action. No sooner had the boarding party returned to Leopard than three broadsides followed to be answered by a single shot. Chesapeake surrendered but Leopard's master Captain Humphreys refused the ship and instead sent the boarding party taking three Americans and a British sailor who was later hanged. The

Chesapeake - Leopard affair was seen by some as a prelude to the War of 1812 but at the time did little more than strain diplomatic relations. Leopard remained on the American station until 1812 when she was converted into a troopship. Two years later the ship grounded in fog on Anticosti Island in the Gulf of St Lawrence on 28 June 1814. Laden with 475 men of the Royal Scots Guards she was bound from England to Quebec, but on this occasion remained on the rocks and became a total loss.

Lion 1

Builders	:	Buesumer Schiffswerft, Buesum, Germany. 1957
Length	:	150 feet
Beam	:	27 feet
Displacement	:	457 tons
Machinery	:	Daihatsu 6 cyl. diesel. 700 hp
Position	:	03°.21'.50" S 40°.07' E

The ship was launched as the Clio for Partenreederei of Hamburg with an M.A.K. 300 hp engine and seven years later sold to Rhein Maas of Hamburg. Over the next twenty-five years she was sold three times, re-engined with a more powerful unit and in 1991 renamed Lion 1 and registered in Valletta. On 26 February 1992 the ship left Mombasa laden with 380 tons of bagged wheat for Somalia. Later that day the main engine failed and the ship drifted ashore near Watamu. Some hours later on the incoming tide the ship refloated but was listing to starboard. The crew found water in the bilges and started the pumps. The list decreased for a while and slowly increased until the starboard deck was awash. In the early hours of the 27th, the Master put the ship aground again to prevent her capsizing. The following day the Murri International tug Barbara arrived and attempted to pull the ship off but failed. The bagged wheat was thrown overboard and on 1 March the ship refloated. Divers patched the holes in the hull and the ship was towed back to Mombasa for repairs. An enquiry showed the causes of the predicament to be human error and an unseaworthy ship.

Mansoor

Builders	:	Rheinstahl Noordseewerke, Emden, Germany. 1958
Length	:	517 feet
Beam	:	67 feet
Displacement	:	12,864 tons
Machinery	:	M.A.N. 6 cyl. diesel. 5,400 hp
Position	:	04°.04'.10" S 39°.41'.20" E

The ship was launched as the Fritz Thyssen for Frigga Seeschiffahrt of Hamburg, and in 1965 renamed Thor. Two years later she was purchased by the East Bengal Steam Ship Co, who renamed her Mansoor. While on a voyage from Cherbourg to Karachi via the Cape of Good Hope the ship stopped at Mombasa for fuel and water. During the evening of 4 February 1971 while approaching the port, the crew became unsure of their position. The ship slowed to a stop and then proceeded at half ahead and grounded shortly afterwards. She was refloated three hours later after deballasting and proceeded into Mombasa escorted by the tugs Ndovu and Ngamia. An inspection by the class surveyor showed some bottom damage but the ship was permitted to sail. The grounding was attributed to the ship approaching too close to the port before picking up a pilot, and relying on the radar picture, while ignoring the navigation buoys that marked the channel. She was sold in 1979 to the Pakistan Shipping Corporation and remained in service until December 1983 when she was sold for breaking at Gadani Beach in March 1984.

Margo

Builders	:	Burntisland Shipbuilding Co. Burntisland, Scotland. 1962
Length	:	483 feet
Beam	:	62 feet
Displacement	:	13,239 tons
Machinery	:	Gotaverken 5 cyl. diesel. 6,300 hp
Position	:	04°.05'S 39°.42'.30" E

The Liberian registered Margo was on a voyage from Hamburg to Dar es Salaam via Mombasa when she grounded on Leven Reef on the evening of 23 July 1977 with 1,870 tons of general cargo. Attempts by the crew to refloat the ship having discharged six hundred tons of ballast were unsuccessful after the main engine overheated due to sand ingested into the sea intakes. The following morning a Lloyds Open Form was signed with the harbourmaster and the tugs Nyangumi and Tewa were sent to assist. The salvage attempt was abandoned by mid morning and a second contract signed with Murri International. The tug Barbara arrived and ran out the starboard anchor and commenced pulling on the rising tide that evening. The attempt was unsuccessful and on the 25th the Nyangumi returned and both tugs together with the ship's engine attempted a second time. With the tide falling the tugs laid off and calculations showed that at least four hundred tons required discharging to reach the stranding draft. The ship was reballasted to hold her on the reef while the landing craft Rampart was brought alongside on the 26th. Despite a heavy swell over three hundred tons of steel was discharged from No. 2, 4 and 5 holds. On the morning of 29th after discharging ballast, two tugs Chuchunge and Nyangumi refloated the ship and towed her into Mombasa. Reloading was completed after a survey showed no damage and she sailed on 4 August. The stranding was attributed to a navigational error. Four months later on 4 December, the ship grounded on the Middle Ground sandbar entering Mina Sulman, Bahrain. After discharging two hundred and fifty tons of bagged cement the ship refloated with the help of two harbour tugs and sailed after a satisfactory diving inspection. In 1980 the ship was sold and renamed Linklove and four years later sold and renamed Comet under the Maltese flag and in December went to Indian breakers at Alang.

Maria Bourboulis

Builders	:	Societe Cant. Nav., Legnano, Italy. 1940
Length	:	228 feet
Beam	:	32 feet
Displacement	:	886 tons
Machinery	:	Twin Franco Tosi 6 cyl. diesel.
Position	:	04°.04'.90" S 39°.40'.10" E

The ship was launched as the Lago Zuai for Societa Anonima Navigazione of Eritrea and in 1955 sold and renamed Valfredda. Three years later she was bought by Captain Bourboulis of Piraeus and possibly named after his wife. While inbound to Mombasa in 1963, the main engine failed and the Master dropped both anchors but the ship drifted on to the reef at the entrance to Kilindini. The Marie Felling was sent to assist and after passing a line, pulled her off and escorted the vessel to a berth. There was no damage and the ship sailed two days later. In 1965 she was sold to another member of the family who renamed her Maria M and traded until 1971 when she was sold to Messrs. Paikonomou of Piraeus who renamed her Irene P. After forty-six years service she was deleted from Lloyds Register and reported broken up.

Marina

Builders	:	T. van Duijrendijk, Lekkerkerk, Holland. 1920
Length	:	264 feet
Beam	:	42 feet
Displacement	:	3,180 tons
Machinery	:	Single triple expansion. 162 nhp

The ship was launched as the Ledaal for the Norwegian owner Brodrene Olsen and changed hands a number of times over the next forty years. In 1962 she was sold to the Lebanese company Vialel Cia. Nav. and renamed Marina. Six days after sailing from Kismayu in Somalia to Basra with a cargo of 2,000 tons of charcoal, smoke was seen coming from No. 2 and 3 hatches. The Master headed for Mombasa where fire-fighting facilities were available. The fire spread and destroyed the hatch boards and one lifeboat by the time the ship arrived in Mombasa on 26 December 1963. The fire service attended the ship and after the fire was out the cargo was offloaded, dried and reloaded. On 4 January when the ship was about to sail the tail shaft jammed and a diver inspected the propeller but found nothing wrong. The following day there were signs of overheating of the charcoal in No. 1 hold. In the meantime an inspection of the stern gland showed it to be damaged and the cause of the problem. The charcoal was off loaded, dried and reloaded. On 12 January the shaft seized again and the cargo was removed from No. 3 and 4 holds to gain access to the propeller shaft and tunnel. The stern gland was repaired and the cargo reloaded and the ship finally left for Basrah on 31 March. Later that year she was sold to the Danish company Paul Bergsoe & Son and broken up at Masnedsund in November.

Melbourne

Builders	:	Messageries Maritime, La Ciota, France. 1881
Length	:	413 feet
Beam	:	39 feet
Displacement	:	3,993 tons
Machinery	:	Single triple expansion. 3,400 ihp
Position	:	04°.04'.40" S 39°.40'.85" E

The Melbourne was one of two sister ships built for the French company Messageries Maritimes and launched on 24 December 1881. The ship entered service in April 1882 with accommodation for ninety First, forty-four Second and thirty-three Third Class passengers on the Marseille to Sydney service via Reunion. After nine years the ship was transferred to the Far East route and with the machinery showing its age was re-engined in 1895. In 1900 she was requisitioned as a troop transport in China and nine years later while on the East African run stranded at the entrance to Mombasa. Early on the morning of 28 March 1909 while entering Kilindini the ship grounded a hundred yards west of the lighthouse. A second company vessel Oxus arrived and placed a towline aboard but also grounded. A third vessel Rovuma arrived and succeeded in refloating the Oxus. During the day four hundred tons of cargo and fresh water were discharged in preparation for the evening high tide. As the tide ebbed the ship began to list and there was concern for the safety of the passengers who were taken ashore and placed in hotels which did a thriving trade. At 5 pm two Uganda Railway divers inspected the ship and found no damage. By that evening a large crowd of onlookers had gathered on the shore. When the ship was once again upright, the Oxus accompanied by the tug Percy Anderson connected a towline. Half an hour later the ship was afloat and proceeded into the port where after taking water and embarking passengers sailed on the 29th. In the stranding enquiry the Captain stated that in the early morning light he had seen a buoy on the port side assumed to be the black turning buoy seen on previous voyages. However since his previous visit the buoy had been moved and replaced by a red one but he had taken the same course and grounded. After service as a troop ship during the First World War the ship was broken up at La Spezia, Italy in 1921.

Minerva

Builders	:	Russell & Co. Port Glasgow. 1897
Length	:	340 feet
Beam	:	45 feet
Displacement	:	3,603 tons
Machinery	:	Single triple expansion. 288 nhp

Minerva was built for the Venus Steam Shipping Co. of Newcastle. In early 1898 the ship was chartered on behalf of the Uganda Railway carrying over 1,650 tons of construction material. On 21 April 1898 the ship arrived off Mombasa and anchored for the night but around midnight dragged her anchor and grounded on Leven Reef. Distress rockets were fired and the railway tug Percy Anderson was sentb to investigate. The ship appeared in no immediate danger. Over the next two days two steamers Canara and Juba assisted the tug in trying to pull her free. Canara was almost stranded herself and afterwards took no further part in the operation. The cruiser H.M.S. Magicienne arrived and her captain decided the cargo should be off loaded. Under the direction of Thomas White, the railway's chief store keeper the cargo was offloaded into a lighter, although due to the rough weather only forty tons could be offloaded at a time. Despite some leaks in the hold and engine room the ship's pumps kept pace with the ingress and by the 29th over 1,000 tons had been landed at Kilindini. On 3 May Magicienne arrived and two anchors were laid out by the tug. That afternoon Magicienne took the tow and the ship's windlass hauled in on the anchor cables and the ship floated free. At the end of May the ship sailed to Calcutta for dry docking. The Railway Committee lodged a claim for salvage which took three years to settle. White received £200 for his efforts in April 1901. In 1899 the ship changed hands and continued as the Minerva until 1909 when she became the Aizkarai-Mendi and in 1915 after a further sale was renamed Luisa for Spanish owners. On 12 April 1918 while on a voyage from Barcelona to Liverpool with general cargo, the ship was torpedoed and sunk by UB 74 six miles south west of Pendeen lighthouse on the Cornish coast.

Miramichi

Builders	:	J.L. Thompson, Sunderland. 1902
Length	:	340 feet
Beam	:	48 feet
Displacement	:	3,624 tons
Machinery	:	Single triple expansion. 329 nhp

The Miramichi was built for the North Atlantic Steamship Co. registered in Bristol. In 1912 she was sold to the Bank Line and on 23 February 1916 caught fire while discharging a cargo of petroleum in Kilindini. A large party of crew from the Australian cruiser H.M.A.S. Pioneer were ferried over to help fight the fire and assist with moving the ship. With the sides buckling and huge volumes of smoke enshrouding the ship they succeeded in raising the anchor and with the assistance of the tug Percy Anderson beached the vessel in Port Reitz where she burnt out. The crew were later commended by the Royal Navy C. in C. East Africa, Rear Admiral Herbert King-Hall for their efforts. Later that year the ship was sold to W. Gowan & Co, and towed to Cape Town for repairs in September 1917. She was bought by the South African Steam Navigation Co. in Durban in 1918 and sold the next year to L. Miglievich and renamed Lilyada. Three years later they sold her to the Italian company Societa di Navigazione Lloyd Adriatic. The ship sank on 14 June 1925 after a collision five miles off Cape Roca, Portugal with the Spanish cargo vessel Cabo Menor while on a voyage from Bona to Rotterdam with a cargo of iron pyrites. The Cabo Menor owned by the Ybarra Line survived and was scrapped in 1963.

Modasa

Builders	:	Swan, Hunter & Wigham Richardson Ltd. Newcastle. 1920
Length	:	465 feet
Beam	:	58 feet
Displacement	:	11,045 tons
Machinery	:	Twin Metrovick steam turbines. 4,000 shp
Position	:	05°.40' S 39°.12' E

The Modasa was named after a small town in Gujerat, India, one of six near sister ships owned by the British India Line carrying 103 First and 81 Second Class passengers. The ship was launched on 24 December 1920 and completed a year later. Most of her pre-war years were spent on the London - Calcutta service but occasionally to East Africa when in 1927 she carried the first maize cargo to London. Three years later during the Prince of Wales's visit to East Africa, he and his retinue were passengers from Beira to Mombasa. In 1933 she arrived at Middlesborough to discharge cargo before proceeding to London for repairs. On board was 450 tons of fuel oil and His Majesty's Customs ruled that as this constituted a coastal voyage, the oil was liable to duty. The row was settled by sailing to Antwerp for repairs, this being a non-coastal voyage. When on passage in August 1935 she sustained minor damage in collision with the steam yacht Latharna that required a stopover in Malta for repairs. Homeward bound from Calcutta in 1937 under Captain J.W. Gilchrist, the ship encountered a violent storm in the Bay of Biscay and hove to for three days with the B.B.C. reporting her overdue. Superficial damage was sustained when the bridge deck and forward ladders to the promenade and boat decks were swept away, together with the derricks and starboard side bulwarks adjacent to No. 2 hold. The most serious damage was structural when the vessel was almost overwhelmed by a huge wave that set the foredeck next to No. 3 hold down eighteen inches. In the t'ween deck the ladders and stanchions had been concertinaed and distorted. Earth moving equipment, loaded at Marseilles splintered the wooden hatch boards, and lodged between the hatch beams. The ship was docked in Smith's dry dock, Middlesbrough for extensive repairs that took three weeks. On completion she sailed direct to Calcutta in ballast in order to meet her next scheduled sailing date on the homeward voyage, which was fully booked for the forthcoming coronation of King George VI. During the Second World War she was requisitioned for the Liner Division in June 1940 and utilised as a Military Store Ship for the first four months of 1941. Those onboard believed they had been attacked by a U-Boat in the Bay of Bengal in December 1942 but the event was later questioned. In 1946 the ship was refurbished to carry 183 single class passengers and returned to service on the London-East Africa route in 1947. In 1951 she was alongside at Mombasa when the port was occupied by six other B.I. ships, Kampala, Karanja, Mantola, Mombasa, Sofala and Tabora on Sunday 16 September known as B.I. Sunday. It was here a year later on 17 November that she suffered a fire which was brought under control with shore assistance and little damage to the ship. On January 23 1954, after unloading her cargo at the Tyne, she proceeded to Blyth where she was sold the following day to Hughes Bolckow Shipbreaking Co. Ltd.

Negba

Builders	:	Shikoku Dockyard, Takamatsu, Japan. 1977
Length	:	490 feet
Beam	:	71 feet
Displacement	:	17,250 tons
Machinery	:	Mitsubishi 8 cyl. diesel. 8,000 hp.
Position	:	03°.38'.50" S 39°.54'.00" E

The Negba ran aground at Kilifi on 10 November 1979 while on a voyage from Durban to Eilat via Mombasa with 16,000 tons of general cargo. Both anchors were laid astern using the ship's cargo gear and the vessel tried three times unsuccessfully using a combination of anchors and the main engine to refloat itself. Three days later the Salvage Association surveyor boarded the vessel to assess the situation. The sounding survey showed the ship aground over a quarter of her length but the ballast tanks were dry. An estimated seven hundred tons of cargo required discharging to regain the stranding draft and the cargo vessel Nabila was chartered by Divecon Mombasa to offload the cargo from No. 1 hold, and relay the anchors in deeper water. The owners meanwhile chartered the salvage tug Guul Victory which left Mogadishu on the 13th to assist, while the double bottom tanks were ballasted to maintain the ship steady on the reef. Around 750 tons had been removed by the 17th and the following afternoon after discharging ballast, the ship refloated using its main engine and the salvage tug. After a hull inspection showed some set up to the forward bottom plating, the vessel reloaded and continued the voyage on the 21st. The stranding was attributed to poor navigation while taking a radar fix. The crew mistook Ras Serani lighthouse at Mombasa for that of Chale Point some thirty miles to the south and continued north until they saw the entrance to Kilifi Creek, assumed it to be Mombasa and grounded. The ship had been built as the Tengco for Japanese owners before being sold to the Israeli shipping company Zim Israel Navigation Co. in 1979. In 1995 the ship was sold to Appolonia Lines of Malta and renamed Appolonia Spirit and later Ionian Spirit before being scrapped in China in 2013.

Nooreen

Builders	:	Rauma Repola, Rauma, Finland. 1962
Length	:	347 feet
Beam	:	49 feet
Displacement	:	4,399 tons
Machinery	:	B & W 5 cyl. diesel. 2,900 hp
Position	:	04°.04'.40" S 39°.42'.80" E

The Nooreen was built as the ice strengthened Aluksne for the former U.S.S.R. and sold in 1990. After two name changes the vessel was renamed Nooreen in 1991. On 12 May 1996 the ship left Mombasa on a voyage to Somalia with a record of mechanical troubles. Two weeks later she suffered a major engine and generator failure off the Somalia coast and began to drift. The following morning an anchor was dropped to prevent the vessel grounding on the reef near Brava. A second tanker Sofia sent by the ship's agents was unable to assist and sailed on. A message was passed to Murri International and the tug Barbara arrived on the 30th. Next morning after cutting the anchor chain as there was no power on board, the pair got under way for Mombasa. Seven days later Barbara contacted Mombasa for assistance. While on the approach to Kilindini the Barbara's engines failed and an anchor was let go to hold both vessels. The combination of tide and wind dragged both vessels before the anchor held, by which time the tug and tow were lying across the entrance channel. The tug Bison 1 arrived and maintained station warning vessels of the situation. Around midnight a cargo vessel approached the channel, and despite a warning from the signal station, Bison and Barbara to wait five miles off, passed between the two ships severing the tow wire. The rogue ship then completed a circuit and returned to await the pilot. The Nooreen drifted northwards and grounded on Leven Reef close to the Globe Star engine block. Later that morning Bison refloated the stranded ship and towed her into African Marine for repair and the Barbara followed shortly after. The enquiry into the sorry saga revealed that the Nooreen had sailed with insufficient crew, safety equipment and a host of mechanical defects, and the stranding was attributed to poor seamanship by all concerned, compounded by the cargo vessel entering Mombasa without a pilot. The Nooreen was sold in 1997 and renamed Ocina and in January 1999 broken up at Alang.

Olympic Rider

Builders	:	Misubishi Nippon H.I. Yokohama, Japan. 1960
Length	:	820 feet
Beam	:	92 feet
Displacement	:	60,000 tons
Machinery	:	Twin Westinghouse turbines. Single propeller. 18,000 shp
Position	:	04°.03'.13' S 39°.43' E

The Liberian registered tanker Olympic Rider was an Onassis owned vessel that had been jumboised six years after completion. The vessel grounded in the Arabian Gulf in 1963 and at the entrance to the Suez Canal in 1966. Ten years later she arrived off Mombasa laden with 51,000 tons of Arabian Light Crude from Umm Said, Qatar. On the afternoon of 12 September while inbound to Kilindini she grounded on Leven Reef and both anchors were let go. That evening the ship refloated using her main engine and the tugs Chuchunge and Simba but swung in the tide and grounded a second time. That evening oil was seen bubbling to the surface and it was suspected the hull had been damaged by one of her own anchors. The oil was monitored as it spread towards Mombasa but it dispersed quickly giving no cause for alarm. The ship was refloated a second time on the 15th using the Chuchunge and Ndovu and discharged the cargo safely. The crack in the hull was repaired with a concrete box and the vessel sailed on the 28th. The stranding was attributed to an error in judgement and the vessel's sluggish response to the rudder after the pilot had ordered a turn to starboard. The ship continued in trade until broken up by Shyeh Sheng Huat Steel at Kaohsiung in February 1979.

Pacific Express

Builders	:	Mitsubishi Heavy Industries, Shimonoseki, Japan. 1981
Length	:	557 feet
Beam	:	89 feet
Displacement	:	22,597 tons
Machinery	:	Sulzer 7 cyl. diesel. 12,949 hp
Position	:	04°.24' S 42°.20' E

The ship was launched as the Pacific Maru for Mitsui OSK of Japan. In 1996 the name changed to Pacific Wind and three years later under the Cypriot flag she was renamed Pacific Express. A further change to Delmas Charcot in 2000 was followed by the vessel being sold to Estelle Shipping Co. Ltd of Cyprus and renamed Pacific Express. On 21 September 2011 the ship was on passage from Bombay to Mombasa with a cargo of steel products and vehicles when it was attacked and set on fire by Somali pirates 190 miles east of Mombasa. After the Italian destroyer Andrea Doria arrived on the scene the pirates fled and the crew were transferred to the warship. The salvage operation was awarded to Tsavliris who sub contracted the operation to Comarco owned Kenya Marine Contractors of Mombasa who despatched the Comarco Osprey and Comarco Falcon with armed guards. A third tug KMC Eland also sailed from Mombasa with armed guards to collect the crew from the Andrea Doria and land them at Mombasa. In the meantime, due to prevailing currents the Pacific Express was drifting to the north and there was concern that she would enter Somalian waters and or go ground. The Comarco Osprey connected her towline and commenced towage to Mombasa. Once the KMC Eland had disembarked the crew, the tug returned to assist the Osprey. The Falcon stood by and supplied fuel and the trio successfully brought the casualty into Mombasa on the 30th. A pilot and the Mombasa harbour tug Kiboko II assisted in bringing the casualty into the anchorage. The vessel was later discharged and as the accommodation and bridge had been totally destroyed in the fire, the vessel was considered a Constructive Total Loss, and sold to Rajendra Shipbreakers of Alang, India where it arrived in tow on 15 March 2012.

Parkgate

Builders	:	Burntisland Shipbuilding Co. Scotland. 1945
Length	:	443 feet
Beam	:	57 feet
Displacement	:	10,000 tons
Machinery	:	Doxford 3 cyl. diesel.2500 hp
Position	:	02°.20' N 51°.14' E

The Parkgate was built for the Ministry of War Transport and launched in July 1945 as the Empire Calshot. In 1946 she was sold to McCowan and Gross Ltd and renamed Derrycunihy. Six years later she became the Argobeam and in August 1955 on a voyage from the United States to Denmark had an engine room fire which was extinguished leaving the vessel with a 40 degree list. After the crew abandoned ship she was towed to Stornaway by the tug Salveda and pumped out before proceeding to Copenhagen for discharge. Repairs were completed in Hamburg where she was purchased by Turnbull Scott & Co. later that year. Five years later on 4 September on a voyage from Khorramshahr to Port Elizabeth in ballast, the master Captain Gibson sent out an emergency call after a main engine failure nine hundred miles north of Mombasa. Heavy seas had produced faults in the machinery, boilers and a shortage of fuel caused by a fractured bulkhead. The Aden based salvage tug Svitzer responded to the call but the Harrison Line vessel Journalist was closer and also heading for Mombasa and arrived at the casualty on the evening of the 7th. The Parkgate meanwhile had drifted a further 160 miles north in the intervening three days. A standard *'no cure, no pay'* was agreed and the following morning a 650 foot tow wire was connected using both ship's anchor cables and the pair set off on the nine day 1,100 mile voyage to Mombasa. On the morning of the 17th the ships arrived off Kilindini and the tow was shortened for the final leg into harbour. The tugs Kongoni and Nyati secured alongside and assisted the ship to anchor. Harrisons were awarded £15,000 for their efforts of which £10,000 went to the owners and £5,000 to the crew. After extensive repairs Parkgate left Mombasa on 15 October but a month later was sold to the Lebanese company Patlem Cia. Nav. and renamed Panagos. Eight years later she set off on her last voyage to the breakers and arrived at Shanghai on 26 September for demolition. The Journalist sailed on until April 1982 when she was sold to breakers at Gadani Beach.

Patna

Builders	:	William Denny, Dumbarton, Scotland. 1871
Length	:	298 feet
Beam	:	33 feet
Displacement	:	1,780 tons
Machinery	:	Single compound. 943 ihp
Position	:	03°.12' S 40°.08' E

The Patna was one of two sister ships built for the British India Line for service on the London - Arabian Gulf service and rigged as a barquentine with two yards on the foremast. There was accommodation for twenty-five First, twelve Second and 1,013 Third class passengers and service commenced in 1873 with occasional pilgrim voyages to Jeddah. After thirteen years service the compound engine began to give trouble and the ship was fitted with a new engine and boiler at the yard of A & J Inglis in Glasgow. The new compound engine although dated when compared with the recently introduced triple expansion engine gave good service during the next fifteen years. In the late 1880s the ship transferred to the East African service and carries the distinction of running aground off Malindi on 30 May 1895 and again the following day off Pemba where she was towed off by the Royal Navy sail steam gunboat H.M.S. Racoon which took the mail on to Zanzibar arriving on 3 June. In the last years of service the ship returned to the Indian coast where she was sold to Bombay breakers in 1901.

Pelion

Builders	:	Nobiskrug, Rensburg, Germany. 1952
Length	:	255 feet
Beam	:	37 feet
Displacement	:	1,744 tons
Machinery	:	M.A.K. 9 cyl. diesel. 1,500 hp
Position	:	03°.16'.30" S 40°.09'.50" E

On 14 April 1958, the German freighter Pelion, grounded on Leopard Reef off Malindi with a general cargo including cement for East and South African ports. The signal station at Mombasa relayed the stranding to the harbour master who despatched the tug Simba. A Lloyds Open Form was signed and the tug stood by. In the meantime the crew disconnected an anchor in preparation to shackle the chain to the towing wire from the tug. As the tide fell, an inspection of the ship showed the rudder had been damaged and bent over to port during the grounding. On the 16th as high water approached the tug closed in towards the reef and a launch took a wire across to the ship. By this time the ship was showing signs of movement as the swell rolled over the reef. Just before high tide the wire rose out of the water as the tug took the strain. Slowly the bows began to swing and within minutes the ship was in deep water and veered to port. The rudder had to be disconnected and centralised to enable the tow to continue. On arrival at Mombasa, the tug Marie Felling assisted the ship to African Marine for repair. A general average was declared on the cargo on 23 April, and the ship sailed for Tanga a month later. In 1962 the ship was sold to Rennies Coasters of South Africa and renamed Induna. On 5 September 1978 she encountered heavy weather off the southern tip of Madagascar and began taking water in the forward hold. When the ship began to sink, two lifeboats were lowered but capsized. The chief officer and second engineer managed to board a life raft and while trying to assist other crew members were blown away from the ship. Twenty-four days later the chief officer was rescued some six hundred miles from where the ship sank by the Greek vessel Constantia, the engineer having died some days before. There were no other survivors.

Putiala

Builders	:	A & J Inglis, Glasgow, Scotland. 1886
Length	:	335 feet
Beam	:	40 feet
Displacement	:	4,000 tons
Machinery	:	Single triple expansion. 2,441 ihp.
Position	:	02°.18' S 40°.55' E

The Putiala was one of a pair of ships launched for the British India Line with a barquentine rig and accommodation for thirty-one First, fifteen Second Class and 1,883 deck passengers. The first fifteen years were spent in service on the coast of India and across the Bay of Bengal to Burma. In 1900 the ship served as a troop transport for the Boxer Rebellion in China and the following year to South Africa for the Boer War. During the next ten years the ship ran aground three times: the first at Beira in December 1903, followed by Lamu in January 1907 when she called at the port for passengers and mail, and Kuwait in February 1912. She was sold on 19 February 1914 to Fratelli Bruzzo for £5,250 and scrapped at Savona, Italy.

Rogo

Builders	:	New England Shipbuilding. Portland, Maine, U.S.A. 1944
Length	:	441 feet
Beam	:	57 feet
Displacement	:	10,912 tons
Machinery	:	Single triple expansion. 2,500 ihp
Position	:	03°.39' S 40°.52' E

The Rogo was a Liberty ship laid down on 24 April 1944 as the Ernest W. Gibson and launched six weeks later, that served with International Freighting Corp. and W. J. Rountree & Co. New York until 1949 when she was laid up. In 1951 she was sold to Three Oceans Corp, New York and renamed Westchester. Two years later she was sold to the Panamanian company Ayalago Cia Nav. and renamed North Pilot. In 1960 after two further name changes she was purchased by Syros Shipping of London and renamed Rogo. On the morning of 25 April 1966, the Mombasa Harbour Master received a call from a hotel at Kilifi regarding a ship aground at the entrance to the creek. The Rogo had grounded a mile from the entrance on a voyage from Beira to Mombasa with a cargo of coal. An aircraft was chartered to investigate and the tug Nguvu dispatched to the scene after a request from the Master for assistance. A wire was passed to the ship but parted and wrapped itself around one of the tug's propellers. While a diver was removing the wire, the ship refloated itself on the incoming tide and proceeded to Mombasa. The cause of stranding was a navigation error in mistaking the entrance of Kilifi Creek for that of Mombasa. Later that year she became the Korthi and in September 1969 was delivered to Japanese breakers at Hirao.

H.M.E.A.S. Rosalind

Builders	:	A. J. Inglis & Co. Glasgow, Scotland. 1941
Length	:	164 feet
Beam	:	27 feet
Displacement	:	545 tons
Machinery	:	Single triple expansion. 950 ihp
Armament	:	1 x 40 mm Bofors gun
		2 x 20 mm Oerlikon guns

The Rosalind deserves a mention as a unique piece of East African maritime history. The ship was an armed trawler of the Shakespeare Class commissioned in the early part of the Second World War and received a battle honour for service in the North Sea. In March 1942 she was adopted by the village of Ystradgynlais, fifteen miles north of Swansea in South Wales. Later that year she became a convoy escort and took part in the Allied landings at Madagascar. After the war the ship remained in East Africa and was handed over to the East African Navy on 7 July 1950 by Sir Edward Twining, then chairman of the East African High Commission. On 13 May 1952 the navy was given the prefix Royal by Queen Elizabeth II, conferred by the new chairman of the High Commission, Sir Evelyn Baring. During the course of her career the ship assisted with taking the Cypriot Archbishop Makarios into exile in the Seychelles, and transporting prisoners to camps in the Lamu area during the Mau Mau Emergency in the 1950s. She also brought relief supplies following hurricane damage at Mtwara in 1955. In 1956 a serious boiler fire earned an African Petty Officer Stoker a British Empire Medal for gallantry with a Governor's commendation to another crew member. Later the ship carried out patrols along the coast engaged in anti ivory smuggling operations, while being a regular visitor to Zanzibar on the occasion of the Sultan's birthday. When Sultan Khalifa bin Haroub died, his son Sultan Abdulla bin Haroub ascended the throne and the ship provided a Guard of Honour for the occasion on 17 October 1960. In June 1961 the ship was detailed to patrol the coast around Pemba and Zanzibar following election riots and brought soldiers of the King's African Rifles to Zanzibar from Dar es Salaam. By December that year the days of the Royal East African Navy were numbered when its disbandment was announced with effect from 30 June 1962. The Navy was sold off in auction and Rosalind bought by African Marine as a harbour based training vessel. Within a few years the ship had been partially cut down and the double bottom lay afloat as a jetty before being scrapped in the 1970s. At the time of the sale she was still burning coal and probably carries the distinction of being the last coal fired warship in the Royal Navy.

Sanko Cherry

Builders	:	Kawasaki Heavy Industries, Sakaide, Japan. 1981
Length	:	780 feet
Beam	:	118 feet
Displacement	:	70,637 tons
Machinery	:	M.A.N. 12 cyl. diesel, 12,100 hp
Position	:	04°.04'.95" E 39°.42'.25" S

On the 18 May 1983, the tanker Sanko Cherry owned by Peacock Tankships of Monrovia was inbound to Mombasa with 58,780 tons of Arabian crude from Ras Tanura, when she grounded on the southern edge of Leven Reef in poor visibility. The main engine was reversed but there was no movement. The salvage contract was taken by the Port Authority with Murri International and United Towing of Hull as sub contractors. Two tugs, El Lamy and Kiboko from the Port Authority were sent to the casualty but a strong south east wind and heavy swell made any assistance difficult. A second attempt with the Murri tug Bison 1 together with El Lamy and Kiboko was abandoned as the tide fell. A sounding survey showed the ship trimmed by the bow. That evening the El Lamy and Bison 1 were positioned astern while Kiboko and the Barbara were secured amidships. Sea conditions were still rough but the effort moved the ship fifty metres astern and caused the vessel's heading to change. The following morning the wind moderated and a diving inspection showed the ship aground under Nos. 2 and 3 tanks. 1,100 tons of crude was transferred from No. 2 to No. 5 tank and the tugs prepared for the evening high tide. With Kiboko and Nyangumi on the port side and Barbara on the starboard and Bison and El Lamy astern, the ship refloated and proceeded into Mombasa. A diving inspection showed some scoring and polishing to the hull. The ship was sold to the Monrovian company Equator Line in 1991 and renamed Equator Express and in 2000 renamed Panoil under the Maltese flag. A year later the name changed to Pebble Beach and in 2004 the ship sustained an engine failure requiring it to be towed to port. In 2005 the ship became the Augusta and after four years trading was scrapped by Xinhui Shipbreaking in Guangdon, China.

Si-Kiang

Builders	:	Ch. Nav de la Ciotat, La Ciotat, France. 1957
Length	:	488 feet
Beam	:	61 feet
Displacement	:	13,800 tons
Machinery	:	B & W 9 cyl. diesel. 8,300 hp.
Position	:	04°.04'.75 S 39°.40'.60" E

The Si-Kiang was one of ten sister ships ordered by Messageries Maritimes to replace the company's ageing Liberty ships, and entered service on the Marseilles to Madagascar and South Africa run carrying cargo and six passengers. While entering Kilindini on 24 February 1964 on a voyage from Le Havre to Cape Town the steering failed. The starboard anchor was let go and the ship swung round with the wind and tide and grounded on the edge of the channel. The tugs Marie Felling and Nguvu were called to assist and two hours later refloated the ship watched by a large crowd on the seashore. The ship entered the port under her own power and berthed alongside for discharging where a diving inspection showed no damage and the ship departed on 4 March. Two years later she was involved in a collision with the coaster Le Tregor, five miles of Cape Gris Nez and rescued the eight crew. On 27 January 1978 the ship was sold to Prince Cia. and renamed Takish H and in 1985 sold to the Turkish breakers Sadikoglu at Alaga with the name changed to Kaleem for the last voyage.

Silago Express

Builders	:	Austin Pickersgill, Sunderland, England. 1974
Length	:	465 feet
Beam	:	65 feet
Displacement	:	14,940 tons
Machinery	:	Sulzer 5 cyl. diesel. 7,500 hp.
Position	:	04°.02'.04" S 39°.43'.50" E

The Silago Express was launched on 21 February 1974 as the Welsh Troubadour for Welsh Overseas Freighters Ltd costing £1.65 million pounds. She was one of a large number of SD14 class of cargo vessels designed by Austin Pickersgill, to replace the Liberty ships of World War II now being scrapped after thirty years service. Six years later the ship was renamed Welsh Jay by Peterhead Shipping and in 1986 sold to Maunland Navigation of the Phillipines and renamed Silago Express. On 9 November 1987 the ship was inbound in ballast to Mombasa from Saleef in South Yemen with grain discharging equipment in containers. Arriving off the port, entry was delayed and the vessel drifted northwards with the current. Late that afternoon the ship was summoned by the port to proceed to the pilot station and made the appropriate change in course. However by nightfall the ship was still to the north and the crew mistook shore lights for those of the leading lights into Mombasa and grounded near the remains of the Kota Menang. The Port Authority was awarded the salvage contract and sub contracted Eagle Tugs with their landing craft Osa Hawk to offload the containers. An attempt to refloat the ship on the 11th was unsuccessful and it was concluded that the ship would have to wait until the high tide on the 18th. The vessel was high and dry at low water and had suffered little damage. To further lighten the vessel 250 tons of fuel oil, diesel and fresh water were removed. Seven days later on the 16th the vessel was refloated by the tug Mwokosi and proceeded into Mombasa to load grain, where the divers reported no damage. The stranding was attributed to a navigation error by the crew in failing to take a regular fix and allow for the northerly current. The vessel continued to trade, and in 1995 was renamed Navira Express and the following year sold and renamed Rena One. On 4 September 1997 with the classification withdrawn the ship arrived at Calcutta for demolition by M.J. Scrap Ltd. who had paid $166.50 per lightweight ton and two months later the task was complete.

Southern Baobab

Builders	:	Ottensner Elsenwerk, Hamburg, Germany. 1952
Length	:	287 feet
Beam	:	39 feet
Displacement	:	1,853 tons
Machinery	:	Twin O.E. 6 cyl. diesels. Single propeller. 1,800 hp
Position	:	04°.04'.50' S 39°.40' E

The Southern Baobab was one of the worlds first bulk cement carriers converted in Hamburg from the German cargo ship Kaspar Robert Moller in 1960 for Southern Line of Mombasa. The arrival of the ship in East African waters saw a huge rise in cement exports from the Baobab cement factory at Bamburi to the Arabian Gulf and islands in the Indian Ocean. Returning from one such voyage to the Seychelles, the ship experienced a sudden blackout while entering the channel into Mombasa on the evening of 27 July 1973. The steering failed and the ship veered to port and grounded on the edge of the channel. The tugs Chuchunge and Simba were sent to assist and shortly before sunrise the next morning the ship was refloated and escorted into port. An enquiry found the cause of the electrical failure to be a faulty windlass starter that short circuited, and tripped the main switchboard circuit breaker. A year later the ship grounded at Astove Island to the north of Madagascar but was refloated and returned to service. The ship was sold in 1975, renamed Baobab and sailed to the Middle East where she was laid up as a floating cement terminal and deleted from Lloyds register in 1978.

Stolt Dimitris

Builders	:	Verolme, Alblasserdam, Holland. 1958
Length	:	600 feet
Beam	:	70 feet
Displacement	:	20,918 tons
Machinery	:	Stork 7 cyl. diesel. 8,600 hp
Position	:	03°.13' S 40°.07' E

Shortly after sunrise on the morning of 8 August 1975 the ship grounded on Leopard Reef off Malindi on a voyage in ballast from Dubai to Mombasa to load molasses. As the sun rose numerous residents reported a vessel aground to the port authorities in Mombasa. With a flooding tide the ship refloated itself after forty-five minutes by discharging ballast and proceeded to Mombasa, where a diving inspection showed some damage and polishing to the hull. At the enquiry held by the port, the Master denied having been aground. Later he blamed the incident on thick fog, bad weather, a strong current and a dark night. The Merchant Shipping Superintendent's report suggested that the Meteorological Office ought to be made aware of the first ever instance of thick fog on the East African coast and the Department of Astronomy should be advised that a competent ship's Master had experienced such a very late sunrise on the day in question! The ship had been launched as the Havprins on 1 February 1958 for P. Meyer of Oslo. Ten years later she was sold and renamed Stolt Eagle and in 1973 sold to Chepalonean Shipping, Piraeus and renamed Stolt Dimitris. They sold the ship after the grounding when she was renamed Queen of Skye and in 1975 she was renamed Siros Trader. Three years later on 5 May the ship was sold for breaking at Brownsville, Texas.

Sunetta

Builders	:	Kanasashi, Toyohashi, Japan. 1975
Length	:	807 feet
Beam	:	125 feet
Displacement	:	87,813 tons
Machinery	:	Kawasaki / M.A.N. 7 cyl. diesel. 20,300 hp.
Position	:	04°.05'.0" S 39°.42'.30" E

The ship was launched as the Carolyn Jane for Agnes Shipping of Singapore and fifteen years later sold to Shell Tankers and renamed Sunetta. On 24 June 1993 the ship arrived off Mombasa with a cargo of 79,218 tons of crude from Fujairah in the United Arab Emirates. The following morning while proceeding towards the pilot pick up point the vessel ran aground. Four tugs were sent out to the ship but were found to have insufficient power for the salvage operation. A Lloyds Open Form was signed on the 25th with the Port Authority and the Smit tug, Smit Lloyd III and the I.T.C. tug Simoom that arrived from Aden. Two lightering vessels, the tanker Nooreen and Ascot were chartered but lightering operations postponed due to rough weather. 10,800 tons was discharged and the ship's starboard anchor run aft as a safety measure. Nine days after stranding with the help of the harbour tugs Faru, Chui, Nduma and Kiboko the ship refloated on the afternoon of 3 July and proceeded into port to discharge. The stranding was attributed to a navigational error. Five years later on 15 May 1998 she arrived at Chittagong, Bangladesh for breaking.

Tenyu Maru 58

Builders	:	Niigata Eng. Co. Niigata, Japan 1974
Length	:	145 feet
Beam	:	25 feet
Displacement	:	284 tons
Machinery	:	Niigata 6 cyl. diesel. 1,250 hp
Position	:	04°.50'.06" S 39°.41'.10" E

The Tenyu Maru 58 was a Japanese trawler that grounded on the northern end of Andromanche Reef while inbound to Mombasa on the evening of 17 March 1978. The tug Ndovu attempted to pull the casualty off but retired with the falling tide. Divecon signed a Lloyds Open Form with the ship's Master and commenced operations by laying the vessels two anchors out behind the ship with a third attached to the stern. Several hours later the vessel began to move with the rising tide, and using the windlass and the stern capstan refloated itself and sailed a week later.

Thorland

Builders	:	Bremer Vulkan, Vegesack, Germany. 1963
Length	:	735 feet
Beam	:	104 feet
Displacement	:	50,230 tons
Machinery	:	Twin B.V. steam turbines, 18,000 shp
Position	:	03°.34'S 47°.15'E

The ship had been built for the Mobil Oil Company as the Mobil Vanguard and sold in 1966 to Thorland Corp. of Panama and renamed Thorland. On the 9 June 1970 she was partially destroyed by a huge gas explosion in No. 9 cargo tank aft of the bridge that peeled open the deck and killed nine of the sixty-one crew. The resulting fire burnt the superstructure and the crew took to the lifeboats. The Swedish ore carrier Bjornrange picked up the distress call and took the survivors to Mombasa. The salvage tug Bremen on station in the port, sailed and located the ship drifting some four hundred miles east of Mombasa. The fire had burnt out and the tug towed the ship towards Mombasa. On arrival some distance off shore, the Harbour Master arrived on the tug Simba and after an inspection around the ship refused permission for it to enter. The damage to the hull was catastrophic with over one hundred feet of deck wrapped over the bridge and sixty feet of the hull side plate missing. The damage was beyond the capability of local repair yards and she was towed into the lee of Pemba island while the Bremen crew rigged pumps and lightened the ship. Ten days after the explosion the ship was towed to Port Amelia in Mozambique pending disposal. On July 10 she was sold to Greek interests and left under tow but broke in half with the fore part sinking, leaving the stern to be towed back to Mocambo Bay, Mozambique. Eight months later on 20 February 1971 the stern departed for Japan under tow of the motor vessel Pati assisted by the salvage tug Svitzer. The stern was joined to the forward section of the tanker Wafra built in 1956 and at the end of September 1971 the ship had been completed as the Achillet. Five years later the ship was purchased by Bu Long Jong Industries of Kaohsiung and arrived for breaking in November.

The after deck peeled forward over the bridge

H.M.S. Turquoise

Builders	:	Earle's Shipbuilding, Hull. 1876
Length	:	220 feet
Beam	:	40 feet
Displacement	:	2,150 tons
Machinery	:	Single horizontal compound. 1,994 ihp
Armament	:	12 x 64 pdr. muzzle loaders. 7 machine guns
Position	:	04°.04'.00 S 39°.40'.00" E

H.M.S. Turquoise was one of six Emerald Class composite screw corvettes completed for the Royal Navy in September 1877 and based on the Pacific station at Valparaiso. In April 1881 the ship was sent to Punta Arenas to assist with the investigation into the loss of H.M.S. Doterel, a sloop destroyed in an internal explosion. Standard dress divers were used to recover the guns and other equipment which received major publicity at the time. Three years later the ship was recommissioned for the Far East and served mainly in India until November 1887 when the ship recommissioned for the East Indies with a new crew under Captain John Brackenbury. Based at Zanzibar the ship and its crew were heavily involved with patrolling the islands on the look out for slave dhows.

On 17 March 1889 the ship was heading into Mombasa and grounded on Andromanche Reef. A message was relayed to the gunboat H.M.S. Algerine in harbour which arrived and assisted with refloating Turquoise two hours after grounding. Divers spent some weeks repairing the hull. Captain Brackenbury and Lieut. Sugden the navigating officer were court-martialled for running the ship aground and found guilty of negligence. Brackenbury was admonished while Sugden was dismissed the ship and later retired from the navy. In December 1889 the ship sailed to Bagamoyo to collect the explorer Henry Morton Stanley returning from an expedition to free the explorer Emin Pasha and on 31st stood by while the grounded French warship Bouvet was refloated at Zanzibar.

The murder of German civilians in the Sultanate of Wituland, north of Mombasa in August 1890 saw the Turquoise involved in a punitive naval expedition with eight other warships and three transports to avenge the deaths of the Germans. The expedition lasted a week during which the crews of the warships destroyed the Sultan's palace at Witu. Turquoise returned to England and decommissioned in 1891 and in January 1892 was sold for breaking.

Winnie

Builders	:	Grangemouth Dockyard Co. Scotland. 1889
Length	:	270 feet
Beam	:	36 feet
Displacement	:	2,532 tons
Machinery	:	Single triple expansion. 161 nhp
Position	:	03°.12'.48" S 40°.13'.00" E

The Winnie was built for C. Nielsen of West Hartlepool and grounded on Pillar Reef, Malindi in the early hours of 18 August 1901 carrying 3,400 tons of coal from Barry, South Wales to Mombasa. A distress message was sent to the ship's agents Smith Mackenzie in Mombasa who were also the Lloyds Agents. They in turn sent a telegram to the cruiser H.M.S. Blanche under Commander Parks lying at anchor in Lamu asking for assistance. Blanche arrived on the afternoon of the 20th and prepared to tow the Winnie off the next morning. The steel wire parted and fouled Blanche's starboard propeller. Having cleared the propeller they laid out the Winnie's anchors to prevent her moving further on to the reef and sailed for Mombasa for additional manilla ropes from the Uganda Railway stores. As they arrived the S.S. Juba departed with labour to discharge the coal. By the time the Blanche returned the weather had deteriorated with heavy seas breaking over the Winnie. Salvage work was impossible until the sea moderated two days later, and the labour commenced throwing coal over the side to lighten ship. Work continued day and night assisted by Blanche's searchlight until the sea picked up and both anchor cables parted driving the ship further on to the reef. When the sea calmed a steadying wire from Blanche was passed to the ship and discharging continued, while Parks took a cutter and surveyed a suitable channel to take the ship out if she continued over the reef. On the 28th steam was raised and at high water the ship slipped over the reef into the northern passage with Parks in command. Despite a damaged rudder the ship steered well enough to make the open sea and that evening Blanche set off with the Winnie for Mombasa, where Parks piloted the ship into Kilindini, and received a letter of thanks from Smith Mackenzie for their efforts. Just over three weeks later a naval court convened in Zanzibar to establish the cause of the stranding. The Master, Captain T. Winder was found guilty of a wrongful act in that he attempted to make port at night without knowledge of his position or the coast and for not taking proper soundings when approaching land. The Winnie was in the opinion of the court not provided with the proper charts for the voyage, and Captain Winder in order to justify his mistake of identifying Malindi for Mombasa, was found guilty of falsifying the log entries produced in court to show that the current was favourable whereas it was adverse. Under the Merchant Shipping Act of 1894 the court suspended Captain Winder's Masters Certificate for a period of three months. In January 1902 the Salvage Association wrote to the Admiralty expressing a desire to award a silver plate and a sum of money to the Blanche. Two months later the Admiralty agreed and in April the Salvage Association wrote to say they were making the necessary arrangements. Winnie was sold eight times with six name changes during the next forty years and as the Lochita she was arrested in Haifa carrying refugees on 25 November 1946 and laid up. Renamed Knesseth Israel she caught fire on 21 August 1949 and was declared a total loss.

Yung Hsiao

Builders	:	Korean Shipbuilding Co. Pusan, Korea. 1969
Length	:	113 feet
Beam	:	25 feet
Displacement	:	320 tons
Machinery	:	Niigata 6 cyl. diesel. 760 hp
Position	:	03°.50' S 39°.51' E

The Yung Hsiao was a Korean trawler that stranded on the reef at Kikambala, thirty miles north of Mombasa in October 1974. The vessel was high and dry at low water enabling Divecon to lay the necessary tow wire from the trawler to a marker buoy anchored in deep water in preparation for the next spring tide. The tug Simba sailed from Mombasa and picked up the tow wire and slowly over the next two hours increased the engine revolutions until the wire rose to the surface. By this time the breakers were sweeping across the reef and the trawler started to move backwards. Half an hour passed as the vessel bumped her way slowly across the shallows, being lifted by the incoming swell. Suddenly without warning the trawler shot backwards over the edge of the reef and almost disappeared as the

stern plunged into a huge wave trough. Seconds later the stern rose out of the breakers with a very wet salvage crew clinging to the ship's railings. The trawler was towed out to sea before transferring the tow from stern to bow for the trip to Mombasa where she was dry docked at African Marine on 14 November.

Zanzibar

Builders	:	J.C. Tecklenborg, Geestemunde, Germany. 1899
Length	:	226 feet
Beam	:	32 feet
Displacement	:	1,270 tons
Machinery	:	Single triple expansion. 90 nhp
Position	:	04°.04'.30" S 39°.40'.80" E

The Zanzibar was the second of three vessels of the same name ordered by the German shipping company William O'Swald for the East African run. The first vessel was lost off the west coast of Zanzibar in 1898. The second ran aground under the lighthouse at Ras Serani near the entrance to the old port Mombasa on the afternoon of 17 April 1900. The following day the British India Line steamer Nevasa attempted unsuccessfully to pull the ship off. A note in the Lloyds Shipping List stated the ship was in a dangerous position. A large quantity of coal was discharged into dhows alongside and on the morning of the 19th she refloated with the help of the Italian gunboat Governolo. After a brief inspection the ship sailed for Zanzibar and Madagascar. Eleven years later the ship was bought by the Italian company Soc. Anon. Vinalcool, renamed Campidano and registered in Cagliari. She changed owners four times in the next twenty years until sold for breaking in 1936.

Miscellaneous wrecks and strandings

Al Azra - The Al Azra, was a wooden-hulled coaster that plied between Mombasa and Zanzibar and ran aground on Diani reef south of Mombasa early on 9 May 2015. It was registered in Zanzibar, with a displacement of 344 tons and a general cargo including plastic shopping bags, rice and cement. The boat had left Mombasa earlier that day for Zanzibar and after the engine stopped the master  decided to beach the craft to effect repairs. By the 14 May the hull had begun to break up and a week later the wood planking was being taken away. Attempts with steel containers to recover the engine were unsuccessful and the wreck abandoned.

Alpha Commander - In the early hours of 23 September 1980 the trawler Alpha Commander inbound to Mombasa with a cargo of frozen fish and twenty-nine crew struck a floating object six miles off Kikambala. Within minutes water was pouring into the hold and efforts to stop the flow were in vain. Half an hour later the engine room was flooded and the pumps unable to cope. A distress call was picked up by the Alpha Challenger which took the vessel in tow to Mombasa. As the trawler was sinking rapidly the crew transferred and just over an hour later she sank in a thousand feet at 03°.57'.30" S 39°.47'.00" E, three miles off Mtwapa. The next day the Murri International tug Bison 1 searched the area but failed to find any trace of the vessel.

Apulia - A twin screw ro-ro cargo vessel launched on 18 July 1980 for the Italian company Lloyd Triestino and entered service in January 1981 on the Italy-Africa route. On 16 November 1983 while entering Kilindini the ship's port propeller was severely damaged on impact with the edge of the main shipping channel. A diving inspection by the author showed one blade missing which was subsequently recovered from the 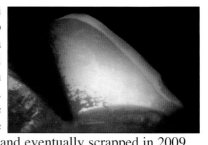 seabed. The ship was later rebuilt as a passenger ferry and eventually scrapped in 2009.

H.M.S. Baia - An Italian steam tug, built as the Baia in 1912 by Cant. Nav. Ruiniti, Ancona, and captured by the Allies at Mogadishu, Somaliland in 1941. Commissioned as H.M.S. Baia in April, she sank between Mogadishu and Mombasa on 3 November 1942.

Caltex Dublin - The 16,600 ton steam tanker touched bottom briefly in the late 1950s when approaching the channel into Mombasa after the north flowing current and heavy swell had taken the ship too close to Leven Reef. It was only the quick thinking of the pilot who called 'Full Ahead' and 'Hard a Port' that saved the day. The vessel was broken up in 1965.

Chance 71 - A Korean trawler aground off Mombasa in 1979 and salvaged by Divecon.

Comrie Castle - Whilst on a voyage from London to Natal the passenger liner Comrie Castle grounded on Leven Reef attempting to enter Mombasa. Anchors were set and no leaks reported. Passengers were taken off and after unloading 700 tons of cargo into lighters, the vessel was re-floated on the 21st and entered Mombasa.

Dae Wang 12 - A Korean trawler ran aground north of Mombasa on 11 May 1978.

Fateh el Khair - A small coaster ran aground in the entrance to Kilindini after steering failure in the 1970s and refloated by the tugs Barbara, Kiboko and Nyangumi.

Gueotec - A French-built deep-sea Tuna Purse Seiner of 1,890 tons, adrift off Mombasa after a main engine gearbox failure in 2004, The tug Comarco Hawk was despatched to assist and towed the vessel into Mombasa for repair.

Hamar - A motorised dhow that capsized off Malindi on 2 March 1991 while carrying refugees from war torn Somalia. This is perhaps the worst passenger casualty on the coast as the vessel was reported carrying at least 900 passengers. 145 bodies were recovered and an estimated 150 are missing.

Ina - A 7,370 ton cargo ship built in 1972 had an accommodation fire at Mombasa while discharging a cargo of fertilizer on the 18 March 1986. The fire destroyed the bridge and accommodation before it was extinguished by the port authorities assisted by the crew of the Royal Navy destroyer H.M.S. Exeter. She was declared a total loss and sold to Al Murtaza Metals of Gadani Beach where she arrived for breaking on 3 December.

Indoyang 18 - A Korean trawler aground off Mombasa in 1975, and refloated by Divecon.

Kherimoyo - A 250 ton Tanzanian vessel carrying sugar, tyres and fifty passengers capsized off Watamu in May 1998 on a voyage from Kismayu to Dar es Salaam.

Kivuna - A trawler aground on the south side of the entrance to Kilindini when the engine failed on 30 October 1979. The Divecon tug Harrier pulled the vessel off on the next high tide.

Kola - On 25 March 1950 a fire broke out in the cargo of hay aboard the ship at Mombasa. The fire was extinguished and the ship returned to service in the Far East. She was a small cargo passenger vessel of 1,466 tons built in 1924 for the British India Line based in Mombasa and used on the East African coastal service.

Kwoo 51 - On 18 April 1978 while anchored in Kilindini, the lookout noticed an adjacent anchored vessel appeared too close for safety. The Master decided to move to a new anchorage and with no pilot aboard grounded the vessel on Mtongwe Reef. After five hours the ship refloated using its own engines and a diving inspection showed no damage. Mtongwe Reef was later removed in a major dredging operation in 1982.

Lee Christine - A concrete hulled trawler sank off shore Kipini at 02°.35' S 04°.37' E

Liza Jane - A wooden coaster that led a charmed life having run aground and sunk on a number of occasions.

Maisho 21 - A Long Liner trawler sailed from Mombasa in 2004 and shortly afterwards experienced turbo charger failure on the main engine and was forced to drop anchor between No. 2 and 3 buoys in the entrance to Kilindini harbour. The Comarco tug Privateer towed the vessel back into Mombasa for repair.

Malik Dinar - A 400 ton Indian vessel aground on Kiwayu Island on a voyage from Bombay to Lamu on 23 June 1998. The ship carrying a general cargo of foodstuff and hardware was salvaged by the Kenya Navy and towed to Lamu for repair.

Miribella III - An 18,000 ton Panamanian tanker on a voyage from Bahrain to Rotterdam in 1968 loaded with diesel fuel experienced engine trouble and called at Mombasa for repairs. On 22 December while passing the Florida Night Club, the ship veered to starboard which a port helm failed to correct. As the bows swung both anchors were let go and the engine reversed but the ship grounded. The tug Nguvu pulled the ship off on the rising tide. The incident was attributed to steering failure.

ML 1057 - A wooden motor launch completed on 30 September 1941 by D. Hillyard of Littlehampton, was lost on 13 October 1944 after detonation of demolition charges in Kilindini.

Nabila - Built in 1962 as the Kronholm, and acquired in 1969 by Southern Line, Mombasa and named Southern Trader. In 1978 she was sold and renamed Nabila and on 14 January 1986 caught fire alongside Southern Engineering. Moved to an anchorage and left to burn out she was declared a constructive total loss and broken up.

Newton - On 8 May 1977 the Newton called for assistance following an engine failure off the Somali coast. The tug Groningen towed the ship into Mombasa where the Doxford main engine bearings were found damaged. The ship remained in service until August 1979 when it was scrapped at Calcutta.

Nyangaku Maru - A Japanese trawler stranded at Kilifi in 1976, and salvaged by Divecon.

Olga Ulyanova - A 13,150 ton Russian cargo ship named after Lenin's sister was on a voyage from London to Dar es Salaam via Mombasa. While approaching the entrance to Kilindini on the evening of 8 June 1978 the ship was advised the pilot would be delayed and should return to the anchorage. The order was ignored and the ship continued in along the leading lights and completed the turn to port onto the Likoni lights. As the ship was passing the Florida Night Club the Master hesitated in view of his proximity to the Likoni ferry. The main engine was put astern and while preparing to drop anchor the bows of the ship grounded on the edge of the channel. Ballast was transferred aft and with the help of the tugs Nyamgumi and Chuchunge the vessel refloated some four hours later having swung round in the tide. A diving inspection showed no apparent damage but the Master was subsequently fined for entering an area that required compulsory pilotage.

Rahmat - A Norwegian built bulk carrier in ballast on a voyage from Dar es Salaam to Mombasa, when the main engine stopped due to fuel starvation on 22 September 2002. The ship drifted over the reef opposite Nyali Beach Hotel and lay in the shallows at 04°.01'.30" S 39°.43'.50" E for some weeks before the Comarco owned Kenya Marine Contractors agreed a lump sum to refloat her in November.

Ricki Nav - A small coaster lost in 1984 between Mombasa and Kismayu.

Seagull - A passenger ferry that usually ran the shuttle service between Zanzibar, Dar es Salaam and Pemba ran aground on Nyali reef, north of Mombasa in April 2008. The vessel was on passage to Mombasa for dry docking with a crew of fifteen and no passengers when strong winds and currents drove it ashore. The ship was subsequently refloated and proceeded for dry docking having sustained damage to the hull.

Shin Jin No. 5 - On 10 July 1978 the Korean trawler grounded off Kilifi and damaged the steering gear and a generator. Shortly afterwards the ship refloated on the incoming tide but unable to steer itself dropped both anchors in view of its proximity to the reef. The radio operator was sent ashore in a small fishing boat and took a taxi to the offices of Murri International in

Mombasa. As they had no salvage tugs available at the time, they subcontracted the port tug Ngamia which arrived on the morning of the 13th. The vessel was refloated that afternoon and towed to Mombasa for repair by African Marine.

Siam Opal – A 32,700 ton general cargo vessel built in 1985 running between Dar es Salaam and Mombasa. In 2009 she broke down off Mombasa and drifted north along the coast with the current. Comarco owned Kenya Marine Contractors were tasked to find and tow her into port and the vessel was located off Malindi. In 2010 the vessel broke down again off Mombasa and

drifted north and was recovered off Malindi once again by Kenya Marine Contractors. Two years later she was sold for breaking at Alang, India.

Southern Pioneer - Completed in 1942 as the August and purchased by Southern Line in 1956. On 11 November 1964 she sustained extensive damage after a gas explosion in a tank while on the slipway at African Marine. Declared a total loss she was beached in Mbaraki creek and eventually broken up.

Theresa Arctic - On 20 June 2017 the 84,040 ton tanker Theresa Arctic grounded off Kilifi. The ship was inbound to Mombasa with 27,500 tons of vegetable oil from Port Klang, Malaysia. A salvage operation was mounted by the Kenya Ports Authority with the assistance of Smit and Comarco. A lightering tanker Theresa Dumai took off some of the cargo and the ship

was refloated and towed into Mombasa on 12 July by Comarco's 14,400 bhp Tug CSC Nelson. After discharge of the cargo the ship was towed to Alang, India for scrap by the CSC Nelson.

Thika - A British India Line steam tug formerly the Empire Minnow built during the Second World War, grounded off Jadini in the early 1950s when on a voyage from Zanzibar to Mombasa. She was refloated, sold and remained in service until the mid 1970s.

Tong Hong 3 - A Korean trawler aground off Mombasa in 1978 and salvaged by Divecon.

Trans Cargo 4 - A 13,000 ton Egyptian freighter carrying a cargo of steel and fertilizer grounded near the remains of the Kota Menang on 8 May 2003. The ship was refloated four days later by port authority tugs in conjunction with the Comarco owned Kenya Marine Contractors.

Twiga - The Port Authority piling barge capsized and sank alongside one of the main shipping berths in Kilindini in 1984. It was salvaged by Divecon using a barge combined with five and ten ton lifting bags.

Ujuzi - A Dutch built fishing trawler originally owned by the United Nations Food and Agriculture Organisation and purchased by Southern Engineering, Mombasa in 1988. On the evening of 24 May 1990 the boat developed engine trouble and another company vessel the Alpha Kilimanjaro towed her from Formosa Bay on the north Kenya coast towards Mombasa. With worsening weather the tow broke a number of times and the vessel grounded on a reef near Malindi that night. The eighteen crew took to the life raft that capsized and pitched them into the sea. The following morning ten bodies were recovered from the beach. The vessel was subsequently refloated and towed to Mombasa for repairs. The enquiry found that part of the cause of the loss of life was the crew abandoning the ship too quickly after the grounding.

Unidentified - Lying on Leven Reef close to the wreck of the Calicut at 04°.04'.80" S 39°.43'.00" E, are the remains of another small ship that came to grief consisting of a small Scotch boiler and parts of the hull.

Unidentified - A small wooden coaster ran aground on Tiwi Reef after engine failure in 1997, not far from the remains of H.M.S. Hildasay. The crew made it through the surf and were taken back to Mombasa.

Unidentified - An early wooden shipwreck that may well be Portuguese has been discovered by divers off Leopard Reef, Malindi containing Chinese and Indian pottery some of which could date back to the 14th Century. Malindi was one of the prime ports for the Portuguese galleons in their trade with India.

Unidentified - The remains of a wreck with pottery from the 15th century discovered off Lamu is thought to be one belonging to the legendary Chinese mariner, Zheng He.

Wiseman - The Wiseman sank in Kilindini harbour and was the subject of a salvage tender offer in the Kenya Gazette of 21 July 1921 under the direction of Captain H.W. Turner, the Port Captain, who three years earlier had been thanked by the Union Castle Line for his part in the salvage of the Comrie Castle.

U-183 - During the Second World War the Type IXc U-Boat, U-183 commanded by Kapitänleutnant Heinrich Schäfer was deployed off the East African coast. U-183 was eventually sunk north of New Guinea by the US submarine Besugo on 23 April 1945.

The Portuguese shipwrecks 1501 - 1670

El Rei - On 8 March 1500 a thirteen ship expedition left Lisbon commanded by Pedro Alvarez de Cabral to gain access to the Far East trade. Six vessels were lost by the time they reached Malindi where they encountered Moorish vessels at anchor. Fearing capture the Moors destroyed their vessels and dumped a quantity of bullion over the side. Cabral traded with India but lost the El Rei on a sandbar off Mombasa and had the wreck burned to deprive the ruler of any benefits but he never the less managed to recover some cannon.

Nossa Senhora de Graca - On 18 April 1542 an expedition of five ships left Lisbon for India commanded by Henrique de Macedo. One ship returned to Portugal while the Graca was wrecked near Malindi with the crew being saved by the remaining three ships.

Flamenga - On 2 April 1557 five ships commanded by Dom Luiz Fernandez de Vasconcellos left for India and the Orient. After rounding the cape they split up and spent time in various ports awaiting the change of monsoon. The Flamenga wintered at Mombasa but shortly after leaving struck a reef and sank in the shallows where most of the cargo was recovered by the survivors.

Aguia - In January 1559 the galleon Aguia commanded by Dom Francisco Barreto with six other vessels left Goa for Portugal laden with treasure and a number of government officials. The fleet sailed together until they ran into a storm off the South African coast. The Santa Maria de Barca began to sink and the captain took the long boat and a number of the more affluent passengers and abandoned ship leaving the remainder to perish. The Aguia and Graca were also damaged but made temporary repairs and continued. Some days later the Graca's hull burst open and the crew and passengers transferred to the Aguia. Worsening weather forced the Aguia to seek shelter for the winter in Mozambique, where a year after leaving Goa, Barreto decided to return for repairs but was wrecked off Mombasa with the loss of over 1,100 lives.

Salvacao - In March 1608 the Salvacao was one of fourteen vessels commanded by Dom Luis de Sousa bound for India. By the time they reached Mozambique for a winter layover, four had been lost and three returned home. The remainder set off in the spring leaving the Salvacao and the Bom Jesus. The latter was captured by Dutch warships while the Salvacao made a run for Mombasa where she was wrecked entering the harbour.

San Filipe - The ship commanded by Dom Martin Afonso sank in 1610 near Mombasa.

Nossa Senhora do Guadalupe - Five ships including the Guadalupe commanded by Joao Soares Henriques sailed for India on 7 April 1614. The Guadalupe was wrecked near Malindi but the crew and a consignment of money in chests was saved.

Santa Amaro - On 21 March 1620 four ships including the Santa Amara commanded by Pedro de Moraes Sarmento sailed for Goa. The Amara and the Nossa Senhora de Paraizo wintered in Mombasa and in May 1621 sailed for India. The Amara ran aground near the harbour entrance and the Paraizo saved the crew, part of the cargo and some of the guns.

Nossa Senhora dos Remedios - In 1670 the Remedios commanded by Captain-Major Simao de Souza de Tavora was one of five ships outbound for Goa when she was wrecked off Mombasa.

Unknown - A caravela under the command of Dom Fernando de Monroy was wrecked at Malindi in 1523. The accompanying ships saved the crew and part of the cargo.

A Deutsche Ost Afrika Line steamer in Dar es Salaam harbour

The Kenya Castle and H.M.S. Ceylon in Dar es Salaam harbour

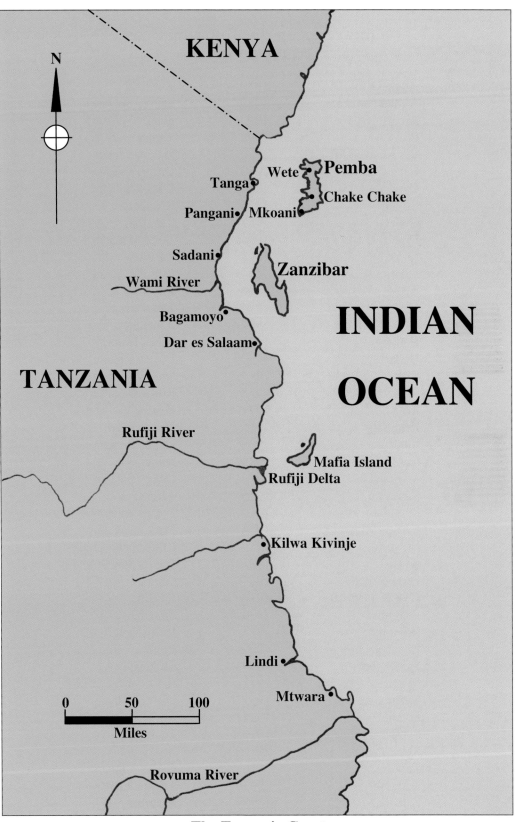

The Tanzania Coast

Shipwrecks on the Tanzania Coast
1499 - 2012

Adele O'Swald	1872	Zanzibar
Almasi	1961	Dar es Salaam
Amaffh One	1990s	Dar es Salaam
Bonsella	1995	Tanga
Canadian Spirit	1990s	Dar es Salaam
Cape Charles	2000	Dar es Salaam
Cape York	1990s	Dar es Salaam
Chyko	1925	Ras Kutani
Colleen	1987	Zanzibar
Dhiran K III	1990s	Dar es Salaam
El Majidi	1872	Zanzibar
Floating Dock	1914	Dar es Salaam
H.H.S. Glasgow	1896	Zanzibar
Glorongay	1974	Zanzibar
Great Northern	1902	Zanzibar
Hedwig	1915	Rufiji Delta
Hodari	1990s	Dar es Salaam
König	1914	Dar es Salaam
S.M.S. Königsberg	1915	Rufiji Delta
Kota Selatan	1971	Pemba
Kronberg	1915	Manza Bay
Lindi	2000	Dar es Salaam
Lord Milner	1929	Dar es Salaam
Marinasi 1	1979	Dar es Salaam
Markgraf	1915	Tanga
Maytham	1999	Dar es Salaam
S.M.S. Möwe	1914	Dar es Salaam
Newbridge	1914	Rufiji Delta
Nyati	1985	Dar es Salaam
Paraportiani	1967	Pemba
H.M.S. Pegasus	1914	Zanzibar
Penguin	1930s	Zanzibar
Rovuma	1915	Rufiji Delta
Royal Sovereign	1960s	Lindi
San Rafael	1499	Mtangata
Skagit	2012	Zanzibar
Slemmestad	1951	Dar es Salaam
Somali	1914	Rufiji Delta
Southern Pioneer	1976	Tanga
Spice Islander 1	2011	Zanzibar
Tabora	1916	Dar es Salaam
Tomondo	1915	Rufiji Delta
Zanzibar	1898	Zanzibar
The Zanzibar Hurricane	1872	Zanzibar

Adele O'Swald

Builders	:	Ernest Dreyer & Co. Reiherstieg, Germany. 1851
Length	:	106 feet
Beam	:	24 feet
Displacement	:	315 tons
Position	:	06°.09'.10" S 39°.09'.40" E

William O'Swald was born in 1798 and began his shipping apprenticeship with the Prussian Overseas Trading Co. of Hamburg and at the age of 24 embarked on a two year round the world trading trip on the sailing ship Mentor. Seven years later in 1831 he founded his own firm with its head office in Hamburg. They first traded with Zanzibar in 1845, and four years later opened an office on the island. His two sons were in turn the company agents in Zanzibar, as were three of their sons. By 1857 the company had thirteen ships, in part due to the success of the export of cowrie shells to West Africa where they were used as currency. One of the ships on this lucrative trade was the Adele O'Swald, a two-masted wooden brig with a cargo capacity of 300 tons. The ship was named after William's wife and built specifically for the Hamburg - Zanzibar trade and had completed nineteen trips to the spice islands at the time of her loss on 19 April 1872. A large number of ships lay at anchor in Zanzibar harbour when a gentle breeze began to blow that increased in ferocity over the next four hours. Small boats and dhows dragged their anchors and were driven ashore. A calm descended for a short while as the eye of the storm passed over the island but within an hour the storm returned with greater force and larger vessels were swamped and stranded. The Adele O'Swald dragged her anchors and capsized on the shore near Malindi. The masts and yards were smashed to matchwood and the hull broken open scattering the cargo of glass in all directions. Captain Scholl and a number of the crew were drowned. Three hours later the storm subsided. The ship was declared a total loss and deleted from the Hamburg ship register on 13 June. The wooden figure head was recovered and now displayed in the Hamburg History Museum. A hundred years later the remains of the wreck were found, with a large number of square glass or '*case*' bottles part buried in the seabed near the entrance to the dhow harbour. They had been designed to be packed closely together to save space and prevent breakage.

Almasi

Builders	:	R. Cock & Son, Appledore, Devon, England. 1898
Length	:	99 feet
Beam	:	22 feet
Displacement	:	150 tons
Machinery	:	Twin N.V. Kromhout 2 cyl. diesel
Position	:	06°.50'.36" S 39°.17'.40" E

The Almasi was one of the last of a dying breed of schooners still plying the Indian Ocean in the late 1950's. The steel hulled vessel arrived in the Seychelles before the Second World War trading around the islands and African mainland with a variety of cargoes and labour for plantations. The ship featured in a number of Indian Ocean travel books including *The Shores of Capricorn*. Her elderly diesel engines left a smoky trail over the azure sea that could be seen for hours before she appeared over the horizon at a sedate five knots. Facilities on board were primitive and passengers either sat on deck or lay in their bunks. She was launched as the topsail schooner Annie Reece for Albert Reece of Sharpness who sold her in 1918. Four years later she was fitted with engines and renamed Diolinda. In 1936 Captain Thomas Voss bought her for £1,750 and with a crew of five left Liverpool on 29 April loaded with cement for the Seychelles. The voyage to Cape Town took over four months where the schooner needed substantial repairs. Voss traded successfully over the next twenty years until his death in 1957 when the Lloyds classification was withdrawn and the ship sold to East African Navigators in Tanganyika. Renamed Almasi, she no longer traded under sail, two masts and the bowsprit having been removed. On 12 November 1961 she arrived in Dar es Salaam from Mombasa with forty-four gallon drums of aviation fuel. At sunrise the next morning the harbour shook as a muffled roar reverberated across the town and a huge fireball soared skywards out of the ship. Four of the crew were incinerated in the blast and two others badly burnt. Years of hard work, neglect and corrosion had eaten the bulkhead between the engine room and hold, and fumes from the fuel were ignited by the blowlamp used to heat the engines before starting. The remains were removed some years later during dredging operations.

Amafhh One

Builders	:	D. W. Kremer & Son, Elmshorn, Germany. 1957
Length	:	205 feet
Beam	:	31 feet
Displacement	:	1,236 tons
Machinery	:	M.A.K. 6 cyl. diesel. 800 hp
Position	:	06°.51'.50" S 39°.17'.85" E

The ship was launched as the Gotaland for Mathias Reederei of Hamburg, trading around the European coast for ten years until sold in 1968 and renamed Walter Kay. Further name changes followed until 1989 when she became the Amafhh One and arrived in East Africa. Like many of the older vessels in the region, a shortage of spare parts and heavy maintenance saw the ship laid up in the upper reaches of Dar es Salaam harbour in the 1990s where she sank some months later. The wreck has since been removed.

Bonsella

Builders	:	De Groot van Slikkerveer, Vliet, Holland. 1960
Length	:	158 feet
Beam	:	25 feet
Displacement	:	480 tons
Machinery	:	Bolens 6 cyl. diesel. 390 hp.
Position	:	05°.07' S 39°.07' E

The Bonsella was the former Bonanza that arrived in Kenya in the 1960's as a coaster and was later fitted with cattle pens on the upper and lower decks. For many years she ran a regular livestock service between the village of Mokowe near Lamu, and the Kenya Meat Commission in Tudor Creek, Mombasa. The ship was sold in the 1980s and converted to carry containers and during loading at Tanga on 27 May 1995, she capsized and lay on her starboard side. The accident was attributed to incorrect weight distribution affecting the stability of the ship. Local personnel succeeded in recovering the containers and returning the vessel to an even keel but failed to refloat her. The salvage contract was awarded to Divecon International who mobilized equipment and personnel from Mombasa, and using a small lighter either side, refloated the vessel and towed her to Mombasa for repair. Sold to new owners, she returned to service under the name Mirage and sank again on 27 June 1998 in Mombasa, but has since been rebuilt and now trading as the Siyama.

Canadian Spirit

Builders	:	Cant. del Tirreno, Genoa, Italy. 1956
Length	:	238 feet
Beam	:	42 feet
Displacement	:	1,306 tons
Machinery	:	Twin Fiat 8 cyl. diesel. 2,054 hp
Position	:	06°.51'.09" S 39°.17'.35" E

The Canadian Spirit was built for Toscano Regionale, Livorno as the Ro-Ro vessel Aethalia, and operated the Italy to Corsica run for many years carrying passengers and up to sixty cars. In 1989 the ship was sold and renamed Pergamus, and a year later sold to Naviero Karemo International of Costa Rica and renamed Canadian Spirit. For over five years the vessel worked as a cargo-passenger ferry between Dar es Salaam, Lindi and Zanzibar. In 1997 the ship was sold to Goldstone Enterprises and laid up at the end of Dar es Salaam harbour where she rolled over and sank in shallow water. The ship has since been scrapped.

Cape Charles / Cape York

Builders	:	Halifax Shipyard, Halifax, Nova Scotia, Canada. 1968
Length	:	156 feet
Beam	:	33 feet
Displacement	:	628 tons
Machinery	:	Deutz 8 cyl. diesel. 1,250 hp.
Position	:	06°.49' S 39°.17' E Cape Charles
		06°.51' S 39°.17' E Cape York

The Cape Charles and Cape York were identical stern trawlers built in Canada for deep sea fishing on the Grand Banks off Nova Scotia. The vessels arrived in Tanzania in the 1990s and after a short period of service were laid up in Dar es Salaam. It was not long before non-ferrous fittings were being removed and the Cape Charles began to list and eventually sank on the afternoon of 8 July 2000. Her sister ship Cape York lies on her starboard side in the upper reaches of the harbour having capsized while being beached for repairs. The hull was later scrapped.

Chyko

Builders	:	Fredrikstad Mek Vaerks, Fredrikstad, Norway. 1905
Length	:	191 feet
Beam	:	33 feet
Displacement	:	712 tons
Machinery	:	Twin triple expansion. 31 nhp
Position	:	06°.55'.80" S 39°.31'.30" E

Launched as the Ipu for the Brazilian company Empreza de Nav. L. Lorentzen, the ship traded from Rio de Janeiro to the Amazon for ten years before being sold to the Union Castle Line for service in Mozambique on the Beira - Chinde run. In 1917 she was requisitioned by the Admiralty until the end of hostilities and in 1924 sold to the Glendenning Steamship Co. and renamed Chyko based at Dar es Salaam. In the early hours of 2 February 1925 the Chyko struck the edge of Fungu Miza reef, thirteen miles south of Dar es Salaam on a voyage from the Rufiji Delta with a cargo of mangrove poles. The water rose rapidly in the engine and boiler room and the Master beached the vessel near Ras Kutani, when the pumps could no longer cope. The fires were extinguished and the crew took to the upper deck and waited to be rescued. One gentleman passenger waded ashore and made his way to Dar es Salaam to raise the alarm. The crew were rescued but the exposed position meant a salvage operation would have been extremely dangerous, and the use of dhows to offload the cargo impossible until the monsoon changed. Since the nearest salvage operatives were at Lorenco Marques, the Lloyds surveyor considered the vessel a total loss. She was stripped of all useful fittings and the remains were eventually washed into shallow water where they can be seen just off the beach. A Court of Inquiry convened on 2 March in Dar es Salaam established the ship was seaworthy and well found. There was only one certificated officer on board which was considered sufficient for the voyage, and the ship grounded on the reef due to an abnormal set of the current, possibly helped by poor steering. The bearing taken at 02.50 of Ras Kanzi light by the standard compass was incorrect and that more bearings should have been taken. The lead was not used and would have been unnecessary had more bearings been taken.

Colleen

Builders	:	Holland
Length	:	120 feet
Beam	:	30 feet
Displacement	:	387 tons
Machinery	:	Musashi 6 cyl. diesel. 500 hp
Position	:	06°.09'.16" S 39°.11'.50" E

In the early 1970s the Dar es Salaam Harbour Authority contracted out the dredging of the entrance channel to the port in a move to improve navigation and on completion of the contract, two of the hopper barges were advertised for sale. They were bought by a local business man and entered service along the Tanzanian coast as the Colleen, (named after his wife) and VDH 12. While on a voyage from Tanga to Zanzibar on 4 June 1987 with a cargo of cement, telegraph poles and a container, the Colleen began taking on water. On arrival in Zanzibar the port pilot requested permission to beach the vessel at Forodhani. This was refused and the Colleen berthed alongside the passenger cargo vessel Mapinduzi. As the vessel continued to settle, the container was offloaded and shortly afterwards she sank. Most of the cargo was removed with the exception of the bagged cement before the vessel was raised and towed three hundred yards to the north, where she sank again and was abandoned as a total loss.

Dhiran K III

Builders	:	Ailsa Shipbuilding, Troon, Scotland. 1960
Length	:	271 feet
Beam	:	39 feet
Displacement	:	2,830 tons
Machinery	:	H. Widdop 8 cyl. diesel. 1,135 hp.
Position	:	06°.51' S 39°.18'.25" E

The ship was launched as the cargo vessel Eastwood for Constantine Lines of Glasgow. Eight years later she was converted into a tanker and sold the following year when the Lloyds Register classification was withdrawn and the name changed to Palmavera. After four more changes of ownership, the ship was transferred to Rapid Investment of Honduras and renamed Dhiran KIII in 1990, operating along the East African coast. Withdrawn from service in the late 1990s the ship was laid up at the end of Dar es Salaam harbour and eventually sank. The wreck has since been removed.

El Majidi

Builders	:	Alexander Stephen & Sons, Glasgow, Scotland. 1863
Length	:	230 feet
Beam	:	32 feet
Displacement	:	1,160 tons
Machinery	:	Single compound. 220 nhp.
Position	:	06°.50' N 50°.00' E

The El Majidi was one of Zanzibar's most famous ships having been the first composite auxiliary screw steamship in the world. Ordered by the shipping company Robertson & Co of Glasgow as the Sea King she was operated by Shaw Savill on behalf of the British government carrying troops to New Zealand. Not long afterwards the ship came to the notice of the American Confederate government which purchased her to replace the C.S.S. Alabama sunk off the French coast on 19 June 1864. The ship was commissioned as the Shenandoah on 19 October under the command of Lt. James Waddell, after installing a mixed armament of muzzle loading cannon off Madeira. During the next fourteen months the raider captured nine American Union flagged vessels, all but two of which were sunk. In January 1865 the ship arrived in Melbourne, Australia for dry docking. Waddell had planned to attack the American South Pacific whaling fleet but learned they had dispersed, and instead headed into the North Pacific intercepting four more Union vessels. As he cruised north the Confederacy collapsed but unaware of the situation he attacked the northern whaling fleet, destroying over twenty vessels. While heading south towards San Francisco for a proposed bombardment of the city, he encountered the English sailing ship

August which relayed news of the Confederate surrender. Waddell, now in command of a stateless ship and worried about being hung as a pirate, had the guns placed in the hold and headed for Liverpool via Cape Horn, where he handed the ship over to the Royal Navy. Thomas Haines Dudley, the United States Consul in Liverpool was tasked with disposing of four Confederate ships handed over to the United States by the British. In April 1866 Dudley sold the Shenandoah for just over £17,000. The U.S. Government, apparently satisfied, then authorised him to sell the others. The following year the ship was sold to the Sultan of Zanzibar, Sultan Ali bin Said, renamed El Majidi and damaged in the Zanzibar hurricane on 15 April 1872. After temporary repairs the ship set sail for Bombay on 10 September with 130 passengers and crew but still leaking badly had to be abandoned and sank a few days later off the Somali coast.

Floating Dock

Builders	:	Blohm & Voss, Hamburg, Germany. 1901
Length	:	212 feet
Beam	:	55 feet
Displacement	:	1,800 tons
Position	:	06°.49'.30" S 39°.18' E

The port of Dar es Salaam increased in importance following the Treaty of Berlin in July 1890, when the town was designated capital of German East Africa, and major shipping companies including the Deutsche Ost Afrika Linie began trading from Europe. Before long there was a requirement for ship repair facilities and a floating dock was towed from Germany capable of accommodating the largest ships entering the port. The dock was the only one of its kind on the east coast, the nearest other facilities being either in Bombay or South Africa. By July 1914 it was evident that the European political situation was leading to war and the German colony prepared for hostilities. War was declared on 4 August and four days later the cruiser H.M.S. Astraea shelled and destroyed the radio station. Korvettenkäpitan Zimmer, the naval commander responsible for the defence of the port, believing it was a prelude to invasion, scuttled the survey vessel Möwe and two days later sank the dock across the harbour entrance. The dock settled at an angle with one side in twenty five feet and the other in fifty. Shortly afterwards the Admiralty ordered

Salvaging the dock with compressed air, 1922

Commander Ingles, Captain of H.M.S. Pegasus to carry out an inspection of the dock. The report was passed to the Perim Island Salvage Co. in Aden with a view to refloating it. However with an increase in hostilities the matter was never finalized and the dock remained in situ until after the war. By 1921 the dock had become a major issue as it was blocking the entrance to the harbour for larger ships. Two salvage companies were asked to quote for the removal but concluded it was not worth salvaging for the scrap value. The dock was eventually refloated in April the following year and moved to one side of the channel by Commander Ingles, now responsible for all salvage operations in the port. There it remained until 1958, when explosive demolition took place for six months. On 15 May 1965 a letter from the East African Railways and Harbours to the Hydrographic Office in Taunton stated that the remains were being removed and the job was eventually completed on 6 July.

The dock lying alongside the shipping channel, 1935

H.H.S. Glasgow

Builders	:	William Denny & Co., Dumbarton, Scotland. 1878
Length	:	210 feet
Beam	:	29 feet
Displacement	:	1,416 tons
Machinery	:	Single compound. 172 nhp.
Position	:	06°.09'.60" S 39°.11'.15" E

During the early 1870s H.M.S. Glasgow was the flagship of the Royal Navy's East Indies Squadron based on the East African coast. Sultan Bargash bin Said, ruler of Zanzibar had visited the ship on a number of occasions and following the loss of his own vessels in the hurricane of 1872, expressed an interest in a new steam yacht on similar lines. Sir William Mackinnon, founder of the British India Line suggested Denny's as a reliable ship builder and the keel was laid on 14 May 1877. She was composite built of four-inch teak planks secured to iron frames with bronze bolts and designated a war sloop with steam machinery designed by Denny. The propeller was located in a well and could be lifted off the shaft when under sail. Launched on 2 March 1878 the ship was named Glasgow after its naval forebear, and the final cost was £32,135. Glasgow arrived in Portsmouth in April to be fitted with an armament of nine pounder muzzle loading guns, a gift from Queen Victoria, before departing on the 17th. On arrival Bargash was rowed out to inspect his new acquisition and was not impressed. Instead of a 250 foot long ship with a fifty foot beam, he received a ship forty foot shorter with two thirds the beam. Glasgow was considered insufficiently elegant for a Royal Yacht and condemned to swing round a buoy in the harbour for the next eighteen years. Bargash died ten years later and his successors also showed little interest in the vessel. On 25 August 1896 Sultan Hamed bin Thuwaini died and Bargash's son Khaled, and a crowd of followers stormed the palace and declared himself the new ruler. This was against the wishes of the British Government who quickly responded with an ultimatum to vacate the palace or face the might of the Royal Navy. He

Glasgow at Zanzibar in the 1890s

refused, and on the morning of the 27th, five warships opened fire and destroyed the palace in a forty-five minute bombardment. Glasgow was sunk after she fired on the flagship H.M.S. St. George. Rear Admiral Harry Rawson the Commander in Chief, had forbidden an attack on the ship unless provoked. A number of shots were fired at the ship along the waterline splintering the hull and Glasgow sank leaving her masts and funnel above the surface. The guns were recovered and three survive to this day: one mounted on a plinth in Zanzibar Stone Town and two at the Dar es Salaam Yacht Club. The wreck lay in front of the palace until 1907 when it was inspected and proposals made to remove it using cables under the hull. The project was shelved until 1912 when the British Resident, John Sinclair ordered its immediate removal as a hazard to navigation. The wreck was broken up by the Perim Island Salvage Co. whose salvage vessel Meyun removed the pieces and dumped them at sea. A year later Glasgow had been reduced to its bottom frames and the job completed. The remains were rediscovered sixty years later with the engine block and propeller shaft and yielded some interesting finds including crockery, cutlery and fuses from the nine pounder shells together with hundreds of iron ballast blocks.

The wreck in 1899, with the Great Northern in the background

Glorongay

Builders	:	F. Curtis, Looe, Cornwall. 1942
Length	:	124 feet
Beam	:	17 feet
Displacement	:	126 tons
Machinery	:	Twin Paxman Ricardo R.P.H. 6 cyl. diesel. 250 hp
Position	:	05°.45' S 39°.25' E

Glorongay was a wooden hulled Fairmile Type B, Rescue Motor Launch, with the Pennant No. 533, one of over six hundred built during the Second World War. They proved to be excellent sea boats fitted with a variety of armament depending on their role, and Hall Scott Defender 1,200 hp. petrol engines as diesel units were unavailable. Her armament consisted of 1 x 3 pdr. gun, 2 x .303 Lewis machine guns and twelve depth charges. Most of her wartime career was spent around Scotland until January 1946 when she was sold by the Small Craft Disposals Unit at Gillingham, Kent. Later that year she was converted into a yacht, and re-engined by the Rowhedge Ironworks and named Rosabelle based at Maldon, Essex. In 1961 the superstructure was modified and the hull lengthened by twelve feet and four years later she was renamed Glorongay. Ten years later she was based in Malta and sailed for the Middle East via the Cape of Good Hope for charter work. Engine trouble and hull damage off the Somali coast forced her into Mogadishu where after negotiations she was sold and towed to Mombasa. After a refit the vessel was placed on charter work including a trip to Astove Island. During a trip to Mafia Island off the coast of Tanzania in 1974, the port propeller and A bracket hit the edge of Luala Reef and she returned to Mombasa for repair. During the voyage north, the yacht took the east coast route round Zanzibar which subjected the damaged bracket to undue stress in the heavy seas. The bracket broke loose from the hull resulting in a major leak beyond the capacity of the bilge pumps. With the vessel settling lower in the water there was little alternative but to beach the yacht on the nearest reef which happened to be the northern tip of Mnemba Island. With the vessel awash the owners mounted a salvage operation but only recovered some of the diving equipment, furniture and contents of the drinks cabinet. Within days Glorongay was a total loss and sections of the double diagonal hull floated ashore to be used as firewood by the villagers. Mnemba is now an exclusive holiday resort and the wreck was rediscovered in the 1990s, however little remains other than the engines, pipe work and ballast.

Great Northern

Builders	:	Denton Gray, West Hartlepool, England. 1870
Length	:	240 feet
Beam	:	32 feet
Displacement	:	1,422 tons
Machinery	:	Single compound. 130 nhp.
Position	:	06°.10'.25" S 39°.08'.55" E

The Great Northern and her crew under Captain Larnder were well known along the coast and her loss on Fungu Chawamba Reef in Zanzibar harbour on 5 December 1902 was widely reported. The telegraph cable to Mombasa had been damaged and the crew spent the day carrying out repairs. That evening while returning to the anchorage near Zanzibar town the ship ran aground and tore a twelve foot hole in the side. The hull filled rapidly and with the weight of a hundred miles of cable quickly settled at an angle leaving the bows and the bridge above the water. Various warships came to the ship's assistance but after an inspection by divers the wreck was declared a total loss. Larnder cabled Lloyds, '*Ship has settled down and Lloyds Agent agrees considering her age and position with half the bottom out, operations to recover the hull would be money wasted. Have arranged to stow all cable recovered on board Nyanza. Am now recovering everything of sufficient value but lighters for cable not available at present*'. By 15 December the cable ends had been prepared for lifting and four days later the recovery commenced. The remainder of the test equipment and useful fittings were also removed and the hull abandoned. Larnder resigned and left Zanzibar for Europe aboard the s.s. Präsident on 13 January 1903. Launched as the Euxine in February 1870, she was sold to Hooper Telegraph Works to be fitted out for cablelaying. During the next seven years the ship was in the Far East and the Mediterranean. In 1879 she was purchased by the Eastern South African Telegraph Co. as a repair ship based at Zanzibar. A major refit was completed in 1892 which included new cable winches and a more powerful triple expansion main engine. She was an elegant

Aground on Fungu Chawamba Reef, January 1903

looking vessel resembling a large private yacht with a single yard on the foremast and schooner rig. To quote a contemporary article, '*She was efficiently fitted for her work as well as the comfort of her staff and crew, and some of the most intricate and delicate electrical appliances in the world were to be found on the ship, and very proud of the fact were the gallant fellows who composed the crew*'. The bows of the ship were visible on the reef until the late 1950s when the rusted remains were cut up. The wreck was rediscovered in the 1970s, and is now a popular dive site with the main engine and part of the hull sloping down to forty feet.

Fifty years later the bows were still visible on the reef

Hedwig

Builders	:	H. Stulcken, Hamburg, Germany. 1913
Length	:	171 feet
Beam	:	27 feet
Displacement	:	571 tons
Machinery	:	Single compound. 300 ihp.
Position	:	08°.55' S 39°.15' E

The Hedwig was built for the Deutsche Ost Afrika Linie and based at Tanga. On 6 August 1914 while on a voyage to India, the ship was directed to intercept the D.O.A.L. liner Markgraf to ensure she headed for Tanga and not Mombasa and internment. In September the Hedwig was armed with a 37 mm gun and transferred to the Rufiji delta as part of the defence force in support of the cruiser Königsberg. When Königsberg arrived in need of fuel, the Hedwig sailed to Lindi to collect two lighters laden with coal from the steamer Präsident. With the destruction of the Königsberg on 11 July 1915, the delta force gradually disbanded and the ship together with the Rovuma and Tomondo was sunk in a backwater on 9 October. They were rediscovered in the early 1920s by Captain Ingles of Pegasus fame who started the Rufiji Delta Trading Co. to export mangrove poles. All three were bought by the company and the Hedwig and the Rovuma scrapped while the Tomondo was repaired and returned to service.

Hodari

Builders	:	Cook, Welton & Gemmel, Beverley, England. 1945
Length	:	191 feet
Beam	:	27 feet
Displacement	:	726 tons
Machinery	:	Single triple expansion. 850 ihp
		Franco Tosi 5 cyl. diesel. 1,300 hp
Position	:	06°.50'.85" S 39°.17'. 95" E

The Hodari was launched as the Isles Class trawler H.M.S. Trodday with the Pennant No. J431. At the end of the Second World War she and hundreds of others were put up for disposal. By July 1959 the ship was laid up in Malta pending scrap but reprieved and converted into a tanker with the addition of an extra forty feet. The steam machinery was replaced and the ship renamed Nicola Jacovitti. She was sold in 1962 and renamed Antonella and Nado after a sale in 1971. Five years later she was bought by Agip Petroleum and renamed Hodari for the Tanzania coastal trade. By 1994 the ship had ceased trading and was laid up and sank alongside the dockyard jetty in Dar es Salaam. The area has now been reclaimed and the wreck removed.

König

Builders	:	Reiherstiegwerft, Hamburg, Germany. 1896
Length	:	403 feet
Beam	:	47 feet
Displacement	:	4,825 tons
Machinery	:	Twin triple expansion. 2,500 ihp
Position	:	06°.49'.30" S 39°.17'.08" E

In July 1890 the British and German governments ratified the Berlin treaty whereby the Sultan of Zanzibar's mainland territory was divided between the two countries to become the colonies of British and German East Africa. The Reichstag in Berlin agreed to subsidise a mail steamship line to German East Africa and the Deutsche Ost Afrika Linie company was founded in Hamburg in 1890, with Adolph Woermannn as director. The steamers ran through the Suez Canal via Zanzibar and Dar es Salaam to Durban. The first ships carried few passengers until 1896 when the Herzog and König entered service capable of carrying sixty-five passengers in First and fifty in Second and Third Class. In 1911 the König entered service on the Zanzibar - Bombay run until 30 July 1914 when she arrived in Dar es Salaam with news of impending hostilities. On 21 October a month after the sinking of H.M.S. Pegasus at Zanzibar by the Königsberg, the cruiser H.M.S. Chatham anchored off the port in search of the raider. The masts of the König, Feldmarschall and Tabora could be seen above the trees and Chatham opened fire at the ships in the belief that the masts were those of the Königsberg. The Germans hoisted a number of white flags and the firing ceased. The Feldmarschall had been hit by a shell that wounded two crew. Having identified the three ships Chatham departed. Five weeks later on 28 November the Navy returned in force determined to disable the vessels. A raiding party consisting of the tug Helmuth and two steam cutters set off to investigate the ships under a cease-fire agreement. The König's engine was disabled by a demolition charge and before long the party came under fire and had to retreat to the safety of the battleship H.M.S. Goliath anchored offshore. Goliath responded by shelling the town and destroying the Governor's palace and a few days later the König was towed to the harbour entrance as a blockship. The ship swung while being scuttled and lay in the shallow water to one side of the entrance. With the increasing importance of Dar es Salaam after the war, Commander

Aground in the entrance, 1919

Ingles, of Pegasus fame was contracted to remove the wrecks in the harbour. The König was the first to be refloated in 1921 and moved to the upper reaches of the harbour. Three years later she was sold for £500 to the local company Jiwanji Brothers who on 13 September sent this request to the Director of Marine, '*Sir, We have the honour to request you that the question of filling up the holes of the wreck may be left aside but we shall be much thankful to you if you will kindly favour us by pumping out the water from it and pulled her to the shore at your earliest convenience. We placed this request before you as we don't know how to lift the anchor hence this request to you. We undertake to pay all cost incurred in respect of this work*'. That same afternoon he replied '*Gentlemen, With reference to your letter of even date, I regret I am unable to pump the harbour dry*'. The ship was subsequently refloated and scrapped.

S.M.S. Königsberg

Builders	:	Imperial Navy Yard, Kiel, Germany. 1905
Length	:	376 feet
Beam	:	43 feet
Displacement	:	3,300 tons
Machinery	:	Twin triple expansion. 12,000 ihp.
Armament	:	10 x 4.1 inch Krupp guns. 8 x 2.1 inch guns
Position	:	07°.52'.13" S 39°.14'.50" E

S.M.S. Königsberg was the first of a number of new city class cruisers ordered from German naval yards in 1903/4. Sea trials commenced on 6 April 1907 but were postponed when the ship became escort to the Kaiser's royal yacht Hohenzollern. Between 1907 and 1912 the cruiser served with the Baltic Fleet and paid a number of visits to England and the Mediterranean. In June 1911 the ship was refitted for the tropics and laid up two years later. In April 1914 she was recommissioned for the German East Africa station under the command of Fregattenkäpitan Max Looff and arrived in Dar es Salaam on 6 June to become the focal point of a local trade fair. With the advent of war in Europe, Looff put to sea on 31 July with orders to become a raider. War was declared on 4 August and two days later the City of Winchester became the first British merchant ship casualty of the First World War when she was intercepted and sunk by the cruiser on 12 August. Coal was in short supply and after exhausting supplies from the collier Somali, Königsberg took refuge in the Rufiji Delta, south of Dar es Salaam awaiting further consignments. Two weeks later on 19 September, coaling was complete and the ship made ready for the long trip back to Germany. That afternoon a report reached Looff of a British cruiser anchored at Zanzibar. The following morning Königsberg appeared at the Zanzibar anchorage and destroyed H.M.S. Pegasus in a brief one sided duel that lasted less than an hour. Some hours later a major engine failure put Königsberg back in the delta again for repair and within a matter of days the damaged machinery was taken overland to Dar es Salaam. The loss of the Pegasus brought a full scale search of the coast and six weeks later on 30 October, Königsberg was discoveered about to leave. A blockade was enforced and the collier Newbridge sunk across one of the delta mouths. To plot the raider's whereabouts a Curtis seaplane was brought from Durban but was shot down shortly afterwards. Two Sopwith seaplanes were shipped out from England in February 1915 with plans to bomb the raider but were soon condemned as unsuitable in the tropics. They were followed by three Short seaplanes that proved little better. Eventually two new Henri Farman and two Caudron landplanes were delivered in June and a base set up on Mafia Island. On 3 June two shallow draft monitors H.M.S. Mersey and Severn arrived and a primitive morse code introduced to coordinate the aircraft spotting with the monitors fire. A month later they were all set for the final showdown on 6 July. The first day's efforts resulted in four hits out of six hundred shots fired. A second attempt on 11th resulted in serious damage and heavy casualties. Looff scuttled the ship and the guns were salvaged and used in the land campaign under Col. Paul von Lettow-Vorbeck. The wreck was bought and sold a number of times during the next fifty years, with salvage operations removing quantities of non-ferrous material. The wreck gradually rolled over on to its starboard side and disappeared into the river bed in 1966. Today there is nothing left other than small pieces of pottery and glass in the bushes adjacent to the site.

The last of the Königsberg, 1965

Kota Selatan

Builders	:	c.v.d. Giessen, Krimpen, Holland. 1938
Length	:	455 feet
Beam	:	62 feet
Displacement	:	8,315 tons
Machinery	:	Twin Werkspoor 8 cyl. diesel. 8,000 hp
Position	:	05°.21'.50" S 39°.49'.50" E

The Kota Selatan was launched as the Straat Soenda, one of a number of sister ships for the Dutch company Koninklijke Paketvaart Lijnen based in Batavia. They were express cargo liners with excellent accommodation for twelve passengers in both double and single cabins. After thirty years service the ship was sold to Pacific International Lines of Singapore and renamed Kota Selatan. During a voyage from Dar es Salaam to Mombasa on 19 May 1971 with 5,000 tons of general cargo, the ship grounded on a reef off the east coast of Pemba. A check of the hatches and double bottom tanks showed water rising rapidly in No. 2 and 3 holds. As the bow settled the ballast pumps were switched on but the inrush of water was too great and with engines at full ahead the ship was driven further on the reef and both anchors let go. The distress call was received by the Mombasa signal station and the German freighter Rudolph Breitscheid that picked up the crew from four lifeboats. In the meantime the ship continued to settle by the bows and the propellers appeared above the surface. The crew were landed at Mombasa and filed a report investigated by the Merchant Shipping Superintendent. An enquiry found the Master at fault, in having set a course too close to the coast, failed to check his position regularly and ignored the 3-4 knot northerly current. On the 23rd the salvage surveyors chartered a plane to investigate the loss, but despite a thorough search of the entire east coast of Pemba, the ship had disappeared. In the vicinity was the fisheries research vessel Manihine which carried out an echo sounder survey of the area and found oil coming to the surface from a depth of over 200 feet.

Kronborg

Builders	:	W. Gray, West Hartlepool, England. 1906
Length	:	343 feet
Beam	:	49 feet
Displacement	:	3,587 tons
Machinery	:	Single triple expansion. 188 nhp.
Position	:	04°.54'.50" S 39°.09'.50" E

The Kronborg was the former Rubens of the Bolton Shipping Company, whose vessels were named after famous painters. On the outbreak of the First World War the ship was impounded in Hamburg and the crew interned. When the cruiser Königsberg was trapped in the Rufiji Delta, plans were implemented to break the blockade and supply coal and ammunition to the warship, and much needed supplies to Colonel von Lettow-Vorbeck's troops. In late 1914 Rubens was altered to represent the Danish freighter Kronborg and departed for East Africa on 19 February 1915 round the Cape of Good Hope. On 8 April off the Madagascar coast, the ship sent out a radio call to the Königsberg that was intercepted and passed to Admiral King-Hall, C. in C. of the Royal Navy squadron on the

Kronborg burning in Manza Bay, 14 April 1915

Fifteen years later

East African coast. Kronborg arrived off Manza Bay north of Tanga on the 14 April but was intercepted by the cruiser H.M.S. Hyacinth which gave chase. The cruiser suffered an engine failure and Kronborg escaped into the bay where the crew beached her and set the timber deck cargo alight giving the impression of destroying the ship. Attempts by Hyacinth's crew to extinguish the fire were unsuccessful and the ship abandoned after a few shells had been fired into her. The Germans returned, extinguished the fire and salvaged the cargo of arms and ammunition but left the coal. Some months later the cruiser H.M.S. Challenger escorted by minesweepers anchored in Manza Bay and sent an armed party to inspect the wreck where it was obvious the cargo had been discharged. It was a costly mistake by the Allies that enabled Lettow-Vorbeck to continue the campaign in East Africa until after the Armistice in 1918. The ship lay there until September 1956 when the Italian salvage company Mawa Handels Anstalt began repairing the numerous holes in the hull. After a seventy day salvage operation the ship was towed to Dar es Salaam by the tugs Simba and Nyati and the 1,600 tons of coal sold to East African Railways and Harbours and the hull broken up for scrap.

Salvage operations in the after hold, 1956

Kronborg enters Dar es Salaam

Discharging the coal after forty years

169

Lindi

Builders	:	Bolsonaes Verft, Molde, Norway. 1974
Length	:	206 feet
Beam	:	40 feet
Displacement	:	854 tons
Machinery	:	Wichman 6 cyl. diesel. 990 hp
Position	:	06°.49'.10" S 39°.17'.20" E

The Lindi arrived in Dar es Salaam in 1980 having been bought by the Tanzanian Shipping Corporation with accommodation for eighteen First, one hundred Second Class passengers and twenty-one crew. After thirteen years trading the ship was surveyed and found to be in a poor state of repair and deemed fit for cargo only. Five years later she was laid up in Dar es Salaam and a survey showed heavy corrosion with numerous cement repairs and leaks. While moored alongside the jetty in 2000 the ship developed a port list that gradually increased until at 08.30 on the morning of 4 October she rolled over and sank on her port side. After some salvage negotiations the vessel was cut down to the low water mark but some of the wreckage remains.

Lord Milner

Builders	:	J. L. Meyer, Papenberg, Germany. 1898
Length	:	172 feet
Beam	:	28 feet
Displacement	:	495 tons
Machinery	:	Twin triple expansion. 755 ihp.
Position	:	06°.45'.90" S 39°.19'.95" E

The Lord Milner was the former German East Africa government steamer Kaiser Wilhelm II used by the Governor before the First World War. She was one of a number of ships disabled by the Royal Navy on 28 November 1914, when a naval party from H.M.S. Goliath investigated the merchant ships anchored in Dar es Salaam, and appears to have been scuttled by the retreating Germans on 4 September 1916. After the invasion of the port by the Allies, the ship was used as a landing stage for other vessels to berth alongside. In 1919 as there was a shortage of small coastal vessels she was repaired and renamed Lord Milner after the British politician Lord Alfred Milner appointed Colonial Secretary after the war. In the absence of other coastal communication, the ship maintained an intermittent passenger and freight service to Kilwa, Mafia and Lindi and north to Tanga and Mombasa. She was an ideal size since the Dar es Salaam entrance channel was still partially blocked by the floating dock and the liner König, making passage for larger ships difficult. The Milner ran aground in 1920 and to lighten the vessel the salvors dumped the cargo of cotton seed over the side believing it to belong to the government. Such was not the case and the government eventually had to settle with the owners. The subsequent secret enquiry on the affair led to correspondence between the editor of the Dar es Salaam Times and the Port Authority as to why it should be held in secret when it was in the public interest to know why the ship stranded. Another tale concerned the race between her and the American ship Chapahua from Mombasa to Dar es Salaam in which the Milner won by a hairsbreadth at the cost of burnt out boiler tubes which possibly spelt the beginning of the end. By 1923 a League of Nations report noted the vessel was unseaworthy and should be replaced. On 6 March 1924 the ship was put up for sale with tenders closing on 30 June. The tender stated the boilers were in fair condition, the engines in good condition and the hull required overhaul. There were no bids and the ship remained in Dar es Salaam until eventually condemned, and sunk on Daphne Reef north of Dar es Salaam in 1929.

Marinasi 1

Builders	:	Fredrikshaven Vaefrt & Tordok, Fredrikshaven, Denmark. 1970
Length	:	213 feet
Beam	:	36 feet
Displacement	:	1,043 tons
Machinery	:	Alpha 8 cyl. diesel. 980 hp
Position	:	06.51'.04" S 39.17'.55" E

The Greek owned Marinasi 1 was the former Merc Selandia owned by the Danish company Mercandia. On 8 January 1979 the ship was on a voyage from Mtwara to Italy and London with a cargo of 1,048 tons of sesame seeds when fire broke out in the engine room. The fire spread to the accommodation and the crew abandoned ship to be picked up by the Dar es Salaam tug Chaza which towed the ship into harbour. The fire was extinguished and the vessel beached. In putting the fire out, the engine room and after hold had flooded and the vessel sank on 10 January leaving the decks awash at low water. A report in Lloyds List in June stated that cargo was being dissipated by the tide. The owners were given two weeks to sign a Lloyds Open Form and Diving Contractors Ltd. awarded the salvage contract. The wreck was refloated on 2 May 1982, towed to Mombasa and scrapped the following year. A section of the ship survives as a storage tank.

Markgraf

Builders	: William Armstrong, Mitchell & Co, Newcastle, England. 1893
Length	: 365 feet
Beam	: 43 feet
Displacement	: 3,680 tons
Machinery	: Single triple expansion. 2,200 ihp
Position	: 05°.03'.53" S 39°.05'.83" E

The Markgraf was the former Mark built for Norddeutschen Lloyd carrying thirty-four First and seventy-nine deck class passengers. In 1902 following service to South America, the ship was sold to the Deutsche Ost Afrika Linie, renamed Markgraf and used on the round Africa trips until 1910 when she was transferred to the Zanzibar - Bombay run. On 24 July 1914 the ship departed Bombay for Tanga where she arrived on 6 August 1914, two days after declaration of war. After discharging cargo the ship was laid up with a proposal to convert her to an armed raider, but rejected on the grounds of cost. On 19 August 1915 a Royal Navy force consisting of the cruiser H.M.S. Challenger, the monitor H.M.S. Severn and two armed whalers Fly and Pickle arrived off the entrance to Tanga harbour. The whalers approached the Markgraf with the intention of boarding and placing demolition charges but the shore batteries were causing some concern and the two retired under heavy fire. Severn having engaged the shore batteries turned her attention to the Markgraf. Opening fire with both 6 inch, and 4.7 inch guns, the ship caught fire and slowly capsized. The force withdrew and Severn opened fire on the port and a barge laden with mines, which blew up in a violent explosion. The ship lay on her side in the harbour until the mid 1950s, when the Italian salvage company Mawa Handels Anstalt cut up the remains.

Maytham

Builders	:	Loland Motorverstad, Liervik, Norway. 1968
Length	:	120 feet
Beam	:	29 feet
Displacement	:	228 tons
Machinery	:	Normo 5 cyl. diesel. 650 hp
Position	:	06°.50'.30" S 39°17'.80" E

The Maytham was the ex Norwegian Ro-Ro vessel Lingen, owned by a local shipping company in Tanzania. On the afternoon of 4 March 1999 the vessel commenced loading six containers for Zanzibar alongside Berth No. 11 in Dar es Salaam. Five containers had been loaded when it was found that there was insufficient space for the sixth. The fourth container was then lifted off the deck, which caused the vessel to list to starboard and the remaining unsecured containers to slide across the deck. With the vessel heeled over at an angle it was impossible to fit the spreader bar to remove a container from the starboard side. The spreader was removed and slings substituted and a second attempt made to remove a container. Unfortunately the engine room access door had been left open and water poured in filling the engine room. The vessel was now being stabilized by its mooring lines which under the increasing tension soon parted and the ship rolled over and sank alongside. The accident was attributed to incorrect distribution of heavy containers and the failure to secure them to the deck. A Note of Protest was given to the owners by the Port Authorities and arrangements made to remove the vessel from the container berth. Divecon International were awarded the contract and using a barge and the Port Authorities two hundred ton floating crane Ndovu, salvaged the containers and other cargo before lifting the vessel and beaching it on 19 April to be later scrapped.

S.M.S. Möwe

Builders	:	Kaiserlichte Werft, Wilhelmshaven, Germany. 1906
Length	:	194 feet
Beam	:	32 feet
Displacement	:	900 tons
Machinery	:	Single triple expansion. 350 ihp.
Armament	:	3 x 2 pdr. guns. 2 x machine guns
Position	:	06°.51'.91" S 39°.17'.83" E

The Möwe was a naval survey vessel that spent four years in the Baltic Sea before arriving in East Africa on 3 May 1911. Under the command of Korvettenkäpitan Zimmer the ship was responsible for a number of major hydrographic surveys along the coast including the Rufiji Delta enabling the Königsberg to use the river to refuel in September 1914. Zimmer had considered arming the vessel with a larger gun and using her as a coastal raider but rejected the idea due to the limited bunker capacity. Four days after war was declared he scuttled the ship in Dar es Salaam following the shelling of the port by H.M.S. Astraea. The wreck was salvaged in 1922 by Commander Ingles and beached at the end of the harbour where it lay for some years before being cut up for scrap.

The salvaged hulk, 1930

Newbridge

Builders	:	William Doxford, Sunderland, England. 1906
Length	:	342 feet
Beam	:	46 feet
Displacement	:	3,737 tons
Machinery	:	Single triple expansion. 313 nhp.
Position	:	07°.47'.16" S 39°.22'.50" E

The ship was ordered by Edward Nicholl & Co. of Cardiff in October 1905 for £34,000 but in February 1906 was requisitioned by the builders while still under construction and resold for £38,000. Launched on 27 April 1906 she was completed in June and registered to John Temperley & Co. of London as the Newbridge. Known as a turret ship she was one of a class of vessels designed to lessen tonnage dues under the Suez Canal system of measurement in that the hull below the water line was considerably wider than the deck. In October 1914 the ship arrived in Mombasa chartered to the Admiralty with a consignment of coal. At the time the Königsberg had recently been located in the Rufiji Delta and the vessel was requisitioned as a blockship across one of the channels. The Newbridge arrived in Zanzibar and by 9 November had been modified for her one way trip with the addition of steel plate around the bridge and anchor windlass, and explosive charges in the engine room. Early the following morning with a crew of naval volunteers the ship sailed into the Ssimba Uranga channel of the delta under heavy fire escorted by the Duplex and four armed steam cutters also protected with hammocks, steel plate and sandbags. At 06.15 the anchors were let go and the raiding party hurriedly disembarked. A torpedo was fired at the ship from a cutter but dived into the river bed and minutes later the charges exploded and a huge column of coal and water rose into the air as the ship sank upright on the muddy bottom. The operation was a success with only two killed and nine wounded, and a number of gallantry awards were made for the action. Königsberg appeared to be imprisoned, however there were two alternative channels that the cruiser could have used, but with a shortage of coal and a number of larger warships outside the delta there was little chance of escape. After hostilities the wreck was bought for its cargo

The scuttling operation, 10 November 1914

of coal by the South African company Irving and Johnson but whether they recovered any is not recorded. By 1930 only the masts and top of the funnel remained and within a few years the remainder had completely disappeared.

The wreck in 1930

Nyati

Builders	:	A. J. Inglis & Co. Glasgow, Scotland. 1951
Length	:	130 feet
Beam	:	30 feet
Displacement	:	359 tons
Machinery	:	Twin triple expansion. 1,530 ihp
Position	:	06°.50'.84" S 39°.17'.95" E

The Nyati (Buffalo) and Simba (Lion) were the last two oil fired steam tugs ordered for the East African Railways and Harbours in the late 1940s. Although mainly used for berthing duties their sea going ability meant they were often used for a variety of tasks including towing and salvage. Simba was based at Mombasa and Nyati at Dar es Salaam and both were in service until the late seventies when increasing boiler maintenance made them uneconomical compared to the contemporary diesel tugs. Simba was scrapped at Mombasa and the Nyati sank alongside the dockyard jetty in Dar es Salaam. The wreck was cut down but remains of the hull and machinery can still be seen today. The area has now been reclaimed for a container port and the wreck removed.

The hull and machinery, 2003

Paraportiani

Builders	:	Lubecker Masch. Ges., Lubeck, Germany. 1927
Length	:	308 feet
Beam	:	44 feet
Displacement	:	4,270 tons
Machinery	:	Single triple expansion. 1,415 ihp.
Position	:	05°.29'.11" S 39°.37'.70" E

The Paraportiani was the former tramp steamer Lica Maersk built for by the Danish company A.P. Moller with its home port at Aarhus. The ship entered service on 23 October 1927 and was fitted with an auxilliary low pressure turbine nine years later. After nearly thirty years service she was sold to the Stern Line in Lubeck and renamed Auriga and later sold and renamed Komminos K. In 1963 she was sold to Paraportiani Shipping and renamed Paraportiani registered in Piraeus. On the evening of 25 October 1967 on a voyage from Galatz in Romania to Jeddah, the ship grounded on Panza Reef at the southern tip of Pemba Island and within hours the forepeak flooded. A distress call was picked up by the Tanga harbour master who chartered a light aircraft and flew over the stranded ship. Laden with 4,000 tons of bagged wheat, she had been inbound to Mombasa for provisions and water. The distress call was also received by the Mombasa signal station and relayed to the Kenya Navy base at Mtongwe. Diplomatic clearance was obtained from the Tanzanian Government to enter their waters and two patrol boats K.N.S. Chui and Simba departed for the casualty. The Zanzibar cargo vessel Afrika also intercepted the S.O.S. and arrived on the scene but the Captain refused assistance. By the following day, both forward holds, engine and boiler room were flooded and the ship had lost all power. Nineteen of the crew took to the lifeboats and rowed ashore where they were arrested and detained by the Green Guard, a local Pemba militia unit. During the confrontation one of the crew was shot in the leg and taken to the local hospital for treatment. Meanwhile the

Aground on Panza Reef, 26 October 1967

Chui sent an inflatable boat to the wreck to collect the remaining crew which later went ashore to locate the others. They too were arrested and taken to Mkoani where the misunderstanding was cleared up with the District Commissioner after Simba returned with two senior police officers from Dar es Salaam. Both patrol boats returned to Mombasa where the injured seaman was treated before the crew were repatriated to Greece. The lack of a suitable salvage tug, the age of the ship and the nature of the cargo

The wreck beginning to settle on the second day

The cylinder heads of the main engine

made any salvage uneconomical and within two days the ship began listing to port and broke up in the heavy seas. The loss was attributed to inaccurate navigation by the crew, having been unable to fix the ship's position due to bad weather and the strong northerly current. The wreck was discovered in the early 1990s, when the aft lifeboat davit was seen protruding above the surface. The hull had collapsed leaving the stern with the four bladed propeller and rudder intact and boiler and engine upright. The main mast lies at an angle above the seabed, with the bow broken off lying on its starboard side. The remains have since been extensively scrapped.

Inspecting the propeller

H.M.S. Pegasus

Builders	:	Palmers Yard, Newcastle on Tyne, England. 1896
Length	:	300 feet
Beam	:	36 feet
Displacement	:	2,135 tons
Machinery	:	Twin triple expansion. 5,000 ihp
Armament	:	8 x 4 inch Q.F. guns, 8 x 3 pdr. guns
Position	:	06°.08'.95" S 9°.11'.65" E

H.M.S. Pegasus was one of eleven Pelorus Class cruisers built for the Royal Navy in the late 19th century. After an uneventful career in the Mediterranean and Australia, the ship was re commissioned in 1913 for the Cape Squadron at Simonstown, South Africa. The squadron commanded by Rear-Admiral King-Hall consisted of three elderly cruisers, H.M.S. Astraea, Hyacinth and Pegasus. At the outbreak of the First World War, Astraea and Pegasus were based at Zanzibar and patrolled the coast until the former was called away for escort duty. Continuous steaming for weeks on end searching for the Königsberg had reduced Pegasus' performance and she required maintenance at Zanzibar on 19 September. In the meantime Königsberg was less than two hundred miles away in the Rufiji Delta having taken on seven hundred tons of coal. Looff received news of Pegasus' whereabouts and arrived off Zanzibar at sunrise the following morning and opened fire. Out gunned and outranged Pegasus was disabled within eight minutes, and the ship reduced to a shambles with thirty-eight killed and fifty-five wounded. Commander Ingles ordered the striking of the colours and the raising of a white flag. Looff ceased fire and departed having fired over two hundred and fifty shells. Attempts to beach the ship with a tug failed and she sank that afternoon in thirty feet leaving the masts above the surface. Ingles organised the recovery of six of the 4 inch guns, which were fitted with carriages in the railway workshops and tested in the grounds of the Marahubi Palace ruins. Two guns were mounted on the Zanzibar seafront as part of the town's defences, while two others were used in the land campaign against von Lettow-Vorbeck. Of the remaining two, one was mounted on the lake steamer Winifred and the other used for the defence of Mombasa.

Pegasus sinking, 20 September 1914

By 1916 the German threat of attack was over and the land campaign guns and Winifred gun were returned to Simonstown and scrapped. After the war the two Zanzibar guns were kept on the sea front as a memorial, but have since disappeared, while the Mombasa gun is preserved outside Fort Jesus, where it can be seen today. Pegasus was abandoned and gradually forgotten until 1955 when the wreck was bought for £500 from the Zanzibar government by the Italian salvage company Mawa Handels Anstalt and broken up. The remains were rediscovered in the 1970s and produced some interesting artifacts but today little remains other than a pile of scrap in an area of poor underwater visibility.

Recovering a 4 inch gun

Test firing the prototype gun at the Marahubi Palace ruins

The surviving Pegasus gun outside Fort Jesus, Mombasa

Penguin

Builders	:	William Simons, Glasgow, Scotland. 1905
Length	:	90 feet
Beam	:	25 feet
Displacement	:	375 tons
Machinery	:	Twin compound engines driving centrifugal pumps
Position	:	06°.10'.64" S 39°.08'.44" E

As a result of increased shipping through the harbour after the First World War, the Zanzibar Government decided in 1919 to build a new wharf capable of taking vessels along side at all states of the tide. Construction commenced in 1920 but required a dredger to deepen the area in front of the wharf as well as backfill the area behind. A pontoon steam dredger built for South African Railways and Harbours was purchased for £20,000 and delivered on 27 February 1922. The Penguin, Hull No. 419, had been one of two used to dredge Durban harbour. All went well until numerous rocks of non Zanzibar origin jammed the dredge pump. A flurry of correspondence showed these to be ballast stones dumped by trading dhows in times gone by. The dredger worked well pumping thousands of cubic yards of sand, until the dredge master resigned and pumping came to a halt. The Crown Agents in London were asked to recruit a suitable replacement, with the proviso that, '*not only should he be familiar with steam machinery, but that he be of sober and steady habits and of strong physique*'. The new man arrived and dredging continued until it was noticed that the material volume had fallen dramatically. The pumps were dismantled and the worn out impellers sent to Bombay for overhaul. Some months later the Penguin returned to service, and by 1929 the task was complete. A survey showed the hull beyond economic repair and should be sold or sunk after the removal of the machinery. Three years later the dredger was still laid up and being considered for further work. Seventy years later the Penguin was discovered lying in 120 feet of water some three miles off the Zanzibar shore, and initially defied attempts to identify it, being described as a barge or a small tug. A recent dive by the author identified it as the Penguin. The tell tale clues being the overboard discharge pipes, twin steam driven delivery pumps and the main suction pipe lying on the sea bed alongside. The large Scotch boiler together with the two compound engines had led to the theory of a tug. Research in the Zanzibar Archives produced sepia photographs of the vessel with a large funnel, pumping material during construction of the main wharf in the 1920s. How the dredger came to be here is unclear but from its present position it may have been sunk deliberately.

Rovuma

Builders	:	F. Krupp, Kiel, Germany. 1894
Length	:	94 feet
Beam	:	17 feet
Displacement	:	115 tons
Machinery	:	Single triple expansion. 260 nhp
Position	:	08°.55' S 39°.15' E

The Rovuma was built for the German East Africa government as a coastal steamer. In September 1914 the ship was armed with two 37 mm guns and transferred to the Rufiji Delta to join the Hedwig and Tomondo. The three vessels comprised part of the delta force and used for communications and transport in support of the Königsberg. With the loss of the cruiser in July 1915 the vessels were sunk in the Mbuni river on 9 October, where they were discovered in the 1920s by Captain Ingles of the Rufiji Delta Trading Company. the Hedwig and Rovuma were scrapped while the Tomondo was salvaged and returned to service. Its fate is unknown.

Royal Sovereign

Builders	:	W. Noble & Sons. Fraserburgh, Scotland. 1936
Length	:	70 feet
Beam	:	20 feet
Displacement	:	60 tons
Machinery	:	Gardner 6 cyl. diesel.
Position	:	39°.12'.30" E 04°.53'.50" S

The Royal Sovereign was a wooden motor fishing vessel sold to the Mauritius Fisheries Research Department after the Second World War and renamed M.F.R.V.1. In November 1949 the vessel was renamed Research and later sold to the East African Marine Fisheries Research Organisation in Zanzibar. In 1958 she was bought by Captain Tom Wheeler and renamed Royal Sovereign. Based in Mombasa the vessel traded along the East African coast carrying a variety of cargoes including beer to Dar es Salaam. In the early hours of 8 November 1960 the ship grounded on Boma Reef, near Tanga while engaged in what was known as the 'Tusker Run'. The assorted cargo consisting of 800 cases of Tusker Beer, 100 cartons of Tenants Beer, 106 bags of rice, 72 cartons of Brandy and four cases of wine and a few tons of corrugated iron. Tom rowed ashore and reported the stranding to the Harbourmaster who offered to refloat the vessel at a price he refused. Being an enterprising individual he decided to salvage the vessel himself. With the assistance of the crew, the beer and spirits were stowed aft and the vessel lightened by throwing the corrugated iron over the side with a marker buoy. Two days later the Tanga pilot boat arrived and passed a line, and on the high water the ship floated off. Six hundred cases of beer had been damaged by oil and diesel during the salvage operation, and on arrival in Tanga were checked by an independent surveyor, who having partaken of a random selection, declared the cargo still drinkable subject to the bottles being relabelled. The corrugated iron was recovered and a general average declared. Tom later sold the vessel and under new owners she ran aground and became a total loss on a reef near Lindi, south of Dar es Salaam and was quickly broken up by local natives for the timber.

San Rafael

Builders	:	Ribeira das Naus, Lisbon, Portugal
Length	:	65 feet
Beam	:	18 feet
Displacement	:	178 tons
Armament	:	20 cannons
Position	:	05°.13' S 39°.15' E

The San Rafael carries the distinction of being one of the earliest recorded shipwrecks on the coast. She was a type of merchant vessel known as a Nao, the Portuguese equivalent of an English Carrack and part of Vasco da Gama's fleet bound for India. Vasco da Gama born at Sines, Portugal in 1469 had served as a naval officer and distinguished himself in West Africa by defending Portuguese possessions against the French. His father had been appointed to lead the expedition but died before it set out. Vasco was appointed commander in his place, and the fleet of four ships, San Gabriel, San Rafael under the command of his brother Paulo, Berrio and a supply vessel left Lisbon on 8 July 1497. The majority of the crew were convicts and treated as expendable. They rounded the Cape of Good Hope on 22 November, and sailed up the east coast with stops at a number of small settlements for provisions and water. One stop was the village of Tongoni, south of Tanga founded in the 14th century where they received a friendly welcome. The next stop was Malindi where he erected a pillar, and they reached Calicut on 20 May 1498. After a difficult period of trading on the Indian coast they set sail for home on 5 October and stopped once again at Malindi on 7 January 1499. Scurvy however was proving to be a killer with over thirty casualties in the past three months. Sailing the vessels with limited crew was now becoming an impossible task and da Gama decided to reduce the number of ships. Six days later they arrived back at Tongoni and during the next fifteen days stripped the Sao Rafael of the trade goods and fittings and removed the figure head. After setting the ship ablaze, the remaining ships set off on the voyage around the cape and arrived back in September 1499 to a hero's welcome. His last trip to India in 1524 as Viceroy ended with his death at Cochin on 24 December and burial in the Franciscan church of San Antonio. In 1539 his remains were returned to Portugal and buried in the Church of Jeronimos in Belem where in 1853 the two foot high ship's figure head was eventually placed after having been widely exhibited.

Skagit

Builders	:	Halter Marine, New Orleans. USA. 1989
Length	:	112 feet
Beam	:	25 feet
Displacement	:	308 tons
Machinery	:	Four Caterpillar V12 diesel. 2,840 h.p
Position	:	06°.17' S 39°.10' E

The Skagit was one of a pair of fast ferries built for service in Puget Sound, Washington State but laid up when there was no funding. They were later operated in the San Francisco Bay area and out of Seattle before being withdrawn from service in 2009. Two years later they were sold to a Canadian company who then sold them to Seagull Sea Transport of Tanzania in 2011 operating between Dar es Salaam and Zanzibar.

On 18 July 2012 shortly before noon the ferry sailed out of Dar es Salaam heading for Zanzibar on what should have been a routine four hour voyage. Designed to carry 230 people the ferry was carrying 291 when it got into difficulties due to heavy weather off Chumbe Island on the south west coast of Zanzibar. Reports stated the vessel

may have lost power and broached across the waves before rolling over. The vessel capsized with the loss of over a hundred passengers and remained upturned for some time before sinking.

The EU Naval Force Somalia Operation immediately redirected a Maritime Patrol and Reconnaissance Aircraft, which was conducting counter-piracy patrols closest to the location of the sinking. From there it conducted several sorties in support of the rescue efforts. Using the aircraft's capabilities, rescue efforts were coordinated, life rafts spotted and tracked. With this support, Tanzanian and other vessels taking part in the rescue mission were guided to the liferafts exact locations, aiding the rescue of reportedly 145 of the ferry's passengers.

Slemmestad

Builders	:	Burmeister & Wain, Copenhagen, Denmark. 1928
Length	:	376 feet
Beam	:	53 feet
Displacement	:	4,295 tons
Machinery	:	Twin B & W 6 cyl. diesel. 490 hp
Position	:	06°.45'.40" S 39°.18'.52" E

The Slemmestad managed by the Norwegian company A.P. Klaveness was on a voyage from Gothenburg to Madagascar when she caught fire off Dar es Salaam on the evening of 27 March 1951. The ship had left the port that afternoon with Captain Richard Crow as pilot. Many years later, he recollected how he had commented to the captain on the rough running of the main engines before leaving the ship to proceed to sea. He returned to his residence at the signal station where some hours later he was told the ship was on fire. Seven miles offshore a fire broke out and the Master advised the port he was returning to the anchorage. The fire spread rapidly through the engine room and up on deck, stranding four of the crew on the aft end who took to a liferaft. The engine stopped and the ship drifted up the coast with the remaining twenty crew, including the captain's wife taking refuge on the foc'sle. They were taken off by Captain Crow who succeeded in placing the pilot boat under the bows, away from the burning cargo which included bitumen, brandy, kerosene, lube oil and matches. Later the harbour tug Empire Linden beached the ship on

The fire damaged bows

Daphne Reef. The following morning the crew in the liferaft were spotted from the air and picked up by a dhow. The fire spread throughout the ship and barrels of bitumen and acetylene cylinders exploded turning the vessel into a large Roman candle. The ship continued to burn until 9 April when the superstructure collapsed and the hull had buckled from the heat. What remained of the ship and cargo were surveyed and declared a total loss and the fire attributed to an explosion that fractured a fuel line and sprayed burning oil around the engine room preventing the fire pumps from being started. There had been a proposal to tow the ship away for scrap but in view of the hull damage the wreck was left. The hull was visible until 1970 when the wreck symbol was deleted from the charts by the Hydrographic Department after reports the remains had sunk. Today the wreck is a popular dive site, with part of the cargo of cement bags still prominent in the remains.

A constructive total loss, 10 April 1951

Somali

Builders	:	Blohm and Voss, Hamburg, Germany. 1889
Length	:	322 feet
Beam	:	40 feet
Displacement	:	2,638 tons
Machinery	:	Single triple expansion. 1,300 ihp
Position	:	07°.51'.33" S 39°.18'.90" E

The Somali was launched as the Osiris for the Deutsche Dampfahrt Gesellschaft and used for some years on the Hamburg - South America run. On 22 August 1901 the ship was sold to the Deutsche Ost Afrika Linie and renamed Somali sailing between Durban and Bombay. Towards the end of July 1914 the ship was anchored at Dar es Salaam awaiting cargo. The cruiser Königsberg had recently departed and would require a supply of coal and Somali was loaded and sailed on 3 August to contact the cruiser. War was declared the following day and two days later Königsberg captured the British merchant ship City of

Aerial view in the mid 1960s

The stern in the 1990s

Winchester. Coal and provisions were transferred to the raider before the ship was scuttled. After a week of steaming around the Gulf of Aden with no further prizes, Königsberg required coal and met Somali at Ras Hafun on the Somaliland coast. A second transfer was arranged at Aldabra Island following a fruitless search for French ships at Majunga in Madagascar. This was the last of the Somali's coal, the only other source being German East Africa. Captain Herm of the Somali suggested taking refuge in the Rufiji Delta while coal was shipped from Dar es Salaam and other ports. After a brief run to Zanzibar in September to destroy H.M.S. Pegasus, Königsberg returned to the delta for engine repairs. At the beginning of November the cruiser H.M.S. Chatham arrived and shelled the Somali, which caught fire and burnt for four days becoming a total loss. During the next forty years the riverbank gradually encroached the wreck and before long the mangroves started growing through the ship. A recent visit showed part of the port side of the hull, bridge, top of the boiler, rudder stock and stem frame still visible in the heavy undergrowth. In recent years large sections have been removed as scrap.

Remains of the bridge superstructure, 2001

Southern Pioneer

Builders   : A/B Norrkopings Varv & Verkstads, Norkoping, Norway. 1955
Length   : 187 feet
Beam   :   29 feet
Displacement   : 498 tons
Machinery   : B & W Alpha 5 cyl. diesel. 600 hp

Position   : 04°.59'.45" S 39°.09'.24" E

On the evening of 31 January 1976 the Southern Pioneer exploded in a huge fireball at Tanga while discharging 1,000 tons of diesel and petrol. Two crew died and five were injured in the blast that destroyed the after end of the ship. The vessel burnt out and sank at its moorings leaving the bow and part of the accommodation above water. During the next two weeks the ship rolled over to port. Divecon were awarded the salvage contract with instructions to remove the remaining fuel and contain any pollution. In the meantime the Salvage Association surveyor's report showed the aft end of the vessel to be a total loss

Spapool alongside the capsized wreck

194

with the decks buckled and the accommodation and bridge completely destroyed. The ex Royal Navy water carrier Spapool lying at Mombasa, was chartered as the salvage support vessel and together with a team of divers refloated the ship upside down on 23 November. Three days later the hulk was towed out to sea and scuttled off Kwale Island in deep water. The ship was launched as the Tankman for Rederi A/B Ostenia, Sweden before being bought by Southern Line and renamed Southern Pioneer II in 1964. The original Southern Pioneer had been declared a total loss after a gas explosion on African Marine's slipway at Mombasa.

Spice Islander 1

Builders	:	Greece. 1967
Length	:	96 feet
Beam	:	37 feet
Displacement	:	836 tons
Machinery	:	Twin Poyaud V12 UD25 diesel. 1,560 horsepower

The Spice Islander was a Ro-Ro ferry launched as the Marianna for Greek owners. She was renamed Apostolos P following a sale in 1988 before being sold to a Honduran company in 2007 and renamed Spice Islande 1. That same year she ran out of fuel off the Somali coast on a voyage from Oman to Tanzania and was aided by the patrolling American destroyer U.S.S. Stout which resupplied her with fuel and food. On 1 September 2007 she was sold to Makame Hasnuu of Zanzibar and renamed Spice Islander I.

On the evening of 9 September 2011 the vessel sailed from Zanzibar town for Pemba Island. She was reported to have been carrying in excess of 800 passengers. Her capacity was 45 crew and 645 passengers. At around 01:00 on 10 September the vessel capsized and sank off the north west coast Zanzibar. Of those on board, 612 were rescued, with 40 of those suffering serious injuries and at least 200 people drowned.

Tabora

Builders	:	Blohm & Voss, Hamburg, Germany. 1912
Length	:	451 feet
Beam	:	56 feet
Displacement	:	8,022 tons
Machinery	:	Twin triple expansion. 4,800 ihp
Position	:	06°.50'.45" S 39°.17'.75" E

The Tabora and General were sister ships built for the Deutsche Ost Afrika Linie shortly before the First World War. The General placed in service in 1911, provided liner service from Hamburg around Africa followed by the Tabora in 1912. The latter carried 116 passengers in First, 112 in Second and 88 in Third Class. On 31 July 1914 the Tabora arrived in Dar es Salaam from Mombasa with news that three British warships were due

The Tabora lying on her port side at the end of hostilities

Curious visitors explore the wreck

in Zanzibar to coal that evening. In the harbour completing coaling was the cruiser Königsberg under the command of Fregattenkäpitan Looff, who on hearing the news sailed that afternoon. Some two hours later the three warships spotted the Königsberg and fell in either side. Looff in a masterful piece of seamanship evaded his escort and disappeared into the night. Four days later war was declared and the Tabora together with the König and Feldmarschall were laid up in Dar es Salaam. On 28 November a naval force consisting of the battleship H.M.S. Goliath, the cruiser H.M.S. Fox together with the Duplex and tug Helmuth anchored off Dar es Salaam, with the intention of disabling the Feldmarschall and König and verifying whether or not Tabora was a Red Cross vessel. The ship was flying a hospital flag and a large Red Cross had been painted on her side but there was little else. The inspecting naval surgeon found a doctor, nurse and patient on board, but on throwing back the sheets the latter was found with his trousers on! On 23 March 1916 H.M.S. Hyacinth and Vengeance arrived off the port and shelled the ship. Struck by nine rounds of high explosive, Tabora heeled over and sank on her port side. Forty years later what remained of the ship was cut up and removed by the Italian company Mawa Handels Anstalt. In the early 1960s the new D.O.A.L. cargo ship Tabora arrived in Dar es Salaam and her Master was presented with the letter R from the original ship's name recovered by the salvage company some years previously.

Tomondo

Builders	:	Joseph L. Meyer, Pappenburg, Germany. 1908
Length	:	82 feet
Beam	:	17 feet
Displacement	:	27 tons
Machinery	:	2 cyl horizontal compound.
Position	:	08°.55' S 39°.15' E

The Tomondo was a shallow draft paddle steamer built for service in the Rufiji River delta. A wood fired locomotive boiler provided steam to two horizontal cylinders driving the paddle wheel, and with a draft of around one foot was ideal for navigation upriver. The arrival of the Königsberg in the river on 3 September 1914, saw the Tomondo become a tender ferrying personnel and stores from the village of Utete around the delta.. After the destruction of the cruiser on 11 July 1915, the Tomondo evacuated the casualties to the field hospital at Nieusteiten and was later used in the salvage of the ten four inch guns and other items from the wreck. As the Allies advanced towards the river, the delta force withdrew and the Tomondo together with the Hedwig and Rovuma were scuttled in the Mbuni River, a tributary of the Kikunya channel on 9 October. Seven years later the wreck was salvaged by Commander Ingles and sold to the shipping company Smith Mackenzie. Records show the vessel was used on the river until the floods of 1930 after which it was laid up in Dar es Salaam and probably scrapped.

Zanzibar

Builders	:	Vulkan, Stettin, Germany. 1883
Length	:	198 feet
Beam	:	29 feet
Displacement	:	982 tons
Machinery	:	Single compound. 100 nhp
Position	:	Unknown

The Zanzibar was the first of three steamers bearing the name, built for the shipping company O'Swald of Hamburg trading around the Madagascar coast. On the night of 24 July 1898 the ship grounded on Newembe Reef, twenty miles north of Zanzibar town on a voyage from Hamburg to Madagascar. The crew were rescued and reported the incident to the owner's agents, who in turn sent a telegram to Lloyds in London who reported the loss in the Shipping List. Within a few days the decks were awash and heavy seas broke open the ship, and as there were no salvage facilities available the wreck was declared a total loss.

The Zanzibar Hurricane - 15 April 1872

The island of Zanzibar lies around two degrees north of the accepted hurricane zone and normally outside any serious weather anomalies, but a change in the weather pattern devastated the island on 15 April 1872. The early morning dawned bright and clear with only a few white clouds scudding gently across a blue sky. Over the horizon to the south west a grey black tropical storm was building up and within an hour the sky was an overcast sullen dark mass of swirling cloud and pouring rain. A strong wind sprang up whipping the otherwise calm blue waters of the harbour into a turbulent boiling cauldron. The harbour was full of vessels of all types at anchor including the Sultan's fleet of six vessels. The rain fell in torrents and the narrow streets quickly filled with a rushing flood of filthy black debris-strewn water carrying all before it. The water undermined the foundations of many houses, and without warning the coral and lime walls collapsed in clouds of dust killing many in an avalanche of rubble. As the wind's fury increased, the palm-thatched roofs tore away leaving gaping holes and mud huts collapsed under the onslaught killing the inhabitants. Trees were uprooted and people fleeing the storm were swept off their feet. At the United Missions Church house the corrugated iron roof was ripped off with a noise that drowned the thunder rumbling above and the rain poured down the staircase like a waterfall. Suddenly with two mournful tolls the bell and tower crashed down. By noon the storm was blowing from the south and at its worst. Out in the harbour the smaller dhows were being overwhelmed by the huge waves and coir anchor ropes unable to take the strain parted leaving the vessels to be blown ashore with such ferocity the hulls splintered the moment they struck. Sailors struggled and died in the tormented sea, their bodies washed ashore and thrown on to the seafront by the pounding surf. Around 1.30 there was a dead calm as the eye of the storm passed over. By 2.30 the wind was blowing from the north and backing west throughout the afternoon. All the ships and over a hundred and fifty Arab and Indian boats and dhows were sunk or stranded, many of them full of cargo. The brig Adele O'Swald was driven ashore as was the London sailing ship Lobelia that lay on its side near the Customs House. The greatest single disaster was the loss of the Sultan's little navy which Seyyid Said bin Sultan, its creator, had taken a special pride and handed on to his successors. The flagship, the frigate El Majidi, previously the Sea King, was seriously damaged, the corvettes Iskandia Shah and Suliman Shah just arrived from Bombay, and the steamers Star and Sultan were completely wrecked. The loss of the fleet was a source of concern to Sultan Bargash bin Said, whose authority over the Arabs along the mainland coast depended upon it. The only vessel to survive undamaged was the 1,100 ton steamer Abydos of London that brought Lt's. Dawson and Henn to look for the explorer Dr Livingstone, and weathered the storm by steaming full ahead on her anchors. That evening the wind died away to a moderate breeze and a deathly silence settled over the island. Over two hundred had died and almost every building had been damaged or lay in ruins. The Mission house was abandoned and the chapel and organ ruined by salt water. Over on the mainland, the village of Bagamoyo saw its entire fishing fleet destroyed with the beach littered with trees and the pathetic remains of dozens of broken craft.

Sir John Kirk, the British Consul wrote, '*The first gust drove in the windows of the Agency and my quarters, broke open doors and threw tables and couches in confusion against the opposite walls.... As the sea rose, sheets of salt spray and rain drifted in at the broken windows and filled the rooms a foot deep with water.... The sea was driven with such force as to undermine and sweep away the whole embankment of stone and double row of wooden piles that protect the foundations of the English, German and American Consulates. The Consular office was burst open by the wind, and a teak chest, in which many valuable documents were preserved, and all pigeon-holes, in which matters of current business were deposited, gutted of their contents. Next morning I recovered in the street many government orders and confidential memoranda together with the bulk of our mail which should have gone next day, but other documents of importance are utterly lost. In my own quarters the floor of the drawing-room was covered with a foot of water in which books, pictures and china formed a confused and sodden heap*'.

The repairs to the Consulate cost £2,000, but that was a trifle compared with the losses of the Arab landowners estimated at between four and five million pounds. At least two-thirds of their clove and coconut plantations had been destroyed, and since new trees would not bear fruit for many years, the loss was incalculable. Zanzibar never regained its full clove production and the bulk of the crop now grows on Pemba.

Strandings and Salvage
on the Tanzania Coast 1883 - 2013

Adjutant	1915	Rufiji Delta
Andreas Boye	1972	Pemba
Ata	1958	Zanzibar
Capitaine Biebuyck	1953	Zanzibar
Comara	1980	Zanzibar
Daphne	1997	Dar es Salaam
Duplex	1914	Dira Reef
Fivi	1997	Dar es Salaam
Fly	1915	Songo Songo Island
Flying Horse	1996	Dar es Salaam
Frierfjord	1969	Tanga
Jamhuri	1967	Dar es Salaam
Jody	1981	Tanga
Juba	1891	Pemba Island
Llandaff Castle	1937	Zanzibar
Manica	1916	Mikindani
Manihine	1978	Zanzibar
Masula	1951	Tanga
Mulbera	1933	Tanga
Nordvaer	1979	Dar es Salaam
Norefjord	1949	Tanga
CEC Pacific 224	2005	Zanzibar
Pemba	1883	Zanzibar
Pentakota	1911	Zanzibar
Phillipias	1977	Latham Island
H.M.A.S. Pioneer	1915	Rufiji Delta
Präsident	1915	Lindi
Rampart	1975	Mafia Island
Roybank	1969	Pemba
SFL Sara	2012	Tanga
Sarah Jolliffe	1915	Pemba
Simla	1883	Zanzibar
Sincerity	1974	Zanzibar
Spalmatori Engineer	1974	Zanzibar
Stanford Buzzard	2013	Mtwara
State of Haryana	1975	Zanzibar
Tanga	1957	Tanga
Tilawa	1942	Zanzibar
Uganda	1952	Dar es Salaam
Umballa	1912	Dar es Salaam
Zambesi	1934	Pangani

Adjutant

Builders	:	Janssen & Schmilinsky, Hamburg, Germany. 1905
Length	:	116 feet
Beam	:	23 feet
Displacement	:	231 tons
Machinery	:	Single compound. 350 nhp
Position	:	07°.47' S 39°.22' E

The capture of the Adjutant off the East African coast by the cruiser H.M.S. Dartmouth on 9 October was the first indication the Königsberg was still in the region. Documents on board showed a delivery of coal to the warship some weeks previously. Adjutant was built as a harbour tug and passenger transfer vessel for the Deutsche Ost Afrika Linie and delivered to Dar es Salaam on 28 December 1905. On the outbreak of war in August 1914 the tug escaped to the neutral port of Beira in Portuguese East Africa but was recalled on 7 October when it was intercepted. Renamed H.M.S. Adjutant the tug was armed with a 3

The burnt out hull on the slipway at Kigoma, 1916

pdr. gun and crewed by men from H.M.S. Pegasus. Königsberg was discovered in the Rufiji delta at the end of October and the tug formed part of the blockade flotilla assembled at the mouth. Together with the tug Helmuth they were used for reconnaissance and mine sweeping duties off the delta. On the morning of 6 February 1915 during a reconnaissance in to the delta, the tug came under heavy fire and was disabled when the steam line to the engine was hit. Leading Seaman Piddock was killed and the remainder surrendered when she drifted ashore. The following day H.M.S. Hyacinth shelled the tug in an attempt to destroy it, but the damage was minimal and a month later, Captain Herm, former master of the Somali, took the tug back to Dar es Salaam. A year later she was dismantled and railed to Kigoma on Lake Tanganyika but never completed. The Allied invasion and withdrawal of German troops from Kigoma, saw the Adjutant destroyed on the slipway on 15 July 1916, and after hostilities the hull was found to be brittle from the fire and scrapped.

Andreas Boye

Builders	:	Nordso Vaeftet, Ringkobing, Denmark. 1962
Length	:	144 feet
Beam	:	25 feet
Displacement	:	450 tons
Machinery	:	B & W Alpha 5 cyl. diesel. 300 hp
Position	:	05°.25' S 39°.45' E

The Andreas Boye was a Danish coaster bound for Mombasa from Sweden with two hundred tons of explosives when she grounded on the southern tip of Pemba on the evening of 18 September 1972. The ship had left Dar es Salaam earlier that day but the lack of navigation lights and the northerly current confused the crew as to their position. The distress call was picked up by the Mombasa signal station and Diving Contractors Ltd. awarded the salvage contract. On 2 October additional assistance was provided by Southern Engineering and Southern Line with the tanker Southern Pioneer and a small tug and barge. The salvage team arrived at Mkoani on 7 October to clear formalities before proceeding to lighten the ship by eighty tons. The vessel was high and dry having run on to a sand bar and damaged the rudder. Five of the crew left the ship and arrived in Dar es

Salaam believing she was a total loss, leaving the Master and a few crew to look after the ship. A survey of the surrounding sand bar and reef showed a narrow channel, the Upembe Passage as the nearest deep water six hundred yards away. Both anchors were laid out to their full extent ahead of the ship and on each successive tide the chains were hauled in and relaid with the ship moving slowly day by day towards deep water. With the onset of neap tides the operation was suspended for ten days until the 19th when the process started once again. The remaining two hundred yards were covered in two days when the ship was refloated and towed to Mkoani. The explosives were re-loaded and the ship towed to Mombasa for repair by the Southern Pioneer. On arrival the cargo was inspected and the ship docked by the tug Simba. Three weeks later she left Mombasa with the balance of cargo for Ethiopia. The ship continued to trade for a further six years until lost after a collision with the Synaftlia on 28 July 1979 off Cape St. Vincent on a voyage to the Mediterranean.

Ata

Builders	:	American Shipbuilding Co. Lorain, Ohio, U.S.A. 1918
Length	:	260 feet
Beam	:	43 feet
Displacement	:	2,875 tons
Machinery	:	Single triple expansion. 274 nhp.
Position	:	05°.51' S 39°.25'.10" E

The Ata was laid down as the War Vigil for the United States Shipping Board but completed as the Lake Harney and sold in 1920 to become a collier for the International Coal Transportation Corp. During the Second World War the ship was chartered to Irish Shipping Ltd. as the Irish Rose and on cessation of hostilities was renamed Mall by Cie National de Nav. of Calais. Eventually after further sales and name changes she was sold to Katana Societa di Navigazione Marittima, Italy in 1957 and re-named Ata. Having discharged a cargo of 250 tons of dates on 20 February 1958, the Ata left Dar es Salaam and the following morning grounded on Mnemba Reef off the east coast of Zanzibar. A message was relayed to Dar es Salaam and the following day the tugs Nyati and Upesi arrived. Lines were secured but they failed to move the ship. That afternoon the Royal East African Navy vessel Rosalind received news of the stranding and proceeded to the site. A second attempt failed and the offer of assistance from the Rosalind was declined. The tugs departed for Dar es Salaam leaving the Ata high and dry on the reef with wisps of steam coming from the funnel. Some days later with no further signs of assistance, the crew abandoned ship and were repatriated. The Ata lay on the reef for two months before a local company George Cohen & Co. bought the wreck and contracted Mawa Handels Anstalt to refloat her. When the salvage crew arrived there was six feet of water in the ship, which together with the ballast in the double bottom was pumped overboard and the ship towed to Mkokotoni on the west coast of Zanzibar on 21 April. Nearly a year later the ship was towed to Dar es Salaam for breaking. By July 1959 demolition was well under way, when on the 24th, a fire broke out as a result of cutting into a fuel tank. Thick black smoke drifted across the harbour while the Port Fire Service struggled to contain the blaze. That evening the fire was brought under control and three months later the last of the Ata was cut up and loaded aboard a ship for Japan.

Capitaine Biebuyck

Builders	:	Swan, Hunter. Newcastle, England. 1942
Length	:	448 feet
Beam	:	56 feet
Displacement	:	7,023 tons
Machinery	:	Triple expansion. 2,500 hp.
Position	:	04°.03'.80" S 39°.39'.10" E

In 1939, the British Ministry of Shipping adopted a standard naming system whereby all merchant ships ordered to be built in Britain to Government account, except very small ship types, would be given the prefix 'Empire' to their name. The Capitaine Biebuyck was launched as the Empire Drayton on 23 October 1941 for the Ministry of War Transport and renamed Belgian Sailor in February 1942 managed by Compagnie Maritime Belge on behalf of the Belgian Government. In 1946 she was sold to the managing company and named after a Captain who lost his life during the war. On a voyage from Mombasa to Dar es Salaam in 1953/4 she grounded on the southwest tip of Zanzibar. The distress signal was answered by the Dar es Salaam tug Empire Linden that succeeded in refloating the ship on the second attempt. There was little damage and the ship departed after a hull inspection. In 1958 she was sold to the Yugoslavian company Kvarnerska Plovidba and renamed Kastav who sold her seven years later to Ivory Shipping Co. of Hong Kong as the Ivory Tellus. After a further five years service the ship made her last voyage to the breakers at Hirao in Japan arriving on 22 April 1970.

Comara

Builders	:	Namura Shipbuilding Co. Osaka, Japan. 1956
Length	:	415 feet
Beam	:	55 feet
Displacement	:	8,089 tons
Machinery	:	Mitsubishi 7 cyl. diesel. 3,300 hp
Position	:	06°.19' S 39°.35' E

The Greek owned motor vessel was on a voyage from Constanza to Dar es Salaam with a cargo of 8,000 tons of bagged sugar, when she grounded five miles north of Ras Makunduchi on the east coast of Zanzibar in the early hours of 28 April 1980. The next morning the self-propelled barge VDH 12 arrived with an offer of help. The refloating attempt was unsuccessful and that afternoon the Murri International tug Bison 1 arrived. After signing a Lloyds Open Form, a line was passed to the ship ready for an attempt on the early morning tide. That was unsuccessful but with a higher tide that afternoon the Comara refloated. A diving inspection showed the bottom had been badly damaged and the tug escorted the ship to Dar es Salaam. After discharging the cargo, the vessel sailed for Mombasa, where dry-docking on 19 June revealed the true extent of the damage to the hull and machinery. Repairs were uneconomic and she was declared a total loss and laid up in Port Reitz for four years. Purchased by Murri International she was sold to ship breakers at Gadani Beach where she arrived on 18 March 1985. The ship had been launched as the Miharu Maru for Nippon Yusen Kaisha and after three further sales sold to Algarve Maritime of Piraeus and renamed Comara.

Daphne

Builders	:	Bremer Vulkan & Rickmers, Germany. 1980
Length	:	560 feet
Beam	:	80 feet
Displacement	:	20,376 tons
Machinery	:	M.A.N. 6 cyl. diesel. 12,390 hp.
Position	:	06°.49' S 39°.19' E

On 10 January 1997 the Maltese owned Daphne grounded near No. 4 channel marker buoy while entering Dar es Salaam channel laden with 13,000 tons of rice. A diving inspection showed the vessel aground amidships. Later that day two harbour tugs, Chui and Mamba, attempted unsuccessfully to refloat the ship. A third tug Kongoni was sub chartered to assist, and after laying the ship's anchors as ground tackle and moving some 200 tons of fuel aft, the ship refloated the next day and proceeded into port to discharge. The stranding was attributed to the vessel entering the channel prior to picking up the pilot and the Master was later fined. Daphne was a composite vessel having been assembled from the center section of the Hapag Lloyd vessel Ludwigshafen mated to a new bow built by Rickmers and stern built by Bremer Vulkan. She was later sold to the Shipping Corporation of Saudi Arabia and renamed Wajdi Arab and sold for breaking at Alang on 17 April 2010.

Duplex

Builders	:	C. Mitchell & Co. Newcastle, England. 1872
Length	:	214 feet
Beam	:	30 feet
Displacement	:	874 tons
Machinery	:	Single compound. 300 ihp.
Position	:	08°.55' S 39°.15' E

The Duplex was a former cable laying vessel owned by the Eastern Telegraph Company and sold to Cowasjee Dinshaw in 1913. Requisitioned by the Royal Navy she became a maid of all work on the East African coast during the First World War armed with two 3 pdr. guns. On 7 November 1914 Duplex accompanied by an armed steam picket boat from the battleship H.M.S. Goliath, and three armed steam cutters approached the mouth of the Simba Uranga in the Rufiji Delta to investigate the German defences, and the possibility of attacking the Königsberg. They were met by heavy fire and after losing a torpedo from the picket boat retired without loss. Three days later Duplex was back in the delta providing covering fire during the sinking of the blockship Newbridge, when a shell exploded on the bridge wounding the captain, Lt. Triggs and three crew. That night under her civilian captain she sailed for Zanzibar with the wounded from the action and grounded on Dira reef. The sky was lit up by exploding rockets as the ship fired off her distress signals and H.M.S. Chatham towed her off on the high water. At the end of November under the command of Commander Henry Ritchie Duplex was due to take part in the investigation of three ships in Dar es Salaam the Feldmarschall, König and Tabora, but since her engine was unreliable she anchored alongside H.M.S. Fox and Goliath. Ritchie led the party in Goliath's steam pinnace accompanied by the tug Helmuth and Fox's steam cutter into port passing the signal station where two white flags flew. Within a short time the truce was broken by a heavy fire, and despite serious wounds Ritchie returned the pinnace along side Goliath. The battleship opened fire and destroyed the Governor's palace and Ritchie became the first naval Victoria Cross winner in the First World War. With Duplex's shallow draft, there was a proposal to fit one of Goliath's 6 inch guns to the foredeck for shore bombardment, but the ship's age and construction made it likely the deck would have buckled under the recoil. However that did not prevent the ship shelling the delta defences with her 3 pdr. guns and at the end of hostilites returned to service and was broken up in Italy in 1931.

Fivi

Builders	:	Kanasashi Co. Ltd, Shimizu, Japan. 1975
Length	:	600 feet
Beam	:	89 feet
Displacement	:	33,653 tons
Machinery	:	B & W 6 cyl. diesel. 11,600 hp
Position	:	06°.47'.06" S 39°.18'.73" E

The ship was launched as the Hydrohos for Greek owners and sold twice before being renamed Fivi in 1993 under Cypriot ownership. On 24 December 1997 the ship arrived off Dar es Salaam carrying 27,000 tons of bulk maize. On New Year's Day she proceeded into the channel and grounded in front of State House. Two harbour tugs were secured to the ship and commenced pulling but abandoned the attempt with the falling tide. A sounding survey round the ship showed that at least 2,000 tons would have to be discharged to achieve the stranding draft. The ship's anchors were laid out and two local cargo vessels chartered for the operation completed on the 14th. The ship refloated with three tugs and proceeded in to discharge the remaining cargo and sailed on the 16th after a bottom survey. In 1999 she was sold to Cavalier Marine and was trading as the Cavalier until 2002 when she was broken up in China.

Fly

Builders	:	Akers Mek Vaerks, Oslo, Norway. 1913
Length	:	104 feet
Beam	:	20 feet
Displacement	:	167 tons
Machinery	:	Single triple expansion. 520 hp
Armament	:	1 x 12 pdr. gun. 2 x 3 pdr. guns
Position	:	8°.32' S 39°.30' E

The Fly was built as the whale catcher Sturmvogel, one of two sister ships, the other being the Seeadler for Deutsche Walfang Gesellschaft, a whaling company based at Luderitzbucht in German South West Africa. With the outbreak of the First World War the German colony was invaded by South African forces and by May 1915 the colony had surrendered. The whaling vessels had been interned at Capetown and the Sturmvogel renamed Fly, became one of a number of small vessels including Childers, Echo, Pickle and Salamander requisitioned by the Royal Navy to assist with patrolling the waters off the East African coast during the blockade of the German cruiser Königsberg. The Fly arrived on station off the Rufiji River delta in early 1915 and on the evening of 9 March ran aground on the reef on the south west corner of Songo Songo island. The cruiser H.M.S. Hyacinth arrived the following afternoon and despatched a steam cutter with additional men to help aboard the Fly. The cutter continued to patrol around the island during the hours of darkness shining a search light. On the afternoon of the 10th Hyacinth sailed for Zanzibar while the smaller cruiser H.M.S. Pyramus arrived. After circling the island and firing on two enemy dhows, the ship anchored close by and a tow wire was passed to the Fly. That evening Pyramus began towing but the attempt was abandoned until daylight. It was suggested lightening ship could assist with refloating and the ammunition and 3 pounder guns were offloaded. Towing began again on the high water on the 12th but the wire parted and had to be relaid. The next day saw the tow resume and that afternoon Fly refloated and was brought along-side Pyramus. Coal and water was supplied and the guns and ammunition reloaded and Fly rejoined the blockade the following day. Fly went on to play a significant part in the blockade and in patrolling the enemy coast after Königsberg had been destroyed. After the war the ship was decommissioned and sold in 1922 to a Norwegian company and renamed Harpun 1. After a number of further sales and name changes the ship was converted into a tug in 1938 by Kaldnes Mekaniske Verksted in Norway and renamed Basen. The vessel was deleted from the shipping register in 1965 and apparently scrapped in the 1970s.

Flying Horse

Builders	:	Lloyds Ship Holdings Pty. Brisbane, Australia. 1989
Length	:	117 feet
Beam	:	43 feet
Displacement	:	179 tons
Machinery	:	Twin Caterpillar V12 diesel. 2,999 hp
Position	:	06°.48'.80" S 39°.18'.60" E

The Flying Horse was one of a new generation of fast catamaran passenger ferries running between Dar es Salaam and Zanzibar and arrived on 15 February 1992. On 4 September 1996 the ferry struck a submerged object while leaving Dar es Salaam, causing a ten foot split in the hull that flooded one of the engine rooms and listed the vessel. To prevent a possible capsize the vessel was grounded on the reef while a diving inspection established the extent of the damage. The harbour ferry Kiomboni was sent to the scene and evacuated the 270 passengers and crew. A temporary repair was carried out by Divecon International and the vessel pumped out and refloated two days later. After an inspection in Dar es Salaam the ferry sailed to Mombasa for repair at African Marine.

Frierfjord

Builders	:	Pennsylvania Shipyards, Beaumont, U.S.A. 1944
Length	:	412 feet
Beam	:	60 feet
Displacement	:	7,967 tons
Machinery	:	Twin Nordberg 6 cyl. diesel. 4,150 hp
Position	:	05°.40' S 39°.12' E

The ship was launched as the Cape Lopez, one of sixty seven American C1-A class of emergency war time vessels fitted with either steam or diesel machinery giving a speed of fourteen knots. In 1947 the vessel was sold to the Norwegian shipping company Den Norske Amerika Linje and renamed Frierfjord, and on 16 August 1969 ran aground at Tanga. Out bound from the port along the channel having dropped the pilot, a vibration was felt and the ship slowed to a stop. Moving slowly astern the ship reached deeper water and set course for Mombasa where the double bottom tanks were inspected. The surveyor recommended fitting a cement box to the damaged area after which the ship continued her voyage. An investigation showed that as one of the navigation buoys was missing, the crew had lost track of their position and the vessel grounded on the edge of the channel. The ship was sold and renamed Ryttersund a year later but lasted a matter of months before being scrapped at Shanghai in January 1972.

Jamhuri

Builders	:	G. Philip & Son, Dartmouth, Devon, England. 1956
Length	:	209 feet
Beam	:	38 feet
Displacement	:	1,542 tons
Machinery	:	Twin British Polar 6 cyl. diesel. 2,240 hp
Position	:	6°.47'.18"S 39°.19'.9" E

The Jamhuri was built as the private yacht and passenger cargo vessel Seyyid Khalifa for the Zanzibar Government. Ordered by the Crown Agents in London in June 1952, she was the largest vessel built on the River Dart and launched on 15 September 1955 at a cost of £330,500. On 3 February 1956 while fitting out in the floating dock, she slipped off the blocks when the dock listed and sank. There was little damage and the ship sailed for Zanzibar in May. The ship was a regular visitor along the coast with occasional use by the Sultan, Khalifa bin Haroub. Following independence from Britain in 1963, and the subsequent revolution she was renamed Jamhuri (Freedom). In the early hours of 20 July

Listing to port in the sunken dock, 3 February 1956

1967 while on a voyage from Zanzibar to Dar es Salaam she grounded six miles outside the port with 295 passengers, fifty crew and a cargo of cement. The tug Simba arrived and after landing the passengers returned to refloat the ship, The attempt was unsuccessful until a second tug Linden arrived from Mombasa. Three days later the cargo was discharged in Dar es Salaam and she was towed to Mombasa for repair at African Marine. The stranding was attributed to the lack of position fixing by the crew, in part due to the intoxication of the Master. In 1978 the Lloyds classification was suspended and five years later she was taken over by the Zanzibar Shipping Corporation and renamed Al Jazirah. Sometime in the 1990s, she was laid up at Chake Chake in Pemba and became a total loss.

Jody

Builders	:	Kockum M/V, Malmo, Sweden. 1960
Length	:	485 feet
Beam	:	61 feet
Displacement	:	8,789 tons
Machinery	:	Kockum 8 cyl. diesel. 7,200 hp.
Position	:	05°.09' S 39°.10' E

The Jody grounded on Fungu Nyama reef on 14 November 1981 on a voyage between Dar es Salaam and Tanga with 2,000 tons of general cargo including sisal and coffee. The Murri International tug Bison 1 arrived from Mombasa and after signing a Lloyds Open Form, attempted unsuccessfully to refloat the ship with her main engine running astern. A sounding survey showed the vessel was out of draft and the need to remove cargo and fuel, and both anchors were laid astern to prevent the vessel moving on the rising tides. The landing craft Rampart lay alongside and ten days later the ship was empty and the cargo transferred to another vessel at Tanga. Over four hundred tons of fuel was transferred to the Rampart and on the high water of the 27th she was refloated by the Barbara and Bison 1 and sailed for Tanga. Two years later the ship was sold for scrap to Bhagwati Shipbreakers at Alang on the west coast of India, who commenced cutting on 10 December 1983. The ship was launched as the Black Osprey for the Norwegian owner Sigurd Herlofson and sold sixteen years later to Cia. Nav. Jody SA. and renamed Jody.

Juba

Builders	:	Ailsa Shipbuilding Co. Glasgow. 1889
Length	:	190 feet
Beam	:	29 feet
Displacement	:	506 tons
Machinery	:	Single triple expansion. 90 hp
Position	:	.04°.50' S 39°.41' E

The steamship Juba was ordered for the Imperial British East Africa Company based in Zanzibar and operated a cargo service along the coast. On 18 February 1891 she sailed out of Mombasa for Zanzibar with some seventy crew and passengers and some hours later grounded on Kigomache Reef at the northern end of Pemba Island. The anchors were laid out astern and unsuccessful efforts made to refloat the ship after the discharge of cargo. Eventually at midnight on the 19th the ship floated off without damage and proceeded to Zanzibar where a court of enquiry was held at the British Consulate on the 25th. The master and mate were found guilty of laying a wrong course and not keeping a good look out. Both had their certificates of competency suspended for a month. A year later on 5 March 1892 with a new master the ship grounded a second time on a reef near Sii Island off Vanga near the Tanzania border. The ship was refloated and a court of enquiry held on board the cruiser H.M.S. Blanche led by Captain Lindley. The stranding was put down to a strong current at right angles to the ship's course and the master was severely reprimanded and cautioned to be more careful in future. The ship was sold to Warden & Co. in 1909 and two years later to the Bombay Steam Navigation Co. of Bombay and scrapped in January 1929.

Llandaff Castle

Builders	:	Workman Clarke & Co. Belfast. Northern Ireland. 1926
Length	:	471 feet
Beam	:	61 feet
Displacement	:	10,786 tons
Machinery	:	Twin quadruple expansion. 6,000 ihp
Position	:	05°.50'.45" S 39°.12' E

The Llandaff Castle entered service with the Union Castle Line on the Africa run on 6 January 1927 with provision for 213 First and 108 Tourist Class passengers. Early on the morning of 21 January 1937, the liner was inbound to Zanzibar from Mombasa when the lookout noticed fishing boats in the water ahead. The ship altered course to port and shortly after ran aground on a sandbar at the southern end of Tumbatu Island. A signal from the master, Captain Fogden requesting assistance, was relayed to Captain Charlewood, the Zanzibar Harbour Master. The inter island steamer Al Hatheri arrived that afternoon with a motor boat to transfer passengers ashore if required and assist with tow ropes. Two lines were passed to the Al Hatheri which anchored awaiting the high tide that evening. In the meantime the Deputy Harbour Master Captain Somers boarded the stranded steamer which had pumped out her ballast tanks to reduce the draft. At 9.45 pm the Al Hatheri took the strain and the Llandaff Castle's starboard engine was run full astern. Somers meanwhile had the seabed sounded around the vessel to discover the ship was three feet deeper by the stern. The forepeak tank was filled and the ship trimmed to an even keel. At 10.40 the ships moved into deep water and the liner proceeded to Zanzibar. Having spoken to Captain Fogden, Charlewood submitted his report to the Zanzibar Secretariat. The stranding was attributed to the ship running too close to Tumbatu Island to avoid a shoal known as Wright Rock, and after turning inshore to avoid the fishing boats, failed to return to a course which would have cleared the sandbar. After discussions between the Crown Agents for the Colonies and the Zanzibar Government a claim for £10,000 was submitted to Union Castle for settlement. The claim was rejected and £5,000 was offered on the grounds that both vessels were in no immediate danger. This in turn was rejected and the original claim resubmitted. A second offer of £6,500 was also rejected and eventually on 20 May an offer of £7,500 was accepted. The salvage crew each received a bonus of a month's salary and the Government wrote to the Crown Agents to express their pleasure at a satisfactory outcome. The ship was converted for troop carrying during the Second World War and took part in the invasion of Madagascar in May 1942. On the 30 November she was hit by three torpedoes from U-177 while on a voyage from Dar es Salaam to Durban, and sank 100 miles south east of Lorenco Marques with two lives lost. The majority of lifeboats were picked up by naval vessels apart from one that landed on the Zululand coast. Local Zulus cared for them until transport arrived and after the war the headman was given a cash reward and three live cows. The compass that he had retrieved from the lifeboat was also returned to the authorities as it did not keep good time and is now on display in the Provincial Council Buildings in Pietermaritzburg.

Manica

Builders	:	Sir James Laing & Sons Ltd., Deptford, London. 1900
Length	:	360 feet
Beam	:	47 feet
Displacement	:	4,120 tons
Machinery	:	Single triple expansion. 530 nhp
Position	:	10°.10' S 40°.16' E

The Manica was built as a tramp steamer for the Ellerman & Bucknall Steamship Co. and between her commissioning and being requisitioned by the Admiralty in March 1915 sailed the world carrying general cargo. While discharging cargo in London the ship was chartered for use by the Royal Navy as a mother ship for a kite balloon. Conversion to operate the kite balloon involved fitting a sloping deck from forecastle to midships, fixing a dynamo to drive a hydrogen compressor and the installation of a winch. A wireless telegraphy house and quarters for the naval officers and men were also added. After service in Gallipoli the ship sailed for East Africa where the balloon was used effectively to spot enemy positions along the German East African coast.

On the early morning of 20 May 1916 while on patrol off the coast near Mikindani, the ship grounded to the north of Ras Sangamku. The two cruisers H.M.S. Challenger and Hyacinth arrived and having laid out both anchors and a wire, Challenger commenced towing mid afternoon and shortly after Manica refloated, but one anchor pennant wire fouled the ship's propeller. This was eventually cleared and the ship proceeded on voyage. In March 1917 the ship left East Africa and sailed for Bombay where she was converted into a tanker and renamed H.M.S. Huntball. In 1919 the ship was sold to Anglo-Saxon Petroleum Co. Ltd. and renamed Phorus. On 24 May 1930 while on passage from Australia to Balik Papan the ship stood by midway between Atamboea and Darwin on the route of Amy Johnson's flight from the UK to Australia. Later that year the vessel was laid up in Hong Kong and on 3 July 1931 arrived at Osaka, Japan for breaking.

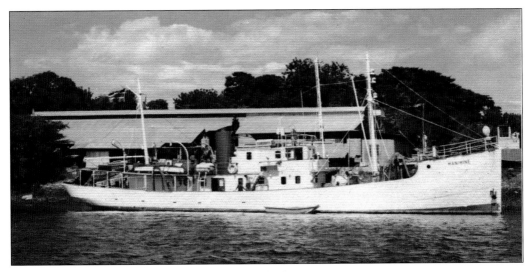

Manihine

Builders	:	Goole Shipbuilding & Repairing Co. Goole, England. 1906
Length	:	118 feet
Beam	:	21 feet
Displacement	:	208 tons
Machinery	:	Single triple expansion steam. 60 nhp
		Twin National Coal & Gas Co. 6 cyl. diesel. 440 hp
Position	:	06°.09'.50" S 39°.11'.25" E

The Manihine was a steel hulled trawler launched as the Coot, one of the Bird class fleet operating out of Aberdeen for Kelsall Brothers & Beeching. During the First World War she was requisitioned by the Admiralty and in 1924 based at Fleetwood before being sold to a private owner in May 1938 and renamed Dorade II. A major conversion to a private yacht entailed the replacement of the steam machinery with two National Oil engines and the fish holds turned into luxury accommodation. During the Second World War the ship was again taken into service by the Royal Navy and used as the Admiral's Barge at Reykjavik, Iceland. After the war she was purchased by Major H.W. Hall and renamed Manihine. During the next eight years Manihine was used for research as far away as the Red Sea before being sold to Singapore as a fisheries research vessel. She changed hands for One Pound in 1961 and joined the East African Marine Fisheries Organisation based in Zanzibar. Three years later ownership was transferred to the East African Common Services Organisation based in Kenya with management and maintenance undertaken by Southern Line and Southern Engineering at Mombasa. In 1976 the vessel was sold to the Institute of Marine Sciences in Zanzibar. During her research voyages, the ship ranged far and wide across the Indian Ocean, and at one time went in search of the fabled prehistoric fish, the Coelacanth. Eventually laid up at Zanzibar in 1976, the vessel became derelict and grounded. In June 1979 she was sold by tender and after an overhaul returned to service as a coastal trader before being beached on the seafront in Dar es Salaam in the late 1980s. Time had taken its toll and with a limited market the remains were cut up. In 1992 she was deleted from Lloyds Register and the hull finally disappeared in 1997.

Masula

Builders	:	Barclay, Curle & Co. Glasgow. 1919
Length	:	449 feet
Beam	:	58 feet
Displacement	:	7,261 tons
Machinery	:	Twin triple expansion. 8,000 ihp
Position	:	05°.40' S 39°.12' E

The Masula was one of a pair of vessels ordered by the British India Line as passenger ships but due to industrial action, were completed as cargo vessels carrying twelve passengers. Although the boilers were adapted for either coal or oil, in service they were coal fired. Less than a year later on a voyage from Australia with grain she arrived at Colombo on 10 June 1920 with four feet of water in No. 1 hold. Part of the cargo was discharged to access some loose rivets that were replaced with bolts by divers. Six years later on the Calcutta - Far East run, a fire in a cargo of cotton destroyed more than half the bales but did little damage to the ship. On 7 June 1930 a fire and explosion in the Mediterranean caused more serious damage but was extinguished with the help of two naval tugs that escorted her into Gibraltar where she was beached. On the voyage home a machinery breakdown on 23 August was repaired while a second vessel stood by. Six years later both ships were fitted with refrigeration for the Australian meat trade. During the Second World War she escaped damage and returned to the East African service in 1946. In 1951 she grounded at Tanga allegedly due to the pilot disembarking before the end of the navigation channel. The ship refloated on the high tide with no damage. By the early 1950s coal firing was outmoded and on 15 April 1952 she was sold to Wheelock, Marden of Hong Kong as the Jolly for £225,000. A year later the ship was purchased by

Villaneuve Shipping of Manilla and renamed Dona Lourdes. On 29 August 1954 she was driven ashore by typhoon Ida at Hong Kong and refloated on 11 September. Severe bottom damage and her age did not justify repairs and after lying at anchor for eighteen months she was sold to Hong Kong Rolling Mills Ltd who began demolition on 25 May 1956.

Mulbera

Builders	:	Alexander Stephen & Co. Glasgow, Scotland. 1922
Length	:	460 feet
Beam	:	60 feet
Displacement	:	9,100 tons
Machinery	:	Twin Parsons turbines. 4,100 shp
Position	:	05°.40' S 39°.12' E

The Mulbera was named after a hill village near the western border of Nepal, and was one of eight 'M' Class boats built for the British India Line. Costing £511,000 she was launched on 14 February 1922 and carried 114 First and 44 Second Class passengers. Unusually the ship was arranged for both coal and oil firing. In 1924 the ship conveyed the Duke and Duchess of York to Kenya and in 1935 was converted to a one class ship carrying 158 passengers. She had an uneventful career apart from a collision on 8 June 1932 with the British steamer Zitella and later that year struck the pier head in the King George V dock in London. The following year she grounded on Ulenge Reef outside Tanga on 22 August. Cargo was discharged into lighters, and the African Wharfage tug Kifaru and B.I. ship Dumra refloated her on the high water two days later with little damage. During the Second World War she was used for passenger carrying under the direction of the Indian government, and after hostilities returned to the India - Australia run until 1949 when she reverted to the East African service. By 1954 she was the last of the class in service and the final voyage in February was marked by a 190 foot paying-off pennant and a rousing farewell at each port. At Dar es Salaam, the Harbour Master sent the following, '*We bid good bye to the Mulbera with deep regret for her own sake and as the last of the M Class steamers which have played such a large part in the development of this territory. Godspeed*'. She arrived at the Royal Albert Docks on the 17 March and was sold on the 26th to Thomas Ward for £64,000 and scrapped at Inverkeithing.

Nordvaer

Builders	:	D.W. Kremer & Sohn, Elmshorn, Germany. 1958
Length	:	161 feet
Beam	:	28 feet
Displacement	:	499 tons
Machinery	:	Klockner Humboldt Deutz, 6 cyl. diesel. 635 hp.
Position	:	06°.48'.90" S 39°.18'.75" E

Built for the Norwegian company Det Nordlanske, the ship was sold in 1968 to the Crown Agents in London and transferred to the Government of the British Indian Ocean Territories, trading to the Seychelles and outlying islands. She was based in Mombasa and managed by Southern Line with maintenance carried out by Southern Engineering. Nordvaer was unique in the region in that she was also a travelling Post Office carrying the stamps of the B.I.O.T. and featured on two stamps in 1969 and 1974. During a departure from Mombasa in 1975 the ship suffered an engine failure and was towed in for repairs including a new crankshaft. In 1978 Southern Line concluded its management contract, when the company sold its shipping interests. The ship reverted to the Seychelles flag and continued to trade until 15 September 1979 when she grounded at Dar es Salaam. On her return to the Seychelles on 9 November, a survey showed the double bottom damage extended over half the vessel's length. Further damage to the variable pitch propeller and stern tube seals made repairs uneconomic and the vessel was put up for sale. There were no takers and the Nordvaer was driven ashore on the island of Desnoeufs as a breakwater and eventually broke up.

Norefjord

Builders	:	Wood Skinner & Co., Newcastle, England. 1919
Length	:	331 feet
Beam	:	46 feet
Displacement	:	3,082 tons
Machinery	:	Single triple expansion. 310 nhp.
Position	:	05°.40' S 39°.12' E

The Norwegian owned Norefjord was on a voyage to the island of Reunion from Oslo with a stop at Tanga. Having discharged cargo the ship was outbound on the evening of 20 March 1949 when she grounded on Ulenge Reef. The African Star arrived and attempted unsuccessfully to refloat the ship before departing. A sounding survey showed the ship aground up to No. 4 hatch with little prospect of refloating until the next spring tide eleven days later. Meanwhile the ship's crew prepared to wait but in the early hours of the 27th the ship refloated herself with the main engine and steamed into Tanga. A temporary certificate of sea worthiness was issued and the ship departed on 31st for Mombasa where a diving inspection showed no damage and four days later the ship sailed. Launched as the War Glade for the British Shipping Controller she was sold in 1920 to Skibs A/S Thoresens Linie as the Norefos. A year later she was sold to the Norwegian company Den Norske Amerikalinje and renamed Norefjord. They sold her in 1949 to A/S Ryvarden who renamed her Ryvarden and in 1958 after two more owners the ship was sold to Pan Norse of Panama and renamed Norse Lady. On 14 August that year the ship grounded at Parigi in the Celebes and was captured by rebels. The ship was refloated and taken to Belang and beached, where on the 22nd she was shelled and set on fire by Nationalist warships. Seven years later the burnt out wreck was refloated and towed to Kaohsiung for scrap.

CEC Pacific

Builders	:	A/S Nordsovaerftet, Ringkobing, 1992
Length	:	290 feet
Beam	:	50 feet
Displacement	:	4,117 tons
Machinery	:	One MaK 6 cyl. 2,692 h.p

The ship was launched as the Arktis Swan, renamed the Arktis Pacific and later as the CEC Pacific. In July 2005 the vessel loaded cargo at the port of Tio in Eritrea destined for Zanzibar. Part of the cargo included two steel pontoon barges loaded using its two heavy lift 50 ton hydraulic pedestal cranes. The first barge was loaded without difficulty but the second took four attempts before it was stowed on deck. After a ten day voyage the ship anchored in Zanzibar on 26 July and the crew prepared the barge for lifting. The barge was lifted off the deck using both cranes but started to swing outboard causing the vessel to list and the two cranes to swing out further. One end of the barge was successfully lowered into the water which transferred the remaining weight on to the second crane. This weight appears to have exceeded the cranes safe working load and the entire crane sheared off its mounting and fell into the sea with the operator in the cab. Fortunately the crane jib came to rest on the barge and the operator managed a successful underwater escape from the cab. Comarco owned Kenya Marine Contractors from Mombasa using the tug Privateer, and a crane barge were awarded the salvage contract to recover the crane and barge. An enquiry after the incident established that the barge was considerably heavier than manifested and buckled the crane structure prior to failing and that following the difficulty in loading at Tio, the weight should have been investigated. Part of the excess weight and swinging was thought to be caused by the free surface effect of water inside the barge. At the time of going to press the vessel continues to trade under the name Pacific 88.

Pemba

Builders	:	A & J Inglis, Glasgow, Scotland. 1877
Length	:	280 feet
Beam	:	31 feet
Displacement	:	1,780 tons
Machinery	:	Single compound. 1,268 ihp.
Position	:	06°.15' S 39°.05' E

The Pemba was one of two sister iron steamers designed for the Bombay - Aden - Zanzibar service, and delivered on 15 September 1877 with a schooner rig and accommodation for twenty-seven First, sixteen Second Class and 1,028 deck passengers. The ship gave excellent service and ran aground twice during her career. The first was at Zanzibar in 1883 where she was refloated after discharging cargo, and the second at Baragua Flats on 13 June 1885 on a voyage from Calcutta to Rangoon. The following year the ship was chartered by the Spanish Compania Trasatlantica to carry passengers and mail from Singapore to Manila after their own vessel Isla de Luzon was disabled off Ceylon. After twenty-five years service she was scrapped at Bombay in December 1902.

Pentakota

Builders	:	A & J. Inglis, Glasgow, Scotland. 1890
Length	:	360 feet
Beam	:	42 feet
Displacement	:	4,620 tons
Machinery	:	Single triple expansion. 2,860 ihp.
Position	:	06°.15' S 39°.05' E

Laid down as the Palaspa she was renamed Pentakota before launching. Like many of the British India Line fleet, the ship spent her early years in the Bay of Bengal. During 1900 she transported troops to China during the Boxer Rebellion and ten years later was transferred to East African waters. On 8 April 1911 the ship grounded in the Zanzibar Channel and three years later at Beira. In September 1914 she was requisitioned to carry Indian troops from Bombay for the ill-fated Allied landing at Tanga on 2 November. At the end of hostilities the ship returned to the Arabian Gulf service, and on 2 September 1920 grounded on the Falha Shoal near Jask flooding No. 1 and 2 holds. After eleven days pumping the ship was refloated and returned to Jask where the bows slowly sank until they rested on the seabed. Temporary repairs enabled her to return to Bombay but the extent of the bottom damage and age of the ship meant she was sold on 28 December for 95,000 rupees and scrapped the following year.

Phillipias

Builders	:	Helsingor Skibs & Msk., Elsinore, Norway. 1954
Length	:	412 feet
Beam	:	53 feet
Displacement	:	6,336 tons
Machinery	:	Helsingor 8 cyl. diesel. 4,200 hp
Position	:	06°.54' S 39°.56 E

The Phillipias was one of two sister ships originally named Belgien and Congo built for the Danish company AS Det Dansk Franske of Copenhagen. After two sales in 1962 she was sold to Santo I Compania Naviera of Piraeus in 1973. The ship grounded on Fungu Kisimkasi in the early hours of 20 June 1977, on a voyage from Karachi to Dar es Salaam and Durban carrying 2,300 tons of general cargo. Otherwise known as Latham Island, this coral outcrop only rises ten feet above the surface, twenty three miles off shore and has been the scene of previous casualties dating back to the age of sail. Four days later the Smit salvage tug Rode Zee arrived and anchored off, but due to the nature of the stranding and the possible time involved, sailed three days later. The prevailing bad weather made any immediate salvage unlikely and some of the crew abandoned ship and proceeded to Dar es Salaam. The Wijsmuller tug Groningen and Murri tug Barbara arrived on the 29th after the salvage was awarded to Murri International and an unsuccessful attempt made to refloat the vessel on 1 July. The high winds and rough seas pounded the ship on the reef causing No. 3 hold to flood, and the bad weather made cargo discharge impossible until the end of August, when the landing craft Rampart arrived and transhipped cargo to Dar es Salaam. The exposed position and uncertain weather made the task extremely difficult and it was not until 13 October that the ship was refloated by the Barbara and Bison 1 and towed to Dar es Salaam to discharge the balance of cargo. In Mombasa, a survey showed extensive bottom damage and considering the age of the ship she was declared a total loss and sold to Pakistani ship breakers at Gadani Beach in May 1979. It was while the ship was aground that an extraordinary saga of cargo mismanagement came to light. The ship was originally destined for Mauritius, Reunion and South Africa with a cargo of rice and beans, but after a delay at Mauritius, the ship received orders to sail for Quelimane in Mozambique to load copper for Bombay. To accommodate the new cargo, the rice for Reunion was offloaded. The copper was discharged in Bombay and additional cargo uplifted for Dar es Salaam, Mauritius, Reunion and South Africa. On arrival at Reunion the ship was arrested for breach of contract. Rice destined for Mauritius was offered instead and the ship sailed for Mauritius where she was arrested for the second time, but released on the understanding that the rice would be retrieved from Quelimane and the ship would sail direct to Durban. The rice was loaded on 16 June and the ship due in Durban on the 21st. The shippers suspected all was not well, when they learned the Phillipias was aground off Dar es Salaam, the owners having decided to offload the Dar es Salaam cargo first.

H.M.A.S. Pioneer

Builders	:	Chatham Dockyard, Chatham, England. 1899
Length	:	300 feet
Beam	:	36 feet
Displacement	:	2,135 tons
Machinery	:	Twin triple expansion. 5,000 ihp,
Armament	:	8 x 4 inch Q.F. guns, 8 x 3 pdr. guns

H.M.S. Pioneer was one of eleven Pelorus Third Class Cruisers ordered for the Royal Navy in the early 1890s and laid down on 16 December 1897. After commissioning, the ship saw service in the Mediterranean until placed in reserve at Chatham on 20 December 1904. The class were condemned by Admiral Fisher in 1905 but reprieved and continued in service. Nine months later the ship sailed for Sydney as part of the Australian Squadron, which also consisted of two other Pelorus Class cruisers H.M.S. Pegasus and Prometheus. On 1 March 1913 the ship was gifted to the Royal Australian Navy as a sea going training ship. On the outbreak of war Pioneer was at Melbourne and detailed for convoy duty, but while off the west coast had to return to Freemantle for engine repairs. On 24 December the Admiralty requested the ship assist with the blockade of the Königsberg in East Africa. She stopped at the Cocos Islands for coal where the crew inspected the wreck of the Königsberg's sister ship Emden destroyed by H.M.A.S. Sydney two months previously, and arrived at Zanzibar on 6 February 1915. Detailed to patrol the coast she grounded at night on a reef off the Rufiji Delta in June but with the aid of a kedge anchor refloated herself. On 6 July Pioneer was engaged in shelling the Rufiji defences while the monitors Severn and Mersey proceeded upstream to attack the Königsberg. The cruiser remained in the area until the end of August when she drydocked at Simonstown for two months. In early 1916 she grounded a second time off Pemba damaging the hull and a propeller blade and sailed to Mombasa for repair. The ship also took part in the bombardment of Tanga and Dar es Salaam prior to the Allied landings and fired her guns in anger for the last time. on 30 July. Three weeks later she sailed for Australia and paid off at Sydney on 7 November, bringing her seagoing career to an end, and the start of six years as an accommodation ship at Garden Island. In May 1923 the ship was handed over to Cockatoo Dockyard and the hull stripped and sold to H.P. Stacey of Sydney for scrap. Eight years later the bare hull was scuttled off Sydney on 18 February 1931.

Präsident

Builders	:	Blohm & Voss, Hamburg, Germany. 1900
Length	:	320 feet
Beam	:	40 feet
Displacement	:	3,310 tons
Machinery	:	Twin triple expansion. 1,500 ihp
Position	:	10°.30'.S 39°.41'.E

The Präsident entered service with the Deutsche Ost Afrika Linie in 1901, on the round Africa trip carrying thirty-one First, thirty-six Second and thirty-two Third Class passengers. In 1907 the ship commenced a new service between Bombay and Durban via Mombasa and Dar es Salaam. On 24 July 1914 the ship left Bombay with a cargo of rice calling at Zanzibar, Dar es Salaam and Lindi. On arrival the ship was discharged and laid up in Lindi creek, war having been declared four days earlier. In September coal from the ship was taken by barge towed by the tug Adjutant to the cruiser Königsberg before she departed for Zanzibar to sink H.M.S. Pegasus. The loss of the latter resulted in the Admiralty ordering the cruisers H.M.S. Chatham, Dartmouth and Weymouth to search the coastline. On 10 October, Dartmouth captured the tug Adjutant bound from Beira to Lindi. Among the ship's papers was a receipt acknowledging delivery of coal. Strongly suspecting the tug and port may have been involved in Königsberg's whereabouts, Chatham anchored off the entrance to Lindi on the 19th and sent a pinnace to investigate. Some three miles upstream lay the Präsident with a white cross painted on the side and a red cross flag at the masthead. Following discussions with the German District Officer a boarding party found there was little on board to indicate a hospital ship, and disabled the main engine removing compasses, chronometers and charts. Among the latter was one of the Rufiji delta surveyed by the Möwe showing the channels to be navigable. The Präsident lay in Lindi until 29 September 1915 when the cruisers H.M.S. Challenger and Hyacinth shelled the port and sank the ship. After the war she was sold to the South African firm Irvin and Johnson who intended to convert her into a whale factory ship. The ship was taken to Cape Town and later moved to Saldhana Bay where she lay until scrapped in 1935. The remains were later filled with earth and became a landing stage.

Rampart

Builders	:	Sir William Arroll, Alloa, Scotland. 1946
Length	:	231 feet
Beam	:	36 feet
Displacement	:	1,017 tons
Machinery	:	Four Paxman Ricardo V12 diesel. Twin screw. 1,800 hp
Position	:	08°.30'.50" S 39°.44' E
	:	03°.21' S 40°.01' E

The Citadel and Rampart ex LCT 4037 were two Mk. VIII Tank Landing Craft ordered for the Royal Corps of Transport for use in the Far East. A number had been ordered but the end of the Second World War in August 1945 resulted in only a few being delivered. By the late 1960s they were placed on the disposal list and two were purchased by Murri

International and based at Mombasa. On 31 May 1975 Rampart was seriously damaged after grounding on Kibondo Island, south of Mafia Island on the Tanzanian coast. She was towed to Mombasa and declared a total loss but subsequently repaired and returned to service. The vessel grounded a second time off the Kenya coast when returning to Mombasa from Songo Songo in Tanzania on 12 June 1976. The radar and steering failed and the combination of current and wind took the vessel north of Mombasa. That evening a flashing light off to port was wrongly mistaken for the entrance to Mtwapa creek and the ship turned about. A lookout spotted waves breaking on a reef and the stern anchor was dropped while the crew waited for daylight. The wire parted and the ship grounded off Watamu village, fifteen miles south of Malindi. The company tug Barbara towed the vessel to Mombasa for repairs and after nearly thirty years service Rampart was sold to local breakers and scrapped at Mombasa in 1993.

Roybank

Builders	:	Harland & Wolff, Belfast, N. Ireland. 1963
Length	:	483 feet
Beam	:	62 feet
Displacement	:	6,378 tons
Machinery	:	H & W. 6 cyl. diesel. 6,700 hp
Position	:	5°.19'.50" S 39°.51'.50" E

The Roybank was one of a number of tramp ships built for the Bank Line of London. In the early hours of 27 September 1969 on a voyage from Lourenco Marques to Mombasa, the bridge lookout noticed a shadow on the port bow. On closer investigation it turned out to be land and the helm put hard a starboard. As the bows swung there was a slight vibration as the bottom grazed the reef and a sounding survey showed water in No. 8 double bottom. A diving inspection in Mombasa, revealed a fracture in the hull that was repaired with a cement box. The report attributed the incident to the ship running too close to the island of Pemba in poor visibility. Ten years later she was sold to Cynthos Maritime of Cyprus and renamed Castor and in 1984 bought by Denner Services of Panama and renamed Byron 1. On 17 January 1985 while at anchor at Kalimenes, Crete, she was driven ashore and sank during a storm on a voyage from Gdynia to India.

SFL Sara

Builders	:	Xiamen Shipbuilding Industry, Xiamen, China. 2011
Length	:	630 feet
Beam	:	105 feet
Displacement	:	57,000 tons
Machinery	:	M.A.N. / B&W 6 cyl. diesel. 12,889 bhp
Position	:	05°.02'.58" S 39°.09'.89" E

The SFL Sara was delivered to her new owners on 21 February 2011 and grounded on Ulenge Reef on the approaches to Tanga on the afternoon of 3 December 2012 with a cargo of clinker for the cement works. The salvage operation was awarded to Comarco owned Kenya Marine Contractors in Mombasa who mobilised the tug Condor . The tug Elizabeth Latigo arrived and began pushing on the starboard side together with the use of the main engine in ahead and astern. All attempts to move the ship failed and the anchor was dropped. Two days later cargo was moved from No.1 Hold to No.2 Hold to begin trimming the vessel by the stern and later that day cargo was discharged from both holds on to a barge alongside. This continued for two days with cargo also being offloaded from No.3 Hold. In the meantime the port anchor had been towed astern by the tug Condor and dropped as part of the ground tackle for the salvage attempt. After further discharging of cargo on the 9th from No.1 and 2 Holds, preparations were made to attempt to refloat the following morning. Deballasting started early and after the arrival of the pilot, the port anchor was slowly heaved in and at 10.30 hrs the SFL Sara was afloat once more. A diving inspection showed minimum damage and the vessel proceeded to Tanga to complete discharge of the remaining cargo and sailed shortly after. The vessel was still trading in 2017.

Sarah Jolliffe

Builders	:	J. Readhead & Sons, South Shields, England. 1890
Length	:	138 feet
Beam	:	25 feet
Displacement	:	333 tons
Machinery	:	Single triple expansion. 900 ihp.
Location	:	5º.45' S 39º.41' E

The Sarah Jolliffe and the T.A Jolliffe were two Liverpool tugs requisitioned in 1915 for service with the Royal Navy to tow three shallow draft monitors H.M.S. Humber, Mersey and Severn to Malta for service at Gallipoli. The Gallipoli plan was cancelled and the Severn and Mersey prepared for the 5,000 mile tow to East Africa to attack the Königsberg. Together with the tugs Blackcock and Revenger and the supply ships Kendall Castle and Trent, the two Jolliffes and the monitors left Malta on 28 April 1915 for Suez. Water and provisions were supplied by the passenger liner Trent, while coal was provided by the collier Kendall Castle. The voyage was not without incident, as the Sarah Jolliffe was shot at while passing through the Suez Canal, and two crew members collapsed from heat exhaustion in the Red Sea. On the final leg from Aden to Mafia Island, the Sarah Jolliffe towing the Mersey ran aground on a reef off the northern tip of Pemba on 1 June. The Mersey was hurriedly disconnected and towed to safety by the Blackcock, while the tug refloated that evening. The flotilla arrived at Mafia Island two days later and prepared for action. On 6 July 1915 the monitors were towed to the mouth of the Rufiji by the tugs, where they proceeded upstream under fire to engage the Königsberg. It was not a success as there was a misunderstanding between the spotter aircraft and monitors. Five days later they returned and within an hour seriously damaged the raider. Unable to return fire, the captain, Max Looff, evacuated the crew and ordered the scuttling of his ship. The Sarah Jolliffe remained on the coast until 1918 after which she returned to European waters and was scrapped in 1924.

Simla

Builders	:	Caird & Co., Greenock, Scotland. 1878
Length	:	281 feet
Beam	:	32 feet
Displacement	:	1,800 tons
Machinery	:	Single compound. 1,100 ihp.
Position	:	06°.14' S 39°.18' E

The Simla was named after the hill town in India so important to the Raj as a retreat during the summer months. She was a one off vessel built for the British India Line entering service on 16 October 1878, rigged as a two masted schooner with accommodation for twenty-seven First, twelve Second Class and 793 deck passengers. She served for a time on the East Africa service and on 12 October 1883 grounded off Zanzibar. Later she carried prospectors from Calcutta to Western Australia during the first gold rush and three years later carried troops from Madras and Calcutta to Chittagong for the Chin Lushai expedition. In May 1894 she collided with the Bombay & Persia vessel King Arthur in the Arabian Gulf and five years later grounded off Bahrain. After twenty-four years service the Simla was sold to Essajee Borah in December 1902 and broken up the following year at Bombay.

Sincerity

Builders	:	Eriksbergs A/B, Goteborg, Sweden. 1949
Length	:	416 feet
Beam	:	58 feet
Displacement	:	8,450 tons
Machinery	:	B & W 7 cyl. diesel. 5,600 hp
Position	:	06°15' S 39°.34' E

The Sincerity was launched as the Lista for A/S Ludwig Mowinckels Rederi and sold eighteen years later becoming the Irene M. She was renamed Sincerity after purchase by Sincerity Shipping of Piraeus in 1970 and abandoned by the crew on 11 July 1974. The vessel developed a thirty degree list off the Tanzanian coast having left Mombasa in ballast for Buenos Aires. The crew alarmed to find that No. 2 hold was taking water put out a distress call which summoned the Italian cargo ship Amerigo Vespucci to their aid. They took off the crew and landed them in Dar es Salaam. The call was also picked up by the Murri tug Barbara which had engine trouble and was unable to help. The ship drifted along the coast until a small fishing vessel put a crew aboard on the 14th and began towing the ship towards Dar es Salaam. However their engine was insufficient to prevent the vessel grounding on the reef at Zanzibar, close to where the Murri salvage crew were working on the stranded Spalmatori Engineer. The landing craft Rampart sailed across to the casualty and commenced pumping. With the water discharged from the hold, the ship regained its trim and was towed into Dar es Salaam. The cause of the list was not a hole in the hull as first thought, but holes in the ballast tank tops which when filled, leaked into the hold affecting stability. Temporary repairs were carried out and the ship sailed for Cape Town on 30 July. Repairs were completed on 16 September and she sailed for South America and ten months later arrived at Gadani Beach for breaking.

Spalmatori Engineer

Builders	:	Bartram & Sons, Sunderland, England. 1950
Length	:	476 feet
Beam	:	62 feet
Displacement	:	10,387 tons
Machinery	:	Doxford 5 cyl. diesel. 5,250 hp
Position	:	06°.18' S 39°.33' E

The ship was launched as the Kieldrecht for the Dutch company N.V. Stoormv before being sold to Greek owners Apiganos Corp. and renamed Spalmatori Engineer. In the early hours of 23 April 1974 she grounded on the east coast of Zanzibar on a voyage from Shanghai via Dar es Salaam to the Red Sea ports with 6,000 tons of general cargo. Attempts to refloat the ship by the crew during the day were unsuccessful and distress calls were picked up by a number of ships but all were unable to help given the position of the ship. The engine room and No. 4 hold flooded as the tide ebbed and the vessel hogged. The crew abandoned the ship and were later flown to Dar es Salaam. Over the next two days the ship swung parallel to the reef and shortly afterwards a surveyor boarded the vessel to assess the damage. The inspection showed heavy buckling of the engine room floor with suspected damage to the rudder and propeller. Murri International was awarded the salvage contract and commenced discharging cargo with their landing craft. After extensive repairs to the hull the ship was refloated and towed to Mombasa in July. A diving inspection revealed the extent of the damage to the underside and she was condemned as a total loss and sold for breaking at Gadani Beach in July 1977.

Stanford Buzzard

Builder	:	Fujian Mawei Shipbuilding, Mawei, China. 2011
Length	:	287 feet
Beam	:	52 feet
Displacement	:	5,115 tons
Machinery	:	4 x Cummins QSK60 diesel electric. 5,400 bhp

The Stanford Buzzard is one of the new generation eco friendly large offshore support vessels built to operate in extreme conditions. One of its features being the ability to withstand pirate attack using an impenetrable command citadel. With its state of the art electronics and bow and stern thrusters it is a huge advance on the original rig supply boats of earlier generations.

In February 2013 the vessel was inbound to Mtwara in southern Tanzania when it missed a navigation way point and crossed the edge of a reef and damaged the side of the hull flooding a fresh water tank. The repair to the hull was undertaken by Subsea Services of Mombasa who dispatched a team of divers and fabricated a steel frame six metres by three which was bolted into the damaged area. Steel plate was in turn cut to fit and floated into place using 200 litre drums for buoyancy and bolted to the frame and the surround sealed and made watertight. The inside of the repair was coated with concrete to complete the seal. The task took five days after which the vessel sailed to Mombasa for drydocking and repair. The tug is still operational in 2017.

State of Haryana

Builders	:	Barclay Curle & Co. Glasgow, Scotland. 1950
Length	:	479 feet
Beam	:	62 feet
Displacement	:	8,590 tons
Machinery	:	Twin Doxford 4 cyl. diesel. 5,900 hp
Position	:	06°.14'.50" S 39°.08'.70" E

The ship was the former Santhia the last of three 'S' Class passenger cargo vessels delivered to the British India Line in November 1950 for service in the Far East. There was accommodation described as comfortable for the twenty-five First and seventy Second Class passengers, while the sixty-eight intermediate were accommodated in four, six and eight berth cabins. In 1960 the ship was placed on the pilgrim run from the Indian sub-continent to Jeddah and four years later when India and Pakistan had a political upheaval, she and another B.I. vessel Dwarka cross transferred passengers of both nationalities, the Indians to the Santhia and the Pakistanis to the Dwarka. After sixteen years service in the Indian Ocean, the ship was sold to the Shipping Corporation of India on 16 December and renamed State of Haryana, sailing between India, the Andaman Islands and latterly East Africa. On the evening of 20 November 1975 while approaching Zanzibar for the pilot, the ship grounded on Nyange Reef. The double bottom tanks and bilges were sounded and found to be tight and some hours later with the rising tide and engines running astern the ship refloated herself and proceeded in to discharge. The stranding was attributed to heavy rain and poor visibility. In 1976 the auxiliary boiler was found to be beyond economical repair and the ship sold to Bombay breakers in January 1977.

Tanga

Builders	:	A/B Gotaverken, Goteborg, Sweden. 1918
Length	:	440 feet
Beam	:	56 feet
Displacement	:	9,270 tons
Machinery	:	Twin Gotaverken 6 cyl. diesel. 835 hp
Position	:	05°.40' S 39°.12' E

The Deutsche Ost Afrika Line passenger cargo ship Tanga grounded on Niule Reef outside Tanga on the evening of 30 November 1957, on a voyage from Hamburg to Beira with general cargo. A Lloyds Open Form was signed with East African Railways and Harbours and their Mk IV Tank Landing Craft arrived and passed a line, but her twin 500 hp Paxman engines were insufficient to make any headway. The LCT returned to Dar es Salaam and the tug Simba arrived from Mombasa on the 1 December. A line was passed to the ship and the tug anchored awaiting high tide. That night the tug crew became aware the ship was drifting down on them and hurriedly took the tow to prevent the ship grounding a second time. As daylight approached the ship was released and sailed to Tanga for a hull inspection by a diver flown down from Mombasa. Other than missing paint the hull was undamaged and the ship sailed for Zanzibar. She was launched as the Bullaren with an open bridge and small funnel for the Gothenburg company Rederi Transatlantic who ran the ship to West Africa and the Pacific. On 13 May 1940 while on charter to the French Government she was captured by the Germans, and after repairs was renamed Tanga and used for U-boat crew accommodation. Four years later while transporting wounded in the Baltic she was damaged and claims of ownership after the war resulted in repairs that were not completed until July 1950. Eleven years later the ship was sold and renamed Pamaru and in August departed from Hamburg for the breakers in Japan with a cargo of scrap metal. Engine trouble off Algeria in September saw the salvage tug Merchantman tow the vessel into Palermo for repairs. While crossing the Indian Ocean in November the ship diverted to Colombo to repair broken piston rings. Both pistons and liners were badly worn and two weeks later on 13 December 1961 the ship anchored in Manila with serious compression problems and an untenable engine room filled with smoke. It was the end of the voyage under power and the tug Atlas was summoned for the tow to Tokyo. After a collision leaving Tokyo she arrived in May for breaking at the Yokohama yard of Amaksu Sangyo.

Tilawa

Builders	:	Hawthorn & Leslie, Newcastle, Yorkshire. 1924
Length	:	471 feet
Beam	:	59 feet
Displacement	:	10,006 tons
Machinery	:	Single quadruple expansion. 5,000 ihp.
Position	:	06°.08'.80" S 39°.11'.70" E

The Tilawa was one of two sister vessels built for the British India Line for service in the Far East. Launched on 20 February 1924 she had accommodation for sixty First, seventy Second Class and 1,356 deck passengers and a 220 crew. The twin funnels appeared too close together for symmetry but this was supposedly to reassure Chinese passengers that there were twin engines. The ship spent fourteen uneventful years in service until requisitioned by the military in September 1939. In November 1940 she was transferred to the Bombay - East Africa run and while entering Zanzibar harbour on the evening of 5 May 1942, grounded on Malindi Spit, north of the dhow harbour. An attempt to refloat her by the American vessel Intent failed and cargo was discharged into lighters. On the 13th a second attempt was successful but resulted in a wire round the propeller. Divers removed the wire while the cargo was reloaded and she sailed a week later for Dar es Salaam. Seven months later on a voyage from Mombasa to Bombay the Tilawa was torpedoed north west of the Maldive Islands on 23 November 1942 by the Japanese submarine I-29. Panic ensued among the steerage passengers who overcrowded the lifeboats, and led to an unnecessary loss of life when the lifeboats were lowered and capsized. About an hour later, the ship was still afloat and the Master, Captain Robinson had just organised the crew and passengers to re-board, when she was hit by a second torpedo and sank at 08°.36' N 61°.08' E. The cruiser H.M.S. Birmingham rescued survivors, but twenty-eight crew and 252 passengers were lost from a complement of 222 crew and 736 passengers.

Uganda

Builders	:	Barclay Curle & Co., Glasgow, Scotland. 1951
Length	:	539 feet
Beam	:	71 feet
Displacement	:	16,907 tons
Machinery	:	Twin Parsons turbines. 11,200 hp

The Kenya and Uganda were said to be the two finest liners ever built for the British India Line with accommodation for 167 First and 133 Tourist class passengers. They entered the East African service in 1952 with the traditional black hull and a white trim line. Later they were repainted with a white hull and a black trim line. On the Uganda's second voyage the port propeller was damaged on 26 November 1952 by a small coral outcrop while anchoring in Dar es Salaam. A diving inspection showed all four blades were damaged and dry-docking was necessary. The nearest was at Diego Suarez in Madagascar and three days later the ship sailed having transferred passengers to the Mulbera. On 3 December the ship docked and four new blades were fitted and repairs completed three days later. The ships maintained a regular service to and from Britain until 1967 when the Uganda was withdrawn and converted to an educational cruise ship. Extensively modernised in Germany with accommodation for 306 passengers and 920 children, she returned to service in 1968. For the next fourteen years the ship's cruises to the Baltic and Mediterranean were extremely popular until on 13 April 1982, one of the cruises came to an abrupt end when she was requisitioned as a hospital ship for the Falklands War. She returned briefly to cruising in 1983, but was re-chartered by the Ministry of Defence until laid up in April 1985. A year later she was delivered to Kaohsiung for breaking but driven ashore in a typhoon where she capsized and broke in half.

Umballa

Builders	:	Denny & Co. Dumbarton. Scotland. 1898
Length	:	410 feet
Beam	:	50 feet
Displacement	:	5,310 tons
Machinery	:	Single triple expansion. 2,462 ihp
Position	:	06°.49'S 39°.19'E

The Umballa was the first of seven similar cargo ships ordered by the British India Line from three different builders, with provision for six passengers in three twin cabins. Launched on 27 October 1897 she was delivered on 25 February 1898 at a cost of £62,400 and entered service on the Australian route. In 1901 she was chartered by the War Department carrying troops to Somaliland for the first expedition against the 'Mad Mullah' between 22 May and 30 July. On 25 February 1912 she grounded at the entrance to Dar es Salaam and refloated after some of the cargo had been discharged. On the outbreak of the First World War the ship carried men of the Lahore Division to France in extremely cramped conditions. She was torpedoed in the boiler room by UB-49 on Christmas Day 1917 on a voyage from Karachi to Naples with a cargo of barley. Fifteen were killed in the explosion and the ship drifted ashore and became a total loss near the village of Prais on the Sicily coast. The ship's bell was subsequently donated to the village church and the ship broken up where she lay.

Zambesi

Builders	:	J.L. Meyer, Papenburg, Germany. 1914
Length	:	131 feet
Beam	:	26 feet
Displacement	:	282 tons
Machinery	:	Single triple expansion. 575 ihp
Position	:	05°.26'S 38°.00'E

The Zambesi was launched as the passenger ferry Seestern for the Cuxhaven Steamer Co. in Germany and operated on the Cuxhaven to Brunsbuettel run. In 1925 the vessel was sold to the salvage company Bugsier and converted to a salvage tug and renamed Nordenham VIII. Two years later in September 1927 she was sold to the Dutch company V.N.S. of 's-Gravenhage and sailed to East Africa. On 29 January 1934 the vessel grounded at Pangani on a voyage from Tanga to Mombasa and after salvage in July was towed to Mombasa and broken up.

Miscellaneous sinkings and strandings

African Queen - An Italian built motor ship of 1,800 tons sunk off the coast.

Anna - A small steamer operating in the Rufiji delta in the late 1920s grounded on a sandbank and remained there until refloated the following season.

Bouvet - An 856 ton wooden composite hull French sailing / steam gunboat built in 1876, ran aground at Zanzibar on 30 December 1889. H.M.S. Turquoise assisted with refloating and the cruiser H.M.S. Cossack towed her back to harbour on 3 January 1890. Returned to France, the ship was scrapped in 1891.

Connie - A French built trawler originally named Formalhaut built in 1964 for Societé de Gerance d'Armemant of La Rochelle. Sold to Dakar in West Africa before arriving in Tanzania. After a period in service in East African waters the vessel was laid up and sank in Dar es Salaam harbour. It has since been removed.

Debbie - A Canadian built stern trawler launched as the Hilda G-77 for Frances Branden Inc. of Corpus Christi. After many years fishing in the Gulf of Mexico it was sold renamed Debbie and brought to Tanzania. After removal of the fishing gear the vessel was converted to carry cargo and ran aground in 2000 at Mchinga Bay between Kilwa and Lindi with a cargo of beer and cement. A salvage attempt by the tug Kongoni was unsuccessful but it was later refloated and laid up in Mombasa.

Dolphin - A 65 foot American built crew boat grounded off Dar es Salaam in the early 1990s carrying passengers on the Zanzibar run.

Ebnesina - An Iranian owned cargo vessel of 1,599 tons grounded at Kilwa in 1979 and refloated by Divecon using the tug Harrier.

Enda - A Canadian built trawler capsized in Dar es Salaam harbour in the 1990s. The wreck has since been removed.

Faith - A small cargo passenger vessel on passage from Dar es Salaam in May 2009 capsized and sank in Zanzibar harbour with seventy-five persons on board of whom six were reported drowned. Reports stated there was a fault with the rudder combined with a major leak in the hull.

First Carrier - A small container vessel sank in 2003 in Msasani Bay.

Fong Ta No. 31 - A Chinese trawler aground on Pemba 8 June 1979. Divecon were awarded the salvage contract and chartered the reefer vessel Aegina   to take the cargo of tuna fish and towed the vessel to Mombasa for repair at African Marine having lost the rudder, both anchors and damaged the hull.

Ibtisaam - A schooner on a voyage from Tanga grounded and sank at the entrance to Dar es Salaam on 8 August 1969. The passengers and crew of eight were rescued by the German vessel Vogtland.

Impala - One of the ex German gunboats supplied to the Tanzanian Government in the 1960s. Converted into a coaster and sank in the late 1970s after it came off the slipway following a refit. Later salvaged and returned to service.

Jalmahavir - A general cargo vessel adrift off Zanzibar in 1979 that was towed into Dar es Salaam by the Divecon Tug Jacaranda.

Mama Mary - Launched as the Helle Frank in 1968 the ship had a number of owners and name changes before arriving in East Africa as the Mama Mary. On 11 January 2000 the ship grounded on a reef five miles east of Mtwara but was salvaged by Comarco and returned to service.

Marvani - A small trading vessel sank in July 1993 while on a voyage from Tanga to Chake Chake in Pemba in which thirty five Tanzanians and five Europeans perished.

Mbudja - A trawler sunk at Dar es Salaam in 1978, salvaged by Divecon and scrapped in the 1990s.

Mohesi - A tug owned by the Dutch company VNS sank off the coast in 1936. Salvaged and towed to Durban, where its engines were returned to Holland and fitted to the tug Upesi I then being built. The hull was sunk off Durban on 26 June 1936.

Moto - An ex Dar es Salaam port tender bought for a development at Bongoyo Island. Sunk as dive site at the northern end around 1997.

Mtwara - A Norwegian built cargo passenger vessel, 682 tons, sank at midnight on 29 June 1990 with the loss of ten lives at 05°.48' S 39°.09' E. The Tanzanian vessel carrying three hundred and sixty tons of general cargo including cars, cement and containers was on a voyage from Tanga to Zanzibar when she collided with the coastal tanker Uhuru coming in the opposite direction three miles off Tumbatu Island off the west coast of Zanzibar.

Nguvu - In 1954 the harbour tug was on a buoy maintenance trip to Mafia Island under the command of Captain Richard Crow. About midnight there was an explosion and fire in the galley which destroyed the wooden superstructure. The bridge was totally consumed leaving a few charred planks and the remains of the

steering wheel. This strange apparition with a helmsman standing on top of a pile of firewood returned to Mombasa, where an enquiry established the cause of the fire to have been contaminated fuel in the paraffin powered fridge.

Nimoyena - An ex World War II wooden hulled motor gunboat smuggling ivory, collided with a dhow at night and sank near Mbweni, Zanzibar in the early 1950s. The remains of the double diagonal planking and twin engines were discovered in the 1970's.

Odysseas - A stern trawler built for Charles Vagelatos of Piraeus and sold to a local fishing company in Dar es Salaam in 1994, sank in heavy seas on 5 April 2000 with the loss of three of the fifteen crew.

Orestes - A wooden hulled topsail ketch built in 1885 fitted with an auxiliary Ruston diesel arrived in Mombasa from England via the Mediterranean in April 1948. It was sold and traded in the Seychelles but later returned to the East African coast and continued to trade until the 1950s, when she sank after striking a reef near Tanga.

Panda II - A cargo vessel sunk off Bongoyo Island in 1999 on a voyage to Zanzibar with a cargo of steel pipe.

Pinguin - A tug reported lost at 05°.30' S 39°.18' E on tow from Dar es Salaam to Mombasa on 24 March 1976.

Pomboo - The former Tanzania Harbour Authority Schottel tug sank in Mtwara harbour in 2009.

Rubin - A Romanian cargo vessel grounded at the entrance to Dar es Salaam on 16 October 1997. The ship had arrived with engine problems and while inbound failed to respond to the helm and grounded at Kivukoni. She was refloated by the tugs Chui and Chatu.

Southern Dawn - A Southern Line motor tanker, 2,000 tons, touched bottom briefly in the 1970s while delivering fuel from Mombasa to the oil storage terminal at Chake Chake in Pemba. Sold and renamed Mayotta.

Tumaini - A trawler that grounded near the village of Kisiju on Kwale Island in southern Tanzania in the 1980s and salvaged by Frank Jansen using the motorised hopper barge Colleen.

Tuna - A small coastal steamer that grounded on a sunken lighter in the entrance to Dar es Salaam in the 1920s. She was towed off by the steamer Duplex that served in the blockade of the Königsberg during the First World War.

Unidentified - South of Zanzibar lies the small coral atoll of Kwale Island. During 1999 and 2000 an underwater survey of the harbour and surrounding area located a number of new finds. One of these was a wooden wreck lying in 120 feet carrying a large quantity of wine bottles and general household china including teapots, cups and saucers.

Unidentified - On the reefs surrounding Latham Island, thirty miles offshore Dar es Salaam, lie the remains of ancient cannon and steel indicating a number of ships have come to grief over the years but little is known about them.

Unidentified - One hundred miles south of Dar es Salaam lies Mafia Island, where a wooden wreck has been reported but not identified.

Unidentified - A reported schooner wreck on the windward side of a coral island near Kilwa Masoko at 08°.54' S 39°.35'.50" E.

Unidentified - A reported schooner or dhow wreck off the NW tip of Bongoyo Island at 6°.42' S, 09°.15'.18" E.

Unidentified - A small trawler was under tow to Bagamoyo in 1995 when the towing bit snapped. The tow line was repositioned around the superstructure which unfortunately sank the vessel.

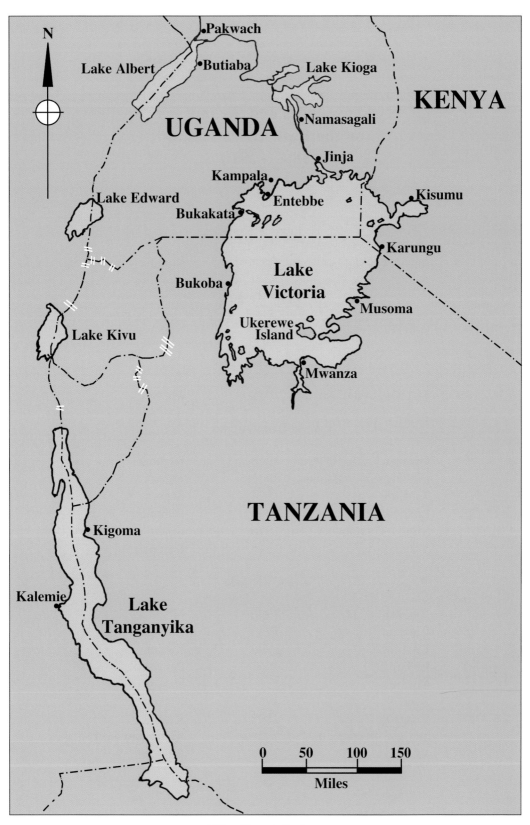

The Great Lakes

Shipwrecks and Strandings
on the East African lakes
1896 - 2010

Lake Albert

Robert Coryndon	1963	Butiaba

Lake Kioga

Grant	1917	Namasagali

Lake Magadi

Magadi Dredge No. 3	1988	Magadi

Lake Tanganyika

Goetzen	1916	Kigoma
Hedwig von Wissman	1916	Kalemie
Kingani	1924	Kigoma
Liemba	1979	Katumbi
Mimi / Toutou	1916	Kalemie
Wami	1916	Kigoma

Lake Victoria

Bukoba	1996	Mwanza
Clement Hill	1936	Bukakata
Kavirondo	1990	Kisumu
Lugard II	1967	Pakwach
Mwanza	1915	Nassoro
Sybil	1967	Kisumu
Usoga	1993	Kisumu
William Mackinnon	1929	Kavirondo Gulf
Winifred	1936	Bukakata

Robert Coryndon

Builders	:	J. Thorneycroft, Southampton, England. 1929
Length	:	207 feet
Beam	:	37 feet
Displacement	:	850 tons
Machinery	:	Twin triple expansion. 800 nhp
Position	:	01°.45'N 31°.20'E

The ship was named in honour of Sir Robert Coryndon, Governor of Uganda from 1918-1922 and Kenya from 1922 until his death on 10 February 1925. During his period in office he had been instrumental in obtaining a loan from the British government to extend the railway to Uganda. Ordered through the Crown Agents in London the ship was built at a cost of £65,250 and bolt assembled before being packed for shipment to Mombasa. Transport to Butiaba on Lake Albert involved nearly a thousand miles of rail, lake and

The remains at Butiaba, 2009

truck before the parts reached the slipway. The hull was launched in November 1930, and completed alongside. Although oil fired, she burnt wood for the first eighteen months until the arrival of oil storage tanks. In service the ship was described as *'Splendid and far too good for the job it performed'*. The panelled dining room and officer's quarters were the finest on the lakes with accommodation for eighteen First and sixteen Second class passengers. As the slipway was incapable of supporting the new ship, a floating dock was built for maintenance and in view of their isolation both the Coryndon and the stern-wheeler Lugard, were fitted with radio to communicate with Nairobi. The Coryndon proved popular and operated across the lake collecting passengers from Butiaba en route to Pakwach for a trip down the Albert Nile and on return collected lighters laden with cotton destined for export via Mombasa. By the early 1960s a new railway was under construction to the lake and in 1963 there was an unprecedented rise in the level that inundated the port and surrounding area. The vessels were laid up at Butiaba and thirty years of prestigious service came to an end. The water tube boilers and engines were removed and installed in the cargo vessel Nyanza at Kisumu and the ship eventually sank alongside the jetty.

Grant

Builders	:	Kincaid & Co., Greenock, Scotland. 1890
Length	:	80 feet
Beam	:	21 feet
Displacement	:	60 tons
Machinery	:	Twin compound horizontal cylinders.

The Grant was the former stern wheeler Kenia ordered by the Imperial British East Africa Company for service on the Tana River, north of Mombasa, based on a report that this was the way into the interior. The February 1891 Engineering Journal had this to say on the vessel, *'The builders have given particular attention to the construction of this vessel, where light draught, strength, and handy sections for shipment or inland transportation are necessary. The craft was sent to Mombasa and there put together. The draught is eighteen inches light and 39 when fully loaded, and at either of these draughts the gear* can arrange the wheel so that the lower floats are just covered. She is fitted with a pair of compound non-condensing engines capable of driving the craft at a speed of ten knots. Steam is supplied at 120 lb pressure by a large locomotive boiler, with a capacious firebox for burning African hardwood. The shaft rods, paddle-wheel, and parts of the machinery are made of mild steel, while all working parts are bushed with gun-metal and easily adjustable to enable the engineer on board to do any overhauling that may be required, engine repair shops being unknown in Africa. The vessel is fitted with a steam windlass and derrick forward which can be used for lifting the anchor, pulling the vessel off banks, or lifting snags as may be required. At the forward end of the upper or awning deck there is placed a powerful kerosene search light immediately over the wheel-house enabling the vessel to be navigated at night. The boiler funnel or smokestack has a spark-catcher fitted on top to prevent burning sparks from the wood fuel escaping and setting fire to the dried grasses, along the river banks. The accommodation for the European officers and passengers is all on the promenade deck and is specially designed with large window, Venetian, and mosquito frames for ventilation, while canvas awnings and screens protect the decks from the tropical heat. A novel means of defence against the native canoes has been provided in the shape of a perforated tube which runs round the vessel underneath the gunwale moulding, and from which, being connected by a pipe and cock to the main boiler, a cloud of steam can be made to envelope the steamer at will. The steam, too, will prevent natives boarding the vessel. A quick-firing Hotchkiss gun has been fitted up forward on the promenade deck. As the carrying capacity of small vessels like the Kenia is necessarily limited, there has been provided a double-ended cargo barge, which the Kenia will tow alongside when more displacement than she possesses in herself is wanted. The barge, like the steamer, is covered from end to end with a light awning shade deck, and both vessels are plated throughout with galvanised steel. The Kenia is provided with three large rudders, the centre one being balanced, and all three are connected to the same yoke or tiller on the promenade deck, while the space aft between the engines supplies room for a comfortable bath room and galley.'

After assembly the steamer sailed to Kipini where the river was found to be unnavigable, and so continued up the coast to the Juba River. Here an uprising in 1893 saw her put to good use by the Royal Navy rescuing two employees of the I.B.E.A. Co. after which the vessel was left under guard. Returned to Mombasa she was used as as floating accommodation until dismantled and sent to Lake Kioga in 1913. Here she was reassembled by Richard Grant and renamed after the explorer James Grant who joined the Royal Geographical Society's expedition in 1860 under John Hanning Speke to discover the source of the Nile. A species of gazelle with long curved horns was also named after him. Once in service the vessel proved troublesome and attempts to modify the original design were a costly failure. The steering was erratic and it would not go astern. The hull was laid up during the First World War and sank on 24 November 1917 while serving as accommodation. Salvage attempts using two barges were unsuccessful and abandoned until 1922 when the machinery and boiler were recovered. The 1918 Uganda Railway annual report summed up the Grant's deficiencies, 'This ship has been a failure from the time she was first put on the lake owing to the lightness of her structure, but it is of the most urgent importance she be replaced'.

Magadi Dredge No. 3

Builders	:	Magadi Soda Company. 1951
Machinery	:	Continuous bucket chain dredger with crusher and slurry pumps connected to the factory via floating pipeline.
Position	:	1°.50'.S 36°17'.S

Lake Magadi is the southern most lake in the Kenya Rift Valley, lying in a catchment of faulted volcanic rocks, north of Tanzania's Lake Natron. During the dry season, it is 95% covered by solid trona (sodium sesqicarbonate and sodium chloride), and is well known for its wading birds, including flamingos. With the completion of the Uganda Railway to Lake Victoria in 1901 attention turned to the lake as a source of sodium carbonate (soda) and a railway line was constructed from Konza on the main line to the lake via Kajiado, a distance of 106 miles. The Magadi Soda Company was formed in 1911 to extract trona which after processing is turned into soda ash for export. The line was completed in 1913, but production was delayed by the First World War as Magadi was close to the border with German East Africa. Production resumed after the war, and high volume exports of almost pure soda ash continue to this day via Mombasa.

Overnight in January 1988 Floating Dredger No.3 suddenly sank into the paddock where it normally floated. This was a saturated solution of sodium carbonate, bicarbonate and sodium chloride. The salvage operation was carried out by Comarco Mombasa on a No Cure/No Pay contract. Specialist diving equipment was hired in to work in the strongly alkaline and toxic liquor. An initial inspection found the dredger resting on the bottom in about twelve feet of liquor with about three feet of liquid above the deck. The intense heat and remote surroundings made the task almost impossible, however it was decided to refloat the dredger using coffer dams in the three lower holds. Once fitted, large submersible pumps were brought in and within a matter of hours the dredge was seen to be lifting off the bottom. The dredge was later repaired and put back into operation. The main reason for the sinking was a wastage of the barge hull shell plate caused by the highly corrosive liquor in which it normally floated.

Goetzen

Builders	:	Joseph Meyer, Papenberg, Germany. 1913
Length	:	232 feet
Beam	:	33 feet
Displacement	:	1,575 tons
Machinery	:	Twin triple expansion.
Position	:	05°.12' S 29°.45' E

The ship was ordered in 1912 by the German East Africa government for service on Lake Tanganyika, and named after a former Governor of the territory, Graf von Goetzen who served from 1901 to 1906. It had been proposed to order three vessels of 1,000 tons each, with the option of fitting diesel engines to burn palm oil but these suggestions were rejected and the vessel fitted for wood firing. Eventually two vessels were ordered but only one was built. She was bolt assembled and completed on 26 November 1913 and afterwards dismantled and shipped to Dar es Salaam arriving in January 1914. Until the completion of the Central Line to Lake Tanganyika in February, it had been impossible to deliver the parts to the new slipway at Kigoma. Construction continued throughout the year with completion set for January 1915. The first sea trials on 8 June 1915 using freshly cut wood were not a success and the following day with dry fuel the speed increased to 8.25 knots. Korvettankäpitan Zimmer, the naval commander on the lake was not impressed with his new acquisition. The ship vibrated at speed, was difficult to steer and had no double bottom in case of grounding. Worst of all the cabins were infested with mosquitoes making life on board a misery. After further modifications including lengthening the funnel by six feet, the ship entered service and ferried troops along the lake. When the Royal Navy sent an expedition to the lake in 1915 to destroy German supremacy, the Goetzen and two other vessels Kingani and Hedwig von Wissman were the main targets. The Kingani was captured and the Wissman sunk. After the destruction of the Königsberg in July, a 4 inch gun from the wreck was fitted on the Goetzen's foredeck, but later

Ready for launching, 1915

removed when it was found to be more use ashore. By early 1916 the Allies were advancing into German territory and a massive campaign of destruction ensued. Bridges, locomotives and rolling stock were systematically destroyed and on 26 July the Goetzen's machinery was greased and she was scuttled off the Malagarasi River south of Kigoma. After the cessation of hostilities in 1918 the Belgians attempted unsuccessfully to salvage the ship. German East Africa became Tanganyika the following year and the Belgians abandoned the operation but were compensated for their efforts. In December 1922 a Royal Navy team headed by Commander Kerr began the second attempt. Little was known about the vessel as all drawings had been destroyed. The proposal was to use compressed air in the ships two holds by extending the hatch coamings downwards to form an airlock under the deck. The initial survey showed the wreck littered with heavy wire hawsers from the previous attempt and the mainmast bent at right angles. Both were removed before the

On the surface, March 1924

coaming plates were fitted and the air compressor started. The results were alarming as air burst to the surface through the deck seams. In the haste to get the ship into service the steel decks had never been caulked, water tightness being achieved by sealing the wooden deck now partly destroyed by immersion and woodborers. Experiments with tallow around the deck seams failed due to the heat of the compressed air. Eventually beeswax proved ideal and slowly in total darkness the divers succeeded in stemming the leaks. As the leaks decreased the water level in the airlock fell, and light was provided by candles also used to find leaks when the flame was sucked through gaps. On completion of the holds, two flexible fifty ton pontoons were attached and inflated but leaked badly and would only hold half their capacity. A trial lift brought the bows to the surface listing to starboard but were sunk while additional pontoons were railed from Dar es Salaam. The two fuel bunkers were sealed and with the pontoons attached and both boilers blown the bows rose again but the result was the same. Kerr took the decision to build two eleven foot diameter steel pontoons using railway jacks to bend the plate. After further set backs the ship finally rose from the depths on 24 March 1924. A year later a refitting party left England and on 16 May 1927 the ship was renamed Liemba and re-entered service on the lake, where she remains to this day.

Hedwig von Wissman

Builders	:	Schiffswerft & Masch. Hamburg, Germany. 1897
Length	:	65 feet
Beam	:	10 feet
Displacement	:	60 tons
Machinery	:	Single compound
Armament	:	1 x 4.7 cm gun, 1 x 3.7 cm gun
Position	:	05°.12' S 29°.45' E

Lake Tanganyika is the deepest and longest of the African lakes and prior to the First World War formed the border between German East Africa and the Belgian Congo. There were few notable vessels on the lake at the time, the Belgians having the Alexander Delcommune and the Germans two small motor boats. There was however a plan to assemble a flotilla at Kigoma and the first vessel launched was the steam pinnace Hedwig von Wissman, named after the wife of Hermann von Wissmann, Governor of the colony in 1895. Originally based at Dar es Salaam between 1900 and 1913, the vessel was dismantled and railed to Kigoma and launched on 12 August 1914. A week earlier the German Commander Lt. Col. von Lettow-Vorbeck had ordered the Kigoma force to attack enemy shipping and attain mastery of the lake. Two days later on the night of the 14th, the Wissman cruised along the Belgian shore and destroyed the telephone line near Uvira, and sank a number of native canoes on the pretext they were used for ferrying troops, and damaged the steamer Alexander Delcommune. In November the launch Kingani arrived in sections from Dar es Salaam and was soon in service. With the destruction of the Delcommune and two other vessels in the south, the Germans now had complete mastery of the lake. It was not long before this state of affairs brought about the most extraordinary

An over dramatic view of the sinking of the Wissman with the Mimi at least three times larger while the Wissman has two funnels and is the size of a small cruiser.

naval expedition in history. Two forty foot motor boats named Mimi and Toutou were shipped from London to Cape Town and then by rail, traction engine and river to the lake arriving at the end of October 1915. A base was set up at Kalemie and a slipway constructed and on 22 December the first boat was launched. Four days later the Kingani steamed past and was captured after a short gun battle and renamed Fifi. The expedition waited for the Germans to investigate the loss and finally on 9 February the Wissman commanded by Oberleutnant Horn appeared and was chased by Mimi and Fifi. The Wissman slowly gained ground on the slower Fifi until the Mimi roared past and began firing. Slowly the Fifi caught up with the duelling pair and fired a 12 pounder shell that burst in the engine room and blew a hole in the side. The Wissman slowed as the bow began to settle and after a duel that had lasted three hours, sank bow first bringing an end to the German supremacy on the lake. A report in Britain stated, '*No single achievement during World War 1 was distinguished by more bizarre features than the successfully executed undertaking of twenty-eight daring men who transported a ready made navy overland through the wilds of Africa to destroy an enemy flotilla in control of Lake Tanganyika*'.

Kingani

Builders	:	J. L. Meyer, Papenberg, Germany. 1894
Length	:	52 feet
Beam	:	11 feet
Displacement	:	45 tons
Machinery	:	Single compound
Armament	:	1 x 37 mm gun
Position	:	05°.30' S 29°.30' E

The Kingani and Wami were two Customs launches named after rivers in Tanganyika, based in Zanzibar until 1913 when they moved to Dar es Salaam. A lack of suitable vessels on Lake Tanganyika saw the Kingani dismantled and railed to Kigoma where it arrived on 10 November 1914. Together with the Hedwig von Wissman, the two ships maintained supremacy on the lake until completion of the larger steamer Goetzen in June 1915. On 26 December 1915, Kingani was patrolling the Belgian coast when it was attacked by the two Royal Navy motor boats Mimi and Toutou brought overland from Capetown. Kingani was captured after a direct hit damaged the gun and steam line to the engine and killed five of the crew. The vessel was towed to Kalemie where after repairs it was renamed H.M.S. Fifi and later took part in the chase and destruction of the Hedwig von Wissman. With a shortage of suitable vessels on the lake after the war, Fifi continued as the mail steamer along the Tanganyika shore until declared obsolete and towed out by the tug Mwanza on 19 October 1924 and sunk with due ceremony.

Liemba

Builders	:	Joseph Meyer, Papenberg, Germany. 1913
Length	:	232 feet
Beam	:	33 feet
Displacement	:	1,575 tons
Machinery	:	Twin Caterpillar diesel. 800 hp
Position	:	06°.00' S 29°.45' E

The ship was the former Goetzen salvaged by the Royal Navy in 1924, and after an extensive rebuild entered service in 1927 with Tanganyika Railways as the Liemba, (the local dialect word for Lake) calling at ports around the shores on a weekly basis. She retained the original steam machinery until 1949 when the wood fired boilers were condemned and replaced with oil fired units during a four year refit. These boilers continued in daily use until 1971 when they were condemned and the ship fitted with twin diesel engines. In the early hours of 15 September 1979 the ship grounded at Katumbi, eighty miles south of Kigoma. The Captain's report of the incident made interesting reading, '*I was awakened by the watchman at 02.47 and directly to switch on the radar, even though there was moon in the sky means that the mainland can be seen clearly. Before the radar is working I hear the land is very close. I ordered the Quarter Master to switch left full rudder and then switch on the echo sounder to see the depth of the lake. But in fact everything was to late the ship has sat and grounded even though we don't feel that the ship has grounded but the speed was zero and the echo sounder also zero, so we are sure the ship is grounded. So we begin to manoeuvre, retreat and ahead but no result. We put two anchors where the water is more deeper and pull the anchors together with two engines on full speed and the two motor boats pushing but no progress. At last we plan to unload the cargo at night but we fail because of the problems. No light can be put on shore because according to the people of Katumbi there are plenty of lions over there. The crew was very tired the whole day. The officers and crew of M.V. Liemba has already done our best to save the ship from stranding even though we are not success yet.*' The vessel was refloated and continues in service to this day having had a major refit in the 1990s.

.

Mimi / Toutou

Builders	:	Thorneycroft, London, England. 1915
Length	:	40 feet
Beam	:	8 feet
Displacement	:	5 tons
Machinery	:	Twin petrol engines. 100 hp
Position	:	05°.12' S 29°.45' E

Shortly after the outbreak of the First World War it came to the Royal Navy's attention that Lake Tanganyika was under German control using three vessels, the Goetzen, Hedwig von Wissman and Kingani. A big game hunter John Lee came up with the idea of using an armed fast motor boat sent overland from South Africa and obtained an interview with the Royal Navy's First Sea Lord, Sir Henry Jackson on 21 April 1915. It would involve shipping the boat on a trailer to Cape Town and then by rail, traction engine and river to Lake Tanganyika, a distance of 9,300 miles. Unfortunately he was not involved and command was given to Commander Spicer-Simson who left London on 15 June 1915 together with two motorboats and crew aboard the Llanstephan Castle. They were the last of eight wooden seaplane tenders built for the Greek Air Force with a speed of nineteen knots. As they had no names Simson christened them Cat and Dog but changed them to Mimi and Toutou much to the expedition members' amazement. After transporting the boats to the end of the railway in Rhodesia, they were faced with a one hundred and twenty mile trek through the bush towed by two traction engines, followed by a second rail journey to the Lualaba River at Sankisia. After a difficult trip down river the boats were railed to the lake where after weeks of trial and tribulation they were launched on 22 December. Four days later the Kingani appeared and was captured and renamed Fifi. The Toutou having sunk in a storm on 24 January 1916 was salvaged but unrepairable as there were no shipwrights or suitable material. The Hedwig von Wissman appeared on 9 February and was sunk by a shell from the Fifi. After the war Toutou was sent to South Africa and used in Victoria docks, Cape Town with a brass plate that read, '*This launch served in the East African campaign as an armed cruiser. Captured and sank three German gunboats with assistance of sister launch Mimi*'.

Wami

Builders	:	J. L. Meyer, Papenberg, Germany. 1893
Length	:	58 feet
Beam	:	11 feet
Displacement	:	45 tons
Machinery	:	Single compound. 85 ihp
Armament	:	1 x 37 mm gun
Position	:	05°.30' S 29°.30' E

The Wami was a wooden hulled Customs launch placed in service at Dar es Salaam on 22 December 1893, both she and her sister vessel Kingani were later based in Zanzibar before returning to Dar es Salaam in 1913. The arrival of the cruiser Königsberg in the Rufiji delta in September 1914, saw the Wami allocated to the defence force protecting the cruiser. In May 1915 she was modified to carry two torpedoes for an attack on the blockading Royal Navy warships but ran aground in the river. After the destruction of the Königsberg in July, the Wami returned to Dar es Salaam on 15 September and was railed to Kigoma in April 1916. With the Allied invasion of the colony, the Germans destroyed the port facilities at Kigoma and the sank the Goetzen. The Wami left Kigoma on 29 July but was sunk by the Belgian vessel Netta and subsequently salvaged and returned to service in the Belgian Congo as the Wapi, the Swahili word for Where?

Bukoba

Builders	:	Belgian Shipbuilders Corp. Ruisbroek, Belgium. 1979
Length	:	195 feet
Beam	:	31 feet
Displacement	:	800 tons
Machinery	:	Caterpillar V16 cyl diesel. 1,035bhp
Position	:	01°.55' S 31°.55' E

The loss of the Bukoba was the worst casualty in the history of maritime operations in East Africa. The ship was built from sections railed to Mwanza on Lake Victoria and commissioned on 26 July 1979. From the outset she was unstable and had to carry additional ballast. In 1984 the Danish Maritime Institute carried out stability tests and recommended that five double bottom tanks should be kept permanently filled with water, which would enable the ship to carry 400 passengers and 35 tons of cargo in safety. A later study recommended increasing the beam, but unfortunately the recommendations were not carried out and in its fifteen years of service the ship only had four surveys and was never officially registered. On the morning of 21 May 1996 the vessel sailed from Bukoba for Mwanza loaded with agricultural produce and a reported 633 passengers. A short while later the ship capsized after encountering heavy weather near Karumo Island, eight miles north west of Bukoba and remained floating upside down with many of the trapped passengers banging on the hull. Local fishermen reported the accident, and three hours later the first vessel picked up 112 survivors. An ill advised rescue effort to release passengers trapped inside, involved cutting a hole in the hull. Three people were recovered before the air rushed out and the vessel sank stern first twenty minutes later in a depth of ninety feet leaving the bow above the surface. A major diving operation was mounted to recover an estimated five hundred bodies using divers from Kenya, South Africa and Tanzania. By 2 June some four hundred bodies had been recovered under traumatic conditions before the President of Tanzania gave the order to cease operations and seal the ship. It was evident from some of the bodies recovered, that a number had survived the capsize and sinking, and continued to live in darkness with diminishing air supplies for at least three days after the event. On 19 December an official announcement by the Tanzanian Government put the final death toll at 869, with the cause being the carriage of an excessive number of passengers, improperly distributed cargo and insufficient ballast. Some two years after the event a set of five stamps was issued by the government depicting the sinking and recovery of bodies.

Clement Hill

Builders	:	Bow MacLachlan & Co. Paisley, Scotland. 1906
Length	:	225 feet
Beam	:	32 feet
Displacement	:	1,100 tons
Machinery	:	Single triple expansion. 635 ihp
Position	:	00°.15' S 32°.03' E

The ship was named after Sir Clement Hill, Permanent Under Secretary at the Foreign Office and Head of the African Department, and a committee member of the Uganda Railway. An elegant looking vessel, she was the largest steamer on Lake Victoria on entering service in March 1907. There was accommodation for twenty First and sixteen Second Class passengers and space for 450 tons of cargo. Winston Churchill on his East Africa visit in 1906, travelled on the ship and referred to it as magnificent, looking rather like a pleasure yacht, with long and spacious decks, baths, electric light, an excellent table and a well selected library. During the First World War the ship remained in service with the Uganda Railway and was escorted by the armed William Mackinnon until a 3 pounder gun was fitted to the foredeck. Unlike the other vessels taken over by the Royal Navy, the '*Clementi*' as she was affectionately known remained in service with the railway for the duration of the war. In 1926 the ship was altered to accommodate fifty passengers on the Entebbe to Kisumu run until the railway reached Kampala in 1931, after which she was relegated to operating the round the lake. Four years later the ship was declared obsolete and withdrawn from service, stripped of machinery and fittings and sunk at Bukakata as a breakwater in 1936.

Kavirondo

Builders	:	Bow MacLachlan, Paisley, Scotland. 1913
Length	:	100 feet
Beam	:	21 feet
Displacement	:	200 tons
Machinery	:	Single triple expansion. 400 nhp
Position	:	00°.02' S 34°.52' E

By 1910 there was a growing need for new vessels to cope with the increase in traffic on Lake Victoria. Early in the new year two passenger cargo vessels Rusinga and Usoga were ordered together with the tug Kavirondo and four lighters. The latter was launched at Kisumu in December 1913, to serve the small ports inaccessible to the larger steamers. With the outbreak of war, the main German vessel on the lake was the tug Muansa, and when a report indicated it was armed, an ancient 9 pdr. muzzle loading saluting gun was fitted to the William Mackinnon then with the addition of sights refitted to the Kavirondo. On 9 September the Germans crossed the border and attacked the town of Kisii some fifty miles from Kisumu. The steamer Winifred embarked a squadron of cavalry intent on landing at Karungu port but found it occupied by the Muansa and withdrew under fire.

They returned the following day with the Kavirondo to find the enemy had withdrawn. The tug together with the William Mackinnon and Sybil were later rearmed with 12 pdr guns and in June 1915 took part in the capture of Bukoba. A year later the tug was part of an expedition to capture the port of Mwanza and after the war returned to towing lighters around the lake. Nearly seventy years later the Kavirondo was laid up at Kisumu. Nine years later the derelict hulk was serving as accommodation and not long afterwards sank alongside. In 2005 the tug was purchased privately and refloated. The superstructure and machinery have been removed and the hull will be lengthened, re-engined and returned to service as a tanker in the near future. The bronze bell in its ornate mounting is presently on display in the Nairobi Railway Museum.

Lugard II

Builders	:	Fleming and Ferguson, Paisley Scotland. 1946
Length	:	180 feet
Beam	:	51 feet
Displacement	:	380 tons
Machinery	:	Single compound. 350 hp
Position	:	02°.29' N 31°.20' E

The Lugard II was ordered in 1946 and entered service in 1948. She was the last side paddle wheel steamer ordered by the Kenya Uganda Railway to operate on the Victoria and Albert Nile but proved larger than the dry dock at Butiaba and had a deeper draft than

planned. With her introduction to service her predecessor Lugard I built in 1927 was withdrawn and laid up. Both were named after Sir Frederick Lugard, (1858-1945) who in 1890 explored Uganda, secured much of it for the British Empire and served as its Military Administrator from 1890-92.

The steamer carrying 28 First Class and 20 Second Class

passengers operated between Pakwach on the Albert Nile and the town of Nimule on the Sudan border and her capacity was supplemented by pushing a barge that provided third class accommodation as well as cargo space.

In 1951 the steamer became the floating base for Katherine Hepburn, Humphrey Bogart and the film crew making 'The African Queen'. The scenes in the film near the Murchison Falls were shot while the vessel was moored close by.

Lugard II was withdrawn from service in 1962 and laid up at Pakwach after Lake Albert rose flooding the port of Butiaba. In 1967 she was offered for sale, but like the other the lake and paddle steamers there were no takers and all fell into disuse and remained where they had been left. The Lugard II woodwork was removed for firewood and other uses leaving a bare skeleton of steelwork rusting slowly into oblivion.

Mwanza

Builders	:	Germany. 1910
Length	:	74 feet
Beam	:	15 feet
Displacement	:	80 tons
Machinery	:	Single compound. 60 nhp
Armament	:	1 x 3.7 cm gun
Position	:	02°.06' S 33°.75' E

Before the First World War the two principal German ports on Lake Victoria were Bukoba and Mwanza, both being areas of considerable produce. With few roads around the lake the steam tug Muansa and three lighters were assembled and placed in service in 1910 trading between the two ports. On the outbreak of the First World War, the tug was requisitioned as a troop transport and armed with two 3.7 cm guns which made it the most powerful ship on the lake as there was no armament immediately available for the British vessels. In September the Muansa towing lighters was used to transport troops to attack the border town of Kisii. The steamer Winifred despatched to investigate had to retreat under heavy fire. The tug continued to pose a threat until 6 March 1915 when it was hunted by the now armed Winifred. Muansa escaped and was scuttled in shallow water by its crew who continued to fire until silenced by the Winifred's heavier armament. The tug was salvaged by the Germans eight days later and returned to service and scuttled a second time on 15 July 1916 after the Allied invasion of the territory. After salvage by the British, she was dismantled and sent to Dar es Salaam in 1917. A demand for vessels on Lake Tanganyika saw the tug dismantled again, railed to Kigoma and placed in service on 17 April 1923 as the Mwanza, carrying passengers and cargo to ports around the lake. On her third voyage the boiler failed and the crew reverted to sail using canvas side screens rigged from the mast. Five days later the intrepid sailors arrived back at Kigoma. After six months of repairs the ship ran trials in January 1924 but a year later was laid up, pending a new boiler, during which a cabin for three first class passengers was added. By 1926 she was back in service with space for thirty deck passengers and thirty tons of cargo but shortly afterwards struck an uncharted rock and was slipped for repairs. Ten years later increasing competition from the Belgians, made the Mwanza uneconomic and she was laid up on 16 June 1938. This was not the end as in 1952 she was fitted with a diesel engine and reportedly sold from railway ownership in 1966.

Sybil

Builders	:	Bow McLachlan, Glasgow, Scotland. 1901
Length	:	189 feet
Beam	:	29 feet
Displacement	:	500 tons
Machinery	:	Twin triple expansion.
		Twin Crossley diesels. 850 hp
Position	:	00°.06' S 34°.45' E

In 1901 when construction of the Uganda Railway was in its last year the Railway Committee ordered two cargo passenger steamers designed by Sir Edward Reed to serve the settlements around the shores of Lake Victoria. One important aspect was that they should not draw more than six feet unladen, but when completed were found to draw seven feet three inches, an excess of twenty one percent. No one admitted the error and the ships went on trial in the River Clyde and then dismantled and shipped to Mombasa. Both were assembled at Kisumu under the direction of Richard Grant of William Mackinnon fame. The first to be launched was the Winifred in 1902, the latter being the Sybil named after a daughter of Sir Francis O'Callaghan, a member of the Railway Committee. Sybil was commissioned in January 1904 under the command of Captain Hutton and transported passengers and cargo across the lake until she grounded. The ship was refloated and in May 1905 hit an uncharted reef near Bukoba. The ship took six months to repair and the anomaly was named Sybil Rocks. Hutton was given three months notice after the second grounding and replaced by William Townsend, formerly Chief the Officer of the Winifred. The outbreak of war in August 1914 saw the British with a flotilla consisting of the tug Kavirondo, Nyanza, Sybil, William Mackinnon and Winifred with the Germans having the Heinrich Otto and Muanza. Weeks of patrolling finally produced a report the Otto was at Bujaga in the Majita Channel, a narrow shallow waterway. Sybil under the command of Lt. Bruce searched a channel south of Musoma and on return to deeper water struck an uncharted rock. With water pouring in he beached the ship at Bujaga Point. A report sent to Kisumu stated the ship had hit a mine. This was later amended by the senior marine engineer to read, *'Sybil holed by an uncharted mine laid by the Almighty c. 4000 BC'*. Over the next two days the ship was stripped of fittings and abandoned after being shelled by the Winifred. The Germans arrived soon after and completed the task by removing anything left of value including the baths and burning the deck. Lt. Bruce received a serious caution and was told to use more *'seamanlike care'* in navigating a vessel. Six months later a salvage party consisting of the Kavirondo, Nyanza, Winifred and a lighter left Kisumu accompanied by two hundred and sixty troops and a diver. The salvage operation took seventy hours and by 18 May 1915 the ship was ready for the long tow to Kisumu. Refitting took a year and the ship resumed service in 1916. Eight years later she was considered obsolete and with engines and accommodation removed converted into a lighter. Some time in the early 1950s the hull was accidentally sunk when a steam crane toppled into the hold and set the cargo alight. The resulting fire was extinguished but in doing so Sybil sank in the mud alongside the jetty. She was rebuilt with twin diesel engines, using a propeller 'A' frame removed from the remains of the Winifred. The ship re-entered service on 12 October 1956 with accommodation for twelve First Class passengers, 150 deck passengers and a capacity of 200 tons of cargo and eleven years later sunk at Kisumu as a breakwater.

Usoga

Builders	:	Bow MacLachlan & Co. Paisley, Scotland. 1913
Length	:	220 feet
Beam	:	35 feet
Displacement	:	1,300 tons
Machinery	:	Single triple expansion. 400 ihp
Position	:	00°.06' S 34°.45' E

The increase in passenger and cargo trade on Lake Victoria in the mid 1900s saw the need for two larger vessels to supplement the overworked Clement Hill, Sybil and Winifred. Two sister ships Rusinga and Usoga named after areas around the lake, were ordered through the Crown Agents in London, with accommodation for twenty four First and sixteen Second Class passengers with 250 on deck and 550 tons of cargo. They were bolt assembled and once all the fittings had been checked, the parts were shipped via Mombasa and reassembled at Kisumu. They entered service in 1914 and 1915 respectively, and were requisitioned by the military as troop transports in the attack on the port of Bukoba on 22 June 1915. A year later Usoga carried troops of the Kings African Rifles in the attack on Ukerewe Island and both ships returned to service around the lake after hostilities. In 1935 Usoga was dry docked for a major refit that increased the First Class passenger accommodation to twenty-eight with a new propeller to improve performance. The commissioning of the new passenger mail ship R.M.S. Victoria in 1961 saw the Usoga relegated to the Mwanza – Bukoba run until laid up at Kisumu alongside the Nyanza in 1975. After years of neglect and removal of internal fittings, the ship sank alongside the jetty in the 1990s and was cut up in 2007, leaving the bottom plates in situ.

William Mackinnon

Builders	:	A. J. Inglis & Co., Glasgow, Scotland. 1890
Length	:	70 feet
Beam	:	16 feet
Displacement	:	70 tons
Machinery	:	Single triple expansion.
Position	:	00°.20'.83" S 34°.09'.75" E

The William Mackinnon was named after the President of the Imperial British East Africa Company and the second vessel after the paddle steamer Kenia, to be ordered by the company for service in East Africa. After bolt assembly she was dismantled together with all the tools and packed into three thousand boxes for shipment to Mombasa. The boxes other than two engine parts all weighed sixty pounds each. The I.B.E.A. went into receivership and the vessel was purchased by the Uganda Railway Committee on 30 January 1895 for the sum of £4,456. The parts were stored in Mombasa until May 1895 when the first loads left for Lake Victoria on the heads of porters. The shipwrights sent to build the vessel returned to England when it was realised at least a year would pass before sufficient parts were available to commence construction. Over the next three years a trickle of odd parts consisting of deck plates and frames arrived at Port Victoria, the projected terminus for the Uganda Railway then under construction from Mombasa. Porters defected, fell ill and died, with the result that the steamer was strewn across the African countryside from Mombasa to the lake. By January 1896 a telegram stated that two hundred loads had arrived, a further one hundred and fifty had left Mombasa and forty-six were lost at Ndi. Many of the copper and brass fittings were stolen by the Nandi tribe and turned into necklaces and anklets. It was obvious that without a skilled shipwright the vessel would never be completed, and the Railway Committee approached the builders and recruited Richard Grant who arrived in March 1898. After a three month wait for porters, he spent the next six months walking across the Protectorate locating parts and moving them to the new terminus at Kisumu. New frames were ordered from the builders to replace those lost, and damaged ones were straightened using a primitive forge, while smaller parts were made in the railway workshops in Mombasa. A slipway was built and the vessel was officially declared to have commenced building on 1 August 1899. Grant was joined by Walter Cowham who had previously worked on the stern wheeler Kenia. They were faced with difficulties when they found that deck plates had been delivered before the frames, but by the end of February 1900, Grant wrote that he had used 10,000 rivets and a month later a further ten thousand. By 15 April they had trial assembled the engine and boilers and on 21 May the hull was launched but stuck on the slipway. She

On the stocks, 1899

eventually floated on 4 June and fitting out was completed by October. After trials the ship was accepted for service with the Uganda Protectorate on 26 November by Charles Hobley. One of the first Masters, Arthur Taylor arrived in May 1901 and served briefly on the ship for three months before being invalided to Mombasa with gastro enteritis and mental disturbance. He was replaced by the First Mate Peter Robin who apparently tried to shoot himself while under the influence and was invalided home. Benjamin Spence followed him in 1902 and after four months was also invalided to Mombasa where he died from the effects of alcohol poisoning. As the boilers were wood fired, the forward hold was used as a bunker, which reduced the capacity for revenue earning cargo. Caroline Kirkland an American woman who wrote of her experiences in East Africa had this to say of the ship. '*The Mackinnon looked harmless that bright November morning. So, unmindful of the horrors that awaited us, we cheerfully embarked. There were an unusual number of passengers, eighteen of us first class. The only cabin was small, containing but two bunks, and was already occupied by the largest cockroaches that ever clattered and rustled about floors and walls. So we seven women and eleven men preferred the small deck, situated astern over the screw, here we had our meals, and the tables being removed, chairs and mattresses were arranged for the night. These were laid as thickly as in an emergency hospital. With our heads in the gunwales, of the ship, and our feet well mixed up in the middle of the deck, we spent what was for some of us eighteen of the most wretched hours of life. At five in the morning some one said to me: "Can't you move out of the rain?" I feebly shook my head. An equatorial downpour was drenching head and shoulders. When morning came, for those who were not too indisposed, plates of unattractive looking food were passed over our prostrate forms. To move for well or ill was out of the question, as we were packed in like sardines. Wind, rain and sun beat on us alike and found us torpid and inanimate. The captain, a good-looking chap who spent the night on the bridge to avoid the sorry spectacle, came and inspected us with a wry face. As there are no lights on the lake travel by night is out of the question, so the steamers pull into some shelter and wait till dawn. From personal experience I can testify to its ability to cause more exquisite human misery than any other vessel of fifty tons in the world'.*

In wartime service with 3 pdr. gun

In an effort to improve cargo capacity and cabin facilities the ship was lengthened to 104 feet and on the outbreak of the First World War armed with a 3 pounder gun and requisitioned by the Royal Navy. However her limited range restricted operations to local defence duties based at Kisumu. After the war the boilers were converted to oil firing and she remained in service until declared obsolete in March 1929 and with due ceremony the hulk was towed into deep water and sunk on 28 July 1929. Today the compass binnacle and an auxiliary boiler can be seen in the Kenya Railways Museum in Nairobi.

Winifred

Builders	:	Bow MacLachlan, Glasgow, Scotland. 1901
Length	:	189 feet
Beam	:	29 feet
Displacement	:	500 tons
Machinery	:	Twin triple expansion.
Position	:	00°.15' S 32°.03' E

The Winifred and her sister ship Sybil were the first passenger cargo vessels ordered for service on Lake Victoria by the Uganda Railway Committee. She was was named after the Honorable Winifred Irby, wife of Sir Harry Johnston, a Special Commissioner of Uganda. The vessel was built at Kisumu under the direction of Richard Grant who had built the William Mackinnon, and launched on 13 February 1902. Under the command of Captain Elliot Farnell the ship was used for survey work until September 1903 when Captain Pringle arrived to inspect the ship following draft and capacity complaints. The inspection lasted three weeks during which it was noted the vessel was drawing just over seven feet instead of six. A new Chief Engineer arrived at Kisumu on 2 August 1903 and was promptly relieved of his position when he fell off the train in an inebriated state. The Winifred entered revenue earning service on 18 November 1903 and became a popular vessel providing a valuable link between Mwanza and Kisumu, with mail carried being occasionally cancelled using an oval ship's stamp. Both the Winifred and Sybil were comfortably fitted with neat little cabins, electric light, an excellent cuisine and officered by a fine class of men from the English colonial service. The first years of service were uneventful until the outbreak of the First World War when she was armed with a Hotchkiss three pounder gun to combat the German tug Muanza. In early September a squadron of

Fitted with a 4 inch gun from H.M.S. Pegasus, 1915

mounted troops embarked and were ordered to Karungu to intercept a retreating enemy force. As she rounded the headland the ship ran into a hail of fire from the Muanza armed with a seven pounder gun. Winifred was outclassed and lucky to escape with a few holes through the accommodation. In 1915 a four-inch gun recovered from the cruiser H.M.S. Pegasus sunk at Zanzibar, was mounted on the foredeck manned by sailors from H.M.S. Hyacinth. The Muanza was chased by the Winifred and scuttled in shallow water with the crew continuing to fire until silenced by the latters heavier gun. Later that year Winifred was sent to shell the partially sunk Sybil abandoned after running aground. In late 1916 the gun was removed and returned to the Royal Navy base at Simonstown. After the war she returned to service, and together with the Clement Hill, were the two preferred passenger vessels on the lake. In 1936 the ship was found to be unseaworthy and sunk to form a breakwater off Luamba Island.

Miscellaneous sinkings and strandings on Lake Victoria

Gigi - A small cargo vessel laden with fish and clothes sank in December 1999 when at least forty passengers died and 102 were rescued.

Heinrich Otto and Schwaben - German steam launches scuttled on 15 July 1916 and later salvaged as British prizes.

Husseni - A small steam tug possibly of German origin that served on the lake from 1915 until declared obsolete and sunk in 1938 as part of the Bukakata jetty in Uganda.

Kabalega - One of theree train fereries operated by Uganda Railways, the other two being Kaawa and Pamba. In the early hours of 8 May 2005, the Kabalega laden with railway wagons on a voyage from Mwanza to Port Bell collided with the Kaawa. The damaged Kaawa returned to port while the holed Kabelega slowly sank some eight miles from the Ssese Islands. There were no casualties and the collision was attributed to poor navigation.

Kenia I - A 42 foot steam launch bolt assembled by Messrs Price Boustead in April 1895 and contracted to the company's subsidiary Boustead Ridley to be delivered to the Uganda Government. She was re-assembled at Nasa across the creek from Mwanza on Lake Victoria and launched on 28 August 1896 but sank and is apparently still there. As the vessel was not delivered they received no payment.

Nyamageni - A cargo passenger ferry carrying over forty passengers from Bukoba to Mwanza sank on 28 April 2006 during a storm. Reports stated that at least twenty-eight are believed to have drowned.

Nyanza - The first cargo steamer built in 1907 for the Uganda Railway. She grounded in the 1950s but refloated herself with little damage and was laid up in the 1970s at Kisumu following the collapse of the East African Community. Twenty years later she was purchased privately and returned to service running cargo on a limited schedule until 2002 when she was laid up once more.

Otter - A motor launch lost in a freak storm on the lake in 1955 with the reported loss of thirty two lives.

Peter - A small missionary motor boat commandeered into military service in August 1914 and sunk at Kigoma on 21 July 1916.

Ruwenzori - A steam launch built by Clark of Brinscombe, Gloucester and delivered to the Church Missionary Society on 23 August 1895. The launch was assembled at Mwanza by Boustead & Ridley and lost off Dweru Island in 1900. Later salvaged and returned to service as the Kampala in 1903 and abandoned in 1913.

Sukuman - A passenger cargo vessel on a voyage from Mwanza to Port Bell in Uganda carrying eight people and 300 tons of fertiliser sank after hitting a rock near Ghana Island in Ukerewe district.

Thor - One of a pair of 270 ton landing craft owned by Kamanga Ferries grounded on Ghana Island on 24 March 2006 while loaded with 300,000 litres of petroleum products.

Ukerewe - A 38 foot steam launch launched at Mwanza in 1899. Sold in 1909 and renamed General Jungblut and captured by the British in 1916. Renamed General Hoskins it sank following a collision after the war.

Ulinzi - A passenger ferry sailing between Mwanza and Ukerewe sank in May 2007.

Umoja - One of two sister Ro-Ro train ferries built for the rail link between Kenya - Uganda and Tanzania grounded in 2002 on a voyage across the lake. It was refloated and returned to service.

Unidentified - A passenger ferry capsized in Uganda waters on 22 July 2010 with a reported death toll of at least fifty people.

Unidentified - A overloaded passenger ferry capsized in July 2010 on Lake Albert with the loss of at least 50 lives.

Walkers - A small vessel carrying assorted cargo capsized and sank in bad weather on 1 April 1995 on a voyage from Kisumu to Musoma.

Tugs in East Africa

Adjutant
Deutsche Ost Afrika Linie, Dar es Salaam

Builders	: Janssen & Schmilinsky, Hamburg, Germany 1905
Length	: 116 feet
Beam	: 23 feet
Displacement	: 231 tons
Machinery	: Single compound. 350 ihp

Amy Konishi
Tanzania Harbours Authority, Dar es Salaam

Builders	: CLEMNA, La Spezia, Italy. 1997
Length	: 104 feet
Beam	: 32 feet
Displacement	: 250 tons
Machinery	: Twin M.W.M. 6 cyl. diesel. 1,600 bhp

Arctic
Bugsier Salvage Co. Hamburg, Germany

Builders	: F. Schichau, Bremerhaven, Germany. 1969
Length	: 286 feet
Beam	: 48 feet
Displacement	: 2,046 tons
Machinery	: Twin Deutz 16 cyl. diesel. 20,000 ihp

Arusha
British India Line, Mombasa

Builders	: Henry Robb, Leith, Scotland. 1951
Length	: 121 feet
Beam	: 32 feet
Displacement	: 346 tons
Machinery	: Single triple expansion. 880 ihp

Banduki
East African Marketing Co. Ltd, Nairobi

Builders	: R. Dunston, Thorne, England. 1945
Length	: 65 feet
Beam	: 17 feet
Displacement	: 54 tons
Machinery	: Single compound. 220 ihp

Barbara
Murri International, Mombasa

Builders	: Halter Marine, New Orleans, U.S.A. 1970
Length	: 110 feet
Beam	: 32 feet
Displacement	: 178 tons
Machinery	: Twin Caterpillar V16 diesel. 3,000 bhp

Bateleur
Eagle Tugs Ltd., Grand Cayman

Builders	: F. Schichau, Bremerhaven, Germany. 1956
Length	: 130 feet
Beam	: 28 feet
Displacement	: 293 tons
Machinery	: Deutz 6 cyl. diesel. 1,900 bhp

Bateleur
Comarco Mauritius Ltd.

Builders	: Imamura Shipbuilding Co. Japan. 1982
Length	: 160 feet
Beam	: 40 feet
Displacement	: 491 tons
Machinery	: Twin Yanmar diesel. 3,200 hp

Betty, Winnie
Eagle Tugs Ltd., Grand Cayman

Builders	: W.J. Yarwood, Northwich, England. 1953
Length	: 84 feet
Beam	: 21 feet
Displacement	: 104 tons
Machinery	: Ruston 6 cyl. diesel. 720 bhp

Bison 1
Murri International, Mombasa

Builders	: D.W. Kremer, Elmshorn, Germany. 1974
Length	: 140 feet
Beam	36 feet
Displacement	: 476 tons
Machinery	: Twin M.A.K. 8 cyl. diesel. 4,300 bhp

Blackcock
Liverpool Towing Co. Liverpool

Builders	: Laird Bros, Birkenhead. England. 1886
Length	: 146 feet
Beam	: 21 feet
Displacement	: 254 tons
Machinery	: Single triple expansion. 1,000 ihp

Black Eagle
Eagle Tugs Ltd., Grand Cayman

Builders	: J. G. Hitzler, Lauenburg, Germany. 1970
Length	: 179 feet
Beam	: 37 feet
Displacement	: 669 tons
Machinery	: Twin M.A.N. V6 diesel. 3,000 bhp

Bremen

Unterweser Reederei, Bremen, Germany

Builders	: A.G. Weser, Bremerhaven, Germany. 1967
Length	: 179 feet
Beam	: 39 feet
Displacement	: 1,182 tons
Machinery	: Twin Deutz 8 cyl diesel. 7,500 ihp

Buganda / Buvuma

Kenya Uganda Railways & Harbours, Kisumu

Builders	: Bow McLachlan, Paisley, Scotland. 1924
Length	: 105 feet
Beam	: 21 feet
Displacement	: 200 tons
Machinery	: Single triple expansion. 400 ihp

Bustard

Kenya Marine Contractors, Mombasa

Builders	: 1974
Length	: 70 feet
Beam	: 17 feet
Displacement	: tons
Machinery	: Single diesel 500 hp

CSC Nelson

Comarco Mauritius Ltd

Builders	: Lindoe Shipyard, Denmark. 1982
Length	: 277 feet
Beam	: 51 feet
Displacement	: 1,955 tons
Machinery	: 4 x MAK 8 cyl. diesel. 14,400 bhp

Chuchunge, Nyangumi - Kenya Ports Authority, Mombasa
Chaza, Nguru, Papa - Tanzania Harbours Authority, Dar es Salaam

Builders	: Robin Shipyard, Singapore. 1974 / 76
Length	: 95 feet
Beam	: 26 feet
Displacement	: 224 tons
Machinery	: Twin Fuji 8 cyl. diesel. 3,200hp

Chatu / Chui

Tanzania Harbours Authority, Dar es Salaam

Builders	: Damen, Gorinchen, Holland. 1991
Length	: 100 feet
Beam	: 30 feet
Displacement	: 308 tons
Machinery	: Twin Deutz 8 cyl. diesel. 5,800 bhp

Chui / Duma / Faru / Nguvu II / Simba II
Kenya Ports Authority, Mombasa

Builders	: Ailsa & Co. Troon, Scotland. 1984
Length	: 119 feet
Beam	: 33 feet
Displacement	: 361 tons
Machinery	: Twin V8 Ruston diesel. 4,870 bhp

Comarco Buzzard
Kenya Marine Contractors, Mombasa

Builders	: Wuxi Shipyard, China. 2000
Length	: 56 feet
Beam	: 16 feet
Displacement	: 144 tons
Machinery	: Twin Yanmar 6 cyl. diesel. 2,400 hp

Comarco Falcon
Comarco Indian Ocean Ltd

Builders	: Tuong Aik Shipbuilders, Sibu, Sarawak. 1998
Length	: 83 feet
Beam	: 24 feet
Displacement	: 149 tons
Machinery	: Twin Caterpillar V12 diesel. 1,344 hp

Comarco Hawk
Comarco Indian Ocean Ltd

Builders	: Guanghzhou Shipyard,Guanghzho,China.1998
Length	: 81 feet
Beam	: 25 feet
Displacement	: 172 tons
Machinery	: Twin Cummins 6 cyl. diesel. 1,200 hp

Comarco Merlin
Comarco Mauritius Ltd.

Builders	: Shangnan Shipyard, China. 19??
Length	: 95 feet
Beam	: 29 feet
Displacement	: 255 tons
Machinery	: Twin Yanmar 6 cyl. diesel. 2,400 bhp

Comarco Osprey
Kenya Marine Contractors, Mombasa

Builders	: Union Naval de Lavant, Valencia, Spain. 1981
Length	: 87 feet
Beam	: 24 feet
Displacement	: 144 tons
Machinery	: Twin Guascor V12 diesel. 1,498 hp

Comarco Swift

Kenya Marine Contractors, Mombasa

Builders	: Osaka Shipbuilding, Japan. 1984
Length	: 120 feet
Beam	: 31 feet
Displacement	: 391 tons
Machinery	: Twin Hanshin 6 cyl. diesel. 2,430 hp

Condor

Comarco Mauritius Ltd.

Builders	: Aukra Bruk AS, Norway. 1974
Length	: 190 feet
Beam	: 40 feet
Displacement	: 1,474 tons
Machinery	: Twin M.A.K. 8cyl diesel. 5,300 bhp

CPC Soave

Consolidated Pipe Contractors, Mombasa

Builders	: Selco Shipyard, Singapore. 1976
Length	: 116 feet
Beam	: 30 feet
Displacement	: 399 tons
Machinery	: Twin M.W.M. 6 cyl. diesel. 1,800 hp

Dar es Salaam

Deutsche Ost Afrika Linie, Dar es Salaam

Builders	: H.C. Stulcken, Hamburg, Germany. 1906
Length	: 94 feet
Beam	: 20 feet
Displacement	: 113 tons
Machinery	: Single compound. 43 nhp

Duma

Tanzania Harbours Authority, Dar es Salaam

Builders	: Damen Shipyards, Cape Town, S.A. 2009
Length	: 68 feet
Beam	: 25 feet
Displacement	: 111 tons
Machinery	: Twin Caterpillar V16 diesel. 2,922 hp

El Lamy

Kenya Ports Authority, Mombasa

Builders	: Damen BV, Gorinchen, Holland. 1983
Length	: 110 feet
Beam	: 32 feet
Displacement	: 354 tons
Machinery	: Twin 8 cyl Ruston diesel. 4,200 bhp

Fast Fox

Cory Towage, United Kingdom

Builders	: R. Dunston, Hessle, Yorkshire. England. 1974
Length	: 120 feet
Beam	: 33 feet
Displacement	: 484 tons
Machinery	: Deutz 8 cyl. diesel. 4,000 bhp

Fish Eagle

Comarco Indian Ocean Ltd., Mombasa

Builders	: J.G. Hitzler, Lauenberg, Germany 1966
Length	: 171 feet
Beam	: 37 feet
Displacement	: 486 tons
Machinery	: Twin M.A.N. V16 diesel. 2,124 hp

Groningen

Wijsmuller, Ijmuiden, Holland

Builders	: Kramer & Booy, Kootstertille, Holland. 1963
Length	: 158 feet
Beam	: 33 feet
Displacement	: 598 tons
Machinery	: Twin Werkspoor 4 cyl. diesel. 4,200 bhp

Harrier

Divecon, Mombasa

Builders	: Kabushiki Kaisha Ishii, Futtsu Chiba, Japan. 1977
Length	: 47 feet
Beam	: 13 feet
Displacement	: 28 tons
Machinery	: Hanshin 6 cyl. diesel. 320 hp

Helmuth

Deutsche Ost Afrika Linie, Dar es Salaam

Builders	: Henry Koch, Lubeck, Germany. 1910
Length	: 55 feet
Beam	: 15 feet
Displacement	: 35 tons
Machinery	: Single triple expansion. 95 nhp

Imara

Tanganyika Port Authority, Dar es Salaam

Builders	: Fleming & Ferguson, Paisley, Scotland. 1931
Length	: 110 feet
Beam	: 28 feet
Displacement	: 290 tons
Machinery	: Twin triple expansion. 1,100 ihp

Kadett
Deutsche Ost Afrika Linie, Dar es Salaam

Builders	: Janssen & Schmilinsky, Germany. 1902
Length	: 116 feet
Beam	: 23 feet
Displacement	: 226 tons
Machinery	: Single compound. 350 ihp

Kavirondo
Kenya Uganda Railways & Harbours, Kisumu

Builders	: Fleming & Ferguson, Paisley, Scotland. 1913
Length	: 100 feet
Beam	: 21 feet
Displacement	: 200 tons
Machinery	: Single triple expansion. 400 ihp

Kiboko
Kenya Marine Contractors, Mombasa

Builders	: Ando Tekkosho, Japan. 1972
Length	: 62 feet
Beam	: 29 feet
Displacement	: 163 tons
Machinery	: Twin Daihatsu 6 cyl. diesel. 600 bhp

Kiboko
Kenya Ports Authority, Mombasa

Builders	: Ailsa & Co. Troon, Scotland. 1977
Length	: 122 feet
Beam	: 33 feet
Displacement	: 392 tons
Machinery	: Ruston V16 cyl. diesel. 3,520 bhp

Kiboko II, Nyangumi II, Simba III
Kenya Ports Authority, Mombasa

Builders	: Damen Shipyard, Gorinchen, Holland. 2004
Length	: 101 feet
Beam	: 30 feet
Displacement	: 313 tons
Machinery	: Twin Caterpillar 16 cyl. diesel. 4,816 hp

Kifaru
African Wharfage Co. Mombasa

Builders	: Bow McLachlan, Glasgow Scotland. 1927
Length	: 125 feet
Beam	: 25 feet
Displacement	: 279 tons
Machinery	: Twin triple expansion. 88 ihp

KMC Eland

Kenya Marine Contractors, Mombasa

Builders	: Eastern Marine Shipbldg, Sibu, Malaysia. 2002
Length	: 80 feet
Beam	: 24 feet
Displacement	: 157 tons
Machinery	: Twin Yanmar 6 cyl. diesel. 1,360 hp

KMC Rhino

Kenya Marine Contractors, Mombasa

Builders	: Ailsa & Co. Troon, Scotland. 1978
Length	: 125 feet
Beam	: 35 feet
Displacement	: 768 tons
Machinery	: Single Ruston V16 cyl. diesel. 3,500 hp

Kongoni

East African Railways & Harbours, Mombasa

Builders	: Scott & Sons, Glasgow, Scotland. 1959
Length	: 105 feet
Beam	: 28 feet
Displacement	: 193 tons
Machinery	: Single Crossley diesel. 1,150 bhp

Leutnant

Deutsche Ost Afrika Linie, Dar es Salaam

Builders	: Gebr. Sachsenberg, Rosslau, Germany. 1912
Length	: 129 feet
Beam	: 25 feet
Displacement	: 340 tons
Machinery	: Twin compound. 43 nhp

Linden

East African Railways & Harbours, Mombasa

Builders	: H. Scarr, Hessle, England. 1942
Length	: 113 feet
Beam	: 27 feet
Displacement	: 245 tons
Machinery	: Single triple expansion. 800 ihp

Mamba

Tanzania Harbours Authority, Dar es Salaam

Builders	: Alblasser, Krimpen, Holland. 1982
Length	: 100 feet
Beam	: 26 feet
Displacement	: 170 tons
Machinery	: Twin Deutz 6 cyl. diesel

Marie Felling
Kenya Uganda Railways & Harbours, Mombasa

Builders	: Earle & Co., Hull, England. 1929
Length	: 104 feet
Beam	: 28 feet
Displacement	: 271 tons
Machinery	: Twin triple expansion. 1,090 ihp

Martial
Eagle Tugs Ltd, Grand Cayman

Builders	: Henry Robb, Leith, Scotland. 1943
Length	: 205 feet
Beam	: 40 feet
Displacement	: 1,136 tons
Machinery	: Twin Atlas Polar 8 cyl. diesel. 4,400 bhp

Martial
Comarco Mauritius Ltd.

Builders	: Astilleros de Huelva, Spain. 1978
Length	: 105 feet
Beam	: 28 feet
Displacement	: 583 tons
Machinery	: Single Deutz V12 diesel. 4,400 bhp

Martial
Comarco Mauritius Ltd.

Builders	: Teraoka Zosen, Japan. 1981
Length	: 188 feet
Beam	: 39 feet
Displacement	: 1,100 tons
Machinery	: Twin Yanmar 6 cyl. diesel. 3,600 bhp

Mississippi
Smit, Rotterdam, Holland

Builders	: J & K Smit's, Kinderdijk, Holland. 1960
Length	: 175 feet
Beam	: 34 feet
Displacement	: 674 tons
Machinery	: Twin M.A.N. 9 cyl. diesel. 2,500 bhp

Mohesi
V.N.S., The Hague, Holland

Builders	: Reiherstieg, Hamburg, Germany. 1924
Length	: 100 feet
Beam	: 25 feet
Displacement	: 185 tons
Machinery	: Single compound. 400 ihp

Mwokozi

Kenya Ports Authority, Mombasa

Builders	: Ferguson Ailsa & Co. Troon, Scotland. 1984
Length	: 135 feet
Beam	: 38 feet
Displacement	: 672 tons
Machinery	: Twin Ruston 12 cyl. diesel. 6,360 bhp

Ndovu / Ngamia

East African Railways & Harbours, Mombasa

Builders	: J. Lamont, Glasgow, Scotland. 1969
Length	: 115 feet
Beam	: 30 feet
Displacement	: 298 tons
Machinery	: Twin Crossley diesel. 2,500 bhp

Nguva / Pomboo

Tanzania Harbours Authority, Dar es Salaam

Builders	: E. Goumas, Salamis, Greece. 1992
Length	: 89 feet
Beam	: 23 feet
Displacement	: 137 tons
Machinery	: Twin Wartsila 4 cyl. diesel. Voith Schneider

Nguvu

Kenya Uganda Railways & Harbours, Mombasa

Builders	: Fleming & Ferguson, Paisley, Scotland. 1925
Length	: 100 feet
Beam	: 22 feet
Displacement	: 179 tons
Machinery	: Single triple expansion. 92 nhp

Nguvu

East African Railways & Harbours, Mombasa

Builders	: J. Thorneycroft, Southampton, England. 1963
Length	: 114 feet
Beam	: 29 feet
Displacement	: 210 tons
Machinery	: Twin Crossley diesel. 2,200 bhp

Nisos Kerkyra

Tsavliris Salvage. Piraeus, Greece

Builders	: Henry Robb, Leith, Scotland. 1945
Length	: 205 feet
Beam	: 40 feet
Displacement	: 1,047 tons
Machinery	: Twin Atlas Polar 8 cyl. diesel. 4,000 bhp

Nyamgumi II

Tanzania Harbours Authority, Dar es Salaam

Builders   : Damen Shipyards, Galati, Romania. 2010
Length   : 92 feet
Beam   : 33 feet
Displacement : 285 tons
Machinery   : Twin Caterpillar V16 diesel. 4,584 hp

Nyati

African Wharfage Co. Mombasa

Builders   : Cox & Co. Falmouth, England. 1899
Length   : 90 feet
Beam   : 19 feet
Displacement : 123 tons
Machinery   : Twin compound. 36 nhp

Nyati / Simba

East African Railways & Harbours, Mombasa

Builders   : A.J. Inglis & Co. Glasgow, Scotland. 1951
Length   : 130 feet
Beam   : 30 feet
Displacement : 359 tons
Machinery   : Twin triple expansion. 1,530 ihp

Percy Anderson

Uganda Railway, Mombasa

Builders   : J.S. Watson, Gainsborough, England. 1896
Length   : 68 feet
Beam   : 14 feet
Displacement : 90 tons
Machinery   : Single triple expansion. 90 nhp

Privateer

Kenya Marine Contractors, Mombasa

Builders   : V.E.B Schiffswerft, Magdeburg, Germany. 1969
Length   : 87 feet
Beam   : 26 feet
Displacement : 232 tons
Machinery   : Single SKL 6 cyl. diesel. 750 hp

Raptor

Comarco Mauritius Ltd.

Builders   : Scheepswerf Waterhuizen, Holland. 1982
Length   : 176 feet
Beam   : 40 feet
Displacement : 1,015 tons
Machinery   : Twin Wichmann 7AXA diesel. 4,400 bhp

Revenger
Elliot & Co. London

Builders	: M van der Kuyl, Slikkerveer. Holland. 1905
Length	: 123 feet
Beam	: 21 feet
Displacement	: 243 tons
Machinery	: Single triple expansion. 900 ihp

Rode Zee
Smit, Rotterdam, Holland

Builders	: Arnhemse, Arnhem, Holland. 1968
Length	: 224 feet
Beam	: 39 feet
Displacement	: 1,312 tons
Machinery	: Twin Werkspoor 6 cyl. diesel. 7,000 bhp

Sea Eagle
Eagle Tugs Ltd, Grand Cayman

Builders	: J.G. Hitzler, Lauenburg, Germany. 1969
Length	: 179 feet
Beam	: 37 feet
Displacement	: 927 tons
Machinery	: Twin M.W.M V16 diesel. 2,740 bhp

Sea Eagle
Comarco Indian Ocean Ltd

Builders	: Jadewerft, Wilhelmshaven, Germany. 1970
Length	: 180 feet
Beam	: 37 feet
Displacement	: 739 tons
Machinery	: Twin M.A.N. V12 diesel. 3,000 hp

Simba
Tanzania Harbours Authority, Dar es Salaam

Builders	: Tille Scheepsbouw, Kootstertille, Holland. 1982
Length	: 100 feet
Beam	: 26 feet
Displacement	: 208 tons
Machinery	: Twin Deutz 8 cyl. diesel.

Sofala
Deutsche Ost Afrika Linie, Dar es Salaam.

Builders	:	1930
Length	: 62 feet	
Beam	: 23 feet	
Displacement	: tons	
Machinery	: ihp	

Svitzer
Svitzer Towage. Copenhagen

Builders	: A/B Gotaverken, Denmark. 1920
Length	: 170 feet
Beam	: 35 feet
Displacement	: 672 tons
Machinery	: Twin M.A.K. 6 cyl. diesel. 3,600 bhp

SVS Morgan
Specialised Vessel Services Ltd

Builders	: Yokohama Shipbuilding, Japan. 1982
Length	: 190 feet
Beam	: 40 feet
Displacement	: 1,053 tons
Machinery	: Twin Yanmar 6 cyl. diesel. 2,760 bhp

T.A. Jolliffe
W & T Jolliffe & Co. Liverpool

Builders	: J. P. Rennoldson, South Shields.England. 1901
Length	: 113 feet
Beam	: 23 feet
Displacement	: 199 tons
Machinery	: Single triple expansion. 650 ihp

Talon
Comarco Mauritius Ltd

Builders	: Yokohama Zosen, Japan. 1981
Length	: 190 feet
Beam	: 40 feet
Displacement	: 863 tons
Machinery	: Twin Yanmar 8 cyl. diesel. 4,200 bhp

Taveta, Tiddler, Toroka,
Kenya Ports Authority, Mombasa

Builders	: R. Dunston, Thorne, England. 1945
Length	: 65 feet
Beam	: 17 feet
Displacement	: 54 tons
Machinery	: Single compound. 220 ihp

Tewa
Kenya Ports Authority, Mombasa

Builders	: Fellows & Co. Great Yarmouth, England. 1973
Length	: 109 feet
Beam	: 28 feet
Displacement	: 217 tons
Machinery	: Ruston Paxman 8 cyl. diesel. 1,760 hp

Thika
British India Line, Mombasa

Builders   : Scott & Sons, Bowling, England. 1943
Length   : 114 feet
Beam   : 30 feet
Displacement : 262 tons
Machinery   : Single triple expansion. 1,032 ihp

Titan
Kenya Marine Contractors, Mombasa

Builders   : Forward Shipbuilding Ent. Sibu. Malaysia. 2001
Length   : 77 feet
Beam   : 24 feet
Displacement : 144 tons
Machinery   : Twin Caterpillar diesel. 1,460 hp

Upesi I
V.N.S. The Hague, Holland

Builders   : N.V. Boele's, Bolnes. Holland. 1937
Length   : 103 feet
Beam   : 22 feet
Displacement : 200 tons
Machinery   : Twin compound. 400 ihp

Upesi II
V.N.S. The Hague, Holland

Builders   : J.G. Broerken, Westerbroek, Holland. 1954
Length   : 115 feet
Beam   : 26 feet
Displacement : 242 tons
Machinery   : Twin Ruston 6 cyl. diesel. 600 bhp

Postscript

Although not strictly part of this book it was never the less intriguing to come across the loss of one's namesake during the course of researching the book. Tucked away in an official Board of Trade publication for 1895 was the report of an enquiry in to the loss of the S.S. Patience. She was an iron steamer built by Raylton Dixon & Co. of Middlesbrough in 1881, brigantine rigged with a length of 225 feet, beam 32 feet and 1,110 gross tons. Fitted with a compound engine she was launched as the Iron Acton and renamed Patience on 12 August 1889 after she was bought by Mr Edwin Harris for £11,500. The report went into great detail about the ship's fixtures and fittings including hold sizes and deck lengths. In March 1894 she underwent a major refit that included an engine overhaul and new funnel. Two months later she sank off Norway but was raised and refitted at a cost of £2,400. On 20 December 1894 the ship was on a voyage from Spain to Stettin under the command of Captain William Plank with a cargo of 1,250 tons of Sulphur, and called in at Portland for coal, water and supplies. That evening she sailed leaving two telegrams addressed to the owners, one from the Chief Engineer read *'Everything working satisfactorily, leaving here at 9 pm. Wishing you a Merry Xmas and a Happy New Year'*. The following day Edwin Harris received a telegram from the Lloyds signal station at Dover informing him, *'Patience passing east. Moderate westerly wind, overcast, mist'*. She was never seen again. The enquiry stated that from all the witnesses accounts she was well found and maintained and left Portland with sufficient freeboard for the voyage in hand. It was impossible to say what caused the loss and any opinion was pure conjecture. However it was common knowledge that on the next day, one of the most sudden and disastrous storms swept over the North Sea, and the ship may have been overwhelmed before the crew had time to respond.

The author alongside his namesake, Bahrain 1982

Acknowledgements

Australia - Peter Charlton, Dave George, David Hawke John Orton, Colin Patience, Mike Tiernan

Bahrain - Christopher Collier-Wright, Maersk Shipping, Ian Rawlinson

Belgium - Piet van Damme

Canada - Barbara and Gordon Mumford

Ireland - Gene Sullivan

Germany - Rolf Hasse, Katrin Buhbut, Andreas Hoppe

Holland - Lisette Aernaudts, Jan Belder, Anton Rijsdijk, Verenigde Nederlandsche Scheepvaart Maatschappy, Rotterdam

Kenya - African Marine and General Engineering Co. - Mombasa, Judy Aldrick, Johnny Antoni, Captain Chris Barnes, Natalie Bland, Bob Brennierson, Monty and Ken Brown, Andy Burnard, Rowena Buxton, Captain Thomaso Castalano, John Carrs, Gordon Cuthbert, The Coast Academy - Mombasa, Captain Henry Dale, Diving Contractors Limited - Mombasa, Divecon International - Mombasa, Peter Doenhoff, The Friends of Fort Jesus Library - Mombasa, Francis and Robert Foster, Linda Furniss, John Gill, Adrian Grimwood, Captain Spike Harding, Bryan Harris, Sue and David Horsey, Kenya National Archives - Nairobi, Kenya Ports Authority - Mombasa, Kenya Railways and Museum - Nairobi, Mike and Sue Keats, Captain Tawib Khamis, Pannayis Lagoussis, Mrs A. Lazar, Lloyds Register of Shipping - Mombasa, George Malcolmson, McMillan Memorial Library - Nairobi, Seif Miskry, Commander Barry Mitchell, Murri International - Mombasa, Charles Odhiambo, Conway Plough, Graham Roberts, the late Edward Rodwell, Carol and Peter Rodwell, Captain Mike Rose, Mike Scarpallini, Robin Schalch, Southern Engineering - Mombasa, Southern Line - Mombasa, Spanfreight Shipping - Mombasa, Roger Tanner, Captain Fred Wahutu, James Willson

New Zealand - Les Ottaway

Serbia - Bane Krstonošić

South Africa - Antony Allen, Robin Stobbs

Tanzania - Sarah Clithero, Stefan Christian, Tony Hughes, Ray Howlett, Colleen & Frank Jansen, Sven Jansen, Jan Newby, Captain Andrew Mattillya, Mike Phillips, Ryan Scholz, Alan Sutton, Captain Khamis Zaunga

United Kingdom - Alan & Jenny Alder, Malcolm Angel & Gulliver's Bookshop - Wimborne, Appledore Maritime Museum, Peter Apsey, John Arnold, Peter Baker, John Barrington-Carver, Brian Benbow, Margaret & Tony Bentley-Buckle, Derek Blackett, Captain Paul Bowes, Clive Brooks, John Brown, Yoland Brown, Anne Browne, Bill Brummage, Sarah Burbridge, Juanita Carberry, Peter Chantry, Geoff Charlewood, Peter Chew, Phyllida and Desmond Cockell, Maureen & Fritz Coers, Joan Considine, Tony Cross, Captain Richard Crow, Captain Henry Dale, Robin Davies, June Dillon, Laurence Dunn, Michael Farrant, Roy Fenton, Steve Le Feuvre, Keith Fitton, Fleet Air Arm Museum - Yeovilton, Foto-Flite, Glynis Furse, Roger Griffiths, The Guildhall Library - London, Allan Hall, Duncan Hawes, Emma Haxhaj, Christopher Hill, Rick Hogben, Rev. Andrew Huckett, The Hydrographic Office - Taunton, The Imperial War Museum - London, Chris Isaac, Barbara Jones, K.J, The Kenya Society, National Archives - London, Richard Larne, Nick Lera, Lloyds Register of Shipping - London, Graham Mackenzie, Moira Macpherson, Beverly Mawby, Fergus McCartney, George Malcolm, Malcolm McCrow, Sam Melesi, Mark Meyer, Graham Mottram, Pam Nightingale, Stephen North, Chris Osborn, Lawrence Patterson, Rick Pearce, Peter Piggott, Poole Maritime Trust, John Prescott, Captain Geoff Pullen, Stephen Reid, Bill Ritchie, Royal Navy Submarine Museum - Gosport, Dave Saywell, Paddy Shields, Nora Shipley, Philip Simons, Peter Singlehurst, Simon Skudder, William Spencer, Joan Steed, Gerald Storer, Captain Phillip Thomas, Captain Keith Trayner, Sheila Unwin, John Walters, Adrian Webb, Jock Whitehouse, Brian Yonge, The Zanzibar Association

United States - Gerry Rilling

Zanzibar - Ali Abdullah, Pat and Gilly Dudgeon, Gary Grieg and One Ocean Divers, Abed and Javed Jafferji, Khamis Khamis, Hamad Omar, Professor Abdul Sharrif, The Zanzibar Archives and Museums

Bibliography

African River Wars, 1914-1916	J. M. Alliston	Naval Hist. Soc. Australia 1996
Afloat & Ashore	Peter Singlehurst	Token Publishing 2006
Battle for the Bundu	Charles Miller	MacDonald 1974
British India Line History	W. Laxon & F. Perry	World Ship Society 1994
British India Line	Duncan Haws	TCL Publications 1988
British India Mail Packets to East Africa	Stephen North	East Africa Study Circle 2002
Channels, Cloves and Coconuts	Clement Charlewood	Western Press 1955
Coast Causerie	Edward Rodwell	Heineman 1972 - 79
Conway's All the World's Fighting Ships		Conway 1979 - 1985
Dictionary of Disasters at Sea	C. Hocking	London Stamp Exchange 1990
Europeans in British East Africa 1888 - 1905	Stephen North	Published by the author 2005
German Mailboats to East Africa 1890 - 1905	Stephen North	Published by the author 2002
Handbook of Tanganyika	G. F. Sayers	Macmillan 1930
Harrisons of Liverpool	Graema Cubbin	World Ship Soc./ Ships in Focus
Henderson Bibby Line	Duncan Haws	TCL Publications 1995
Hitler's Grey Wolves	Lawrence Patterson	Greenhill Books 2004
India Directory	J. Horsborough	W.H. Allen 1864
Jane's Fighting Ships	Fred. T. Jane	Marston 1910 - 1920
Königsberg - A German East African Raider	Kevin Patience	Zanzibar Publications 2001
Lloyds Register of Shipping		Lloyds Register 1866 - 2013
Lloyds Casualty Returns		Lloyds Register 1920 - 2013
Lloyds Weekly Shipping Index		Lloyds Register 1880 - 1910
Military Operations in East Africa		H.M.S.O. 1930
Mimi & Toutou Go Forth	Giles Foden	Michael Joseph 2007
My Reminiscences of East Africa	P. von Lettow-Vorbeck	Hurst and Blackett 1925
Official History of the War	J. S. Corbett	Longmans 1920 - 31
Palm Line	L. Dunn / P. Heaton	P.M. Heaton 1994
Permanent Way Vol. I & II	M. F. Hill	E.A.R.& H. 1949
Reports of Enquiries into Wrecks		Board of Trade 1883 - 1972
Royal Navy ships log books		1890 - 1945
SD 14 - The Full Story	John Lingwood	Ships in Focus 2004
Sea Safari	Peter Kohler	P.M.Heaton 1995
Severn's Saga	E. Keble Chatterton	Hurst and Blackett 1938
Some African Highway's	Caroline Kirkland	D. Estes 1908
Steam and Quinine on Africa's Great Lakes	David Reynolds	South Africa 1996
Steam in East Africa	Kevin Patience	Heineman 1976
Tanganyika Guerilla	J. R. Sibley	Ballantine 1971
The Big Gun Monitors	N. Buxton	Tynemouth 1978
The Lake Steamers of East Africa	Bill Dennis	Runnymede 1996
The Phantom Flotilla	Peter Shankland	Collins 1968
The Königsberg Adventure	E. Keble Chatterton	Hurst and Blackett 1937
Tip and Run	Edward Paice	Weidenfeld & Nicolson 2007
Tufani	Vice Admiral Max Looff	Verlag 1936
Uganda	Marion Browning	Uganda Trust 1998
Union Castle Line	Duncan Haws	TCL Publications 1990
Wartime disasters at sea	David Williams	Patrick Stephens 1997
Zanzibar and the Loss of H.M.S. Pegasus	Kevin Patience	Zanzibar Publications 1995
Zanzibar, Slavery and the Royal Navy	Kevin Patience	Zanzibar Publications 2000

Magazines / Journals / Periodicals

Coastweek, Kenya

The C.M.S. Gleaner, 1870s

Daily Nation, Kenya, 1961 - 2005

East African Railways & Harbours Magazine, 1953 - 1960

East African Standard, Kenya, 1909 - 2003

Illustrated London News, 1872

Kenya - Past and Present

Kenya Gazette, 1904 - 1920

Marine News

Sea Breezes

Ships in Focus

Ships Monthly

Spear, East Africa Railways Corporation, 1960 - 1969

Tanganyika Notes and Records, 1925 - 1958

The Times, 1909 - 1910

Zanzibar Gazette, 1896 - 1914

Public & Private Sources

Church Missionary Society Archives - London

Comarco Marine Salvage Records - Mombasa

Divecon Limited Salvage Records - Mombasa

Fort Jesus Archives - Mombasa

Guildhall Library - London

Imperial War Museum - London

Kenya Merchant Shipping Records - Mombasa

Kenya National Archives - Nairobi

Kenya Port Authority Records - Mombasa

Kenya Railways Photographic Archives - Nairobi

Kenya Railways Museum Records - Nairobi

Lloyds Register of Shipping - London

Murri International Salvage Records - Mombasa

National Archives - London

Southampton Civic Centre Maritime Library

Tanzania National Archives - Dar es Salaam

Tanzania Harbour Authority Records - Dar es Salaam

World Ship Society

Zanzibar Archive Records - Zanzibar

The Internet

www.facebook.com

www.ian.coombe.tripod.com

www.naval-history.net

www.shipsnostalgia.com

www.uboat.net

www.friendsofmombasa.com

www.merchant-navy.net

www.plimsoll.org

www.shipspotting.com

www.worldnavalships.com

www.wrecksite.eu

About the Author

Kevin was resident in East Africa for many years with a keen interest in the maritime and transport history of the region. While serving in the Royal Air Force he qualified as a scuba diver and researched shipwrecks around Malta and Cornwall. On returning to Kenya in the 1970s, he dived and researched shipwrecks that led to an archive of material that formed the basis of this book. A move to the Middle East in 1977 saw the beginning of a career in commercial diving and marine salvage based in Bahrain. Five years later he returned to Kenya as Managing Director of Diving Contractors Ltd. (Divecon Ltd) in Mombasa and was actively involved in salvage work along the East African coast. In 1984 he returned to Bahrain and established Tech Dive, and was responsible for a number of successful salvage operations around the Arabian Gulf. The publication of an article on East African wrecks, began five years of research that culminated in the first edition of this book published in 2006. Ten years later additional ship casualties and information presented an opportunity to update and reprint the book in colour.

Publications by the Author.
Steam in East Africa - 1976
Zanzibar and the Shortest War in History - 1994
Zanzibar and the loss of H.M.S. Pegasus - 1995
Zanzibar and the Bububu Railway - 1995 / 2001
Zanzibar, Slavery and the Royal Navy - 2001
Steam Twilight - 1996
Königsberg - A German East African Raider - 1997 / 2001
Shieldhall - A Clyde Banana Boat - 2001 / 2003
Shipwrecks and Salvage on the East African Coast - 2006 and 2018
Numerous articles in military / maritime publications, including After the Battle magazine, Britain at War magazine, Kenya Regiment journal, Medal News magazine, Naval Historical Collectors Research Association journal, Orders & Medals Journal, Old Africa magazine, Shipwreck journal and the Internet.

Edited and published :
Monuments to Courage by David Harvey - 1999. The graves of Victoria Cross heroes. 1856-1999
Child of Happy Valley by Juanita Carberry - 2009. A childhood in Kenya. 1925-1942

Edited :
Railway to Nowhere by Stephen Mills - 2013. Building the Lunatic Line across Kenya. 1896-1901
Hope in the Darkness by Dr Abdul Aziz Hamza - 2011. Loss of the motor vessel Seistan at Bahrain. 1958
My Life - A Memoir by Anthony Bentley-Buckle - 2013
Kenya Pioneer Chronicles by Errol Trzebinski and Stephen Mills - 2015. 1914 - 18 chapter

Presented with the French Chevalier of the Order of Merit in 1999 for research into the causes of the two Air France DC-4 airliner crashes at Bahrain in 1950.

Awarded the Lord Lewin Memorial Prize in 2003 and 2009 for articles based on research in Zanzibar on Royal Navy operations on the East African coast in the Naval Historical Collectors Research Association Journal.

Index

Adele O'Swald	143	Buyuk Ana	73
Adhara	62	Calicut	20
Adjutant	203, 276	Caltex Dublin	134
African Queen	244	Canadian Spirit	147
Afton	63	Cape Charles	148
Agia Marina	11	Cape York	148
Aguia	139	Capitaine Biebuyck	206
Ahmadi	12	Cetriana	58
Al Amin	64	Chakdara	74
Al Azra	134	Chance 71	134
Alpha Kilimanjaro	16	H.M.S. Chatham	75
Almasi	144	Chenab	76
Alpha Commander	134	Cheog Yang 31	77
Amafh One	145	Chrysovalandou Dyo	78
Amy Konishi	276	Chatu/Chui	278
Andreas Boye	204	Chaza/Nguru/Papa	278
Anna	244	Chuchunge/Nyangumi	278
Ann W	65	K.N.S. Chui	79
Apulia	134	Chui/Duma/Faru/Nguvu II/Simba II	279
Arab Trader	17	Chyko	149
Arctic	276	City of Agra	80
Arusha	276	City of Shanghai	81
Aspia	66	Clement Hill	262
Ata	205	Colleen	150
Atlantic Maru	67	Comara	207
Aventura	18	Comarco Buzzard	279
H.M.S. Baia	134	Comarco Falcon	279
Banduki	276	Comarco Hawk	279
Barbara	276	Comarco Merlin	279
Baron Cawdor	68	Comarco Osprey	279
Bateleur	69, 277	Comarco Swift	280
Bente Dania	19	Comrie Castle	134
Bernora	70	Condor	280
Berwick Castle	71	Connie	244
Betty, Winnie	277	Costoula	82
Beverly Mawby	292	Dae Wang 12	134
Bison 1	277	Dania	21
Blackcock	277	Daphne	208
Black Eagle	277	Dar es Salaam	280
Bonsella	146	Debbie	244
Bouvet	244	Derna	22
Bremen	278	Dhiran K III	151
British Patience	290	Dolphin	244
Buganda/Buvuma	278	No. 203 Dong Sung	85
Bukoba	261	Duma	280
Burma	72	Duplex	209

H.M.S. Durban 86	Indoyang 18 135
Ebnesina 244	Jalmahavir 245
Ekali 87	Jamhuri 214
KMC Eland 283	Jean Laborde 93
El Lamy 280	Jody 215
El Majidi 152	Juba 216
El Moaiz 88	Johangella 94
El Rei 139	J S Danube 95
Enda 244	Kabalega 274
Eva 89	Kadett 282
Faith 244	Kavirondo 263, 282
Fast Fox 281	Kenia 1 274
Fateh el Khair 134	Kestrel 96
Fish Eagle 23, 281	Khalaf 97
Fivi 210	Khandalla 98
Flamenga 139	Kherimoyo 135
Floating Dock 153	Kiboko 282
Fly 211	Kiboko II, Nyangumi II, Simba III . . 282
Flying Horse 212	Kifaru 282
Fong Ta 31 244	Kingani 257
Frierfjord 213	Kivuna 135
Funguo 24	Kola 135
Gigi 274	Kongoni 283
H.H.S. Glasgow 155	König 162
Globe Star 25	S.M.S. Königsberg 164
Glorongay 157	Kota Menang 37
T.C.G. Gökçeada 90	Kota Selatan 166
Goetzen 253	Kronborg 167
Grant 250	Kwoo 51 135
Great Northern 158	Lagada Star 99
Groningen 281	Langsleescot 100
Gueotec 135	Lavest 42
Hamar 135	Lee Christine 135
Harrier 31, 281	H.M.S. Leopard 101
Hedwig 160	Leutnant 283
Hedwig von Wissman 255	Liemba 258
Heinrich Otto 274	Linden 283
Helmuth 281	Lindi 170
Highland Lassie 32	Lion 1 102
Highly 1 91	Liza Jane 135
H.M.S. Hildasay 33	Llandaff Castle 217
Hodari 161	Lord Milner 171
Husseni 274	Lugard II 264
Ibtisaam 245	Magadi Dredge No. 3 252
Imara 281	Maisho 21 135
Impala 36, 245	Malik Dinar 135
Ina 135	Mama Mary 245
Indian Resolve 92	Mamba 283

Manica 218
Manihine 219
Mansoor 103
Margo 104
Marla Bourboulls 105
Marie Felling 284
Marina 106
Marinasi 1 172
Markgraf 173
Martial 284
Martial 284
Marvani. 245
Masula 220
Maytham 174
Mbudja 245
Melbourne 107
Mimi / Toutou 259
Minerva 108
Mirage 43
Miramichi 109
Miribella III 135
Mississippi 284
ML 1057 136
Modasa 110
Mohesi 245, 284
S.M.S. Möwe 175
SVS Morgan 288
Mtongwe 44
Mtwara 245
Mulbera 221
Mwanza 265
Mwokozi 285
Nabila 136
Nairobi 45
Ndovu/Ngamia 285
Negba 111
CSC Nelson 278
Newbridge 176
Newton 136
Ngamia 46, 285
Nguva 285
Nguvu 245
Nimoyena 245
Nisos Kerkyra 285
Nooreen 112
Nordvaer 222
Norefjord 223
Nossa Senhora de Graca 139

Nossa Senhora de Guadalupe 139
Nossa Senhora dos Remedios 139
Nyamageni 274
Nyamgumi 278
Nyamgumi II 286
Nyangaku Maru 136
Nyanza 274
Nyati 178
Nyati 286
Nyati/Simba 286
Odysseas 245
Olga Ulyanova 136
Olympic Rider 113
Orestes 246
CEC Pacific 224
Pacific Express 114
Panda II 246
Paraportiani 179
Parkgate 115
Patna 116
H.M.S. Pegasus 182
Pelion 117
Pemba 225
Penguin 185
Pentakota 226
Percy Anderson 286
Peter 274
Phillipias 227
Pinguin 246
H.M.A.S. Pioneer 228
Pomboo 246, 285
Präsident 229
Privateer 286
Putiala 118
Rafaela 47
Rafiki 48
Rahmat 136
Ramora Bay 49
Rampart 230
Raptor 286
Revenger 287
KMC Rhino 283
Ricki Nav 136
Robert Coryndon 249
Rode Zee 287
Rogo 119
H.M.E.A.S. Rosalind 120
Rovuma 186

Royal Sovereign 187
Roybank 231
Rubin 246
Ruwenzori 274
Said Mohamed 50
Saint Michael 51
Salama 48
Salvacao 139
San Filipe 139
San Rafael 188
Sanko Cherry 121
Santo Antonio de Tanna 52
Santo Amaro 139
SFL Sara 232
Sarah Jolliffe 233
Sea Eagle 287
Sea Eagle 287
Seagull 136
Shakwe 53
Shin Jin No.5 137
Siam Opal 137
Si-Kiang 122
Silago Express 123
Simba 287
Simla 234
Sincerity 235
Skagit 189
Slemmestad 190
CPC Soave 280
Sofala 287
Somali 192
Southern Baobab 124
Southern Dawn 246
Southern Pioneer I 137
Southern Pioneer II 194
Spalmatori Engineer 236
R.F.A. Spapool 54
Spice Islander 1 195
Stanford Buzzard 237
State of Haryana 238
Stolt Dimitris 125
Sukuman 274
Sunetta 126
Sussex 56
Svitzer 288
Sybil 266
Tabora 196
T.A. Joliffe 288

Talon 288
Tanga 239
Taveta, Tiddler, Toroka 288
Tembo 57
Tenyu Maru 58 127
Tewa 288
Theresa Arctic 137
Thika 137
Thika 289
Thor 274
Thorland 128
Tilawa 240
Titan 289
Tomondo 198
Tong Hong 3 137
Trans Cargo 4 137
Tumaini 246
Tuna 246
H.M.S. Turquoise 130
Twiga 137
U-183 138
Uganda 241
Ujuzi 138
Ukerewe 274
Ulinzi 275
Umballa 242
Umoja 275
Unidentified 58, 138, 246, 275
Unknown 139
Upezi I 289
Upezi II 289
Usoga 268
Walkers 275
Wami 260
William Mackinnon 269
Winifred 272
Winnie 131
Wiseman 138
Yung Hsaio 132
Zambesi 243
Zanzibar 133
Zanzibar 199
The Zanzibar Hurricane 200